The Holiday from Hell

The Re-Enlightenment Two

A Spiritual Journey

Carole and David McEntee-Taylor

'The only limit to our realization of tomorrow will be our doubts of today. Let us move forward with strong and active faith.'
Franklin D. Roosevelt (1882 - 1945)

Other books by the same authors

The Re-Enlightenment – A Spiritual Handbook
Fantine Press 2007
See page 371 for more details

Copyright © 2007 Carole and David McEntee-Taylor
All rights reserved.

No part of this publication may be reproduced, stored in a retrieval system or transmitted in any form or by any means, electronic, mechanical, photocopying, recording or otherwise without the prior permission of the copyright holder.

ISBN: 978-0-9559888-0-6

Preface

In the last book we explained how we are not just physical beings but a spirit that has taken a physical body. Our spirit has chosen to do this to allow us to experience a range of emotions and events that will help us evolve spiritually. To do this our physical bodies need somewhere to exist physically and the place we come to is the earth. It is here that we experience the emotions and events that we can only theorise about whilst in our peaceful spiritual home. It is such a complete change from our spiritual existence that it could be described as a holiday. After all, we choose to go on holiday and we chose our destination because of what it has to offer. We also use our holidays to try different things and to think about how we can make changes in our lives. It is the perfect opportunity to have a break from work and spend time with our loved ones.

Our holiday from spirit is no different in that respect. Our spirit chooses our destination for what it has to offer us in terms of our spiritual development. It allows us to experience things we can't experience as Spirit and it gives us the opportunity to make decisions that will influence our future spiritual development. It also allows us to experience the sensations of being physically close to our loved ones. The main difference is that the holidays we take on the earth plane as physical beings are intended to make us feel relaxed and to rejuvenate and energise ourselves. Our holiday from spirit normally has completely the opposite effect and can very often be described as The Holiday from Hell! But it doesn't have to be like that – there is another way.

Have you ever wondered why the world is like it is? Why there are such disparities between rich and poor? Have you ever wondered why we as individuals and communities seem to keep repeating the same mistakes? Why it is that anti Semitism and racism thrives and why the messages put out by the major religions seem to lead to wars and conflict instead of the peace and love that they preach? Have you ever wondered why some people interpret spiritual messages of love as messages of hate and persecution and more importantly, perhaps, why other people would believe that this is the correct interpretation?

The Holiday from Hell asks why, in the 21st Century, we are still fighting over events that happened or supposedly happened centuries earlier. It sets out to examine and explain the roots of current conflicts and asks whether the past is as important as we think it is, or whether we, as individuals and communities should leave the past behind and begin to live in the present. One of the ways it does this is by looking at several explanations for our existence. There are many gaps in our knowledge of the past and almost as many theories put forward to explain them as there are mysteries. Some set out to disprove religious accounts of our beginnings; others try to find proof to back up these religious accounts. Some are based purely in science, others are assumed to be science fiction. The aim of this book is not to say that any of these theories or explanations are right or wrong but to ask whether it really matters. Many of the differences in these explanations are based purely on differences in interpretation and perception and are a result of the life experiences of those doing the interpreting. Throughout the centuries our societies and their values have gone through continual changes and many theories reflect the mores and values of the time in which they were written. Our scientific knowledge is also constantly improving which makes it easier to prove or disprove some of the earlier theories about our existence. There is nothing wrong with a healthy curiosity about our beginnings but we should also remember that we are here to live this life; to experience the here and now. We are often told that the present is a gift – and that we should live in it and appreciate it. Another expression claims that 'the past is another country' and as such should be treated like that. In other words many of today's problems could be resolved if we left the past in the past and concentrated on the present.

As we have said, our spiritual evolution does not happen in isolation. It is not only closely integrated with our physical evolution but also with the spiritual and physical progression of every other living being on the planet. The Re-Enlightenment was an introduction and concentrated on us as individuals. The Holiday from Hell not only continues this examination but expands to include our individual physical journey as well. It also examines our common physical and spiritual evolution because we are not just isolated individuals; we are part of a community. Therefore, everything we think, say and do impacts on someone else and vice versa.

So how do individuals become part of a community? For individuals to form a community there must be some kind of glue that binds them together- that gives them this sense of shared identity. This could be either a sense of or actual shared geographical territory. In other words they live in the same area and within the same physical boundary. If they live within this boundary or area they may well have a shared history ie: the same things that have happened to them will have happened to their neighbours and would have been seen and experienced in the same way. They may also share the same language and even the same dialect. These are the cultural and social things that bind individuals into communities. If the community does have its own territory it may also have its own system of government. All these things will shape the community's view of themselves and the world outside their community and all of these things are essentially political.

But there are other communities who may not live within the same territory or share the same language. They may not share the same history or live under the same type of government; nevertheless they consider themselves to be a community because they share the same religious beliefs. Thus the world has both political communities and religious communities and some that are both. Any solution to the problems facing the world must take this into account because the problems that divide us are both political and religious and both have their origins in the distant past.

But why are we still fighting over things that apparently happened centuries ago? Are they really relevant today or have they become so entangled with our idea of our own identity that we are unable to move past them? If we took a fresh look at the origins of these conflicts would this allow us to move forward? The answer to this probably lies in how the investigation is carried out and whether it encourages us to change our understanding of our political and religious history. It is this attempt to change our perceptions that underpins this book.

The Holiday from Hell describes our spiritual journey from the beginning of our holiday on the earth plane to the end of our time in this physical body. It sets out to argue that in understanding the origins of our physical, political and religious beginnings we have the beginnings of harmony and an end to the differences that divide us. Because we are mind, body and spirit and are all of these things intertwined, we can only understand one if we understand all and the only way we can really do this is to look at our existence from a physical, emotional and spiritual view.

As with our spiritual journey through life, our journey through this book has a Beginning, a Middle and an End. As in life, where we start as children, then progress through adolescence to become adults, in the book we start as spiritual children, progress to our spiritual adolescence and then become spiritual adults. There are also three themes running throughout the book that have a massive impact on how we live our lives. These are identity, change, and control.

Identity, Change and Control

Who we are and how we see ourselves has a huge influence on the way we interact with other people. If we see ourselves as isolated individuals we will become selfish and introverted; only looking out for our own interests and not seeing others' problems as any of our concern. However, if we see ourselves as part of a community, we have to be careful that our community does not strengthen itself by making others 'outsiders'. This is just as harmful as being an isolated individual. The answer is that we all have to change the way we see ourselves. Somehow we have to move beyond this narrow vision of who we are and begin to see ourselves as a world community. We all have to realise that everything we do impacts on someone somewhere else in our world and that something as simple as changing our perception of who we are is the only way forward if we don't want to keep repeating the mistakes of the past.

However, change is something we often find quite difficult to deal with yet how we react to change is another aspect of our lives that has a huge impact on our ability to interact with others. Everything eventually changes; because everything is temporary and nothing ever remains the same, the one thing we do have to get used to and adapt to during our time here, is change. Unfortunately, instead of seeing change as an opportunity, we often see it as a threat and react accordingly.

The third theme is control. If we see ourselves as individuals we see ourselves as being in control of our lives and the events within our lives. When things happen that we have no control over, which is inevitable, we react in negative ways. The same applies to communities and nations which are, after all, just the sum of the individuals within them.

If we consider these three aspects of our lives together we can see how important they are and how much influence they have on how we live our lives and how we interact with others.

The first section begins with our interpretation of how we start on our spiritual journey. It continues by looking at the physical, religious and political aspects of that stage of the journey. The second section begins with a brief introduction and then offers our interpretation of this part of our spiritual journey. This is followed by a look at the physical, religious and political aspects of this stage of our journey. As most journeys have a rest stop we have included two chapters of questions and answers on spiritualism, mediumship and healing in the middle section to give you a chance to have a break before starting the final section which looks at The End of our spiritual journey.

Although it may seem that we are critical of many of our political and religious institutions we have tried to emphasise that it is the institutions we are critical of and the way they have evolved, rather than the individuals within them. After all, if we are writing a book that suggests change is needed, we have to outline where we think the problems lie. We cannot do this unless we look at them critically and although we have tried to be as constructive as possible in our criticism our passion sometimes gets the better of us! We hope that any criticism we have made is seen in the constructive way that it is meant.

The final thing to add before we start our holiday is to say that we have tried to make this as easy to read as possible but we have to include a certain amount of detail to support the theories that we are explaining. As with The Re-Enlightenment we cannot emphasise enough that we do not expect you to take our word or believe everything we say. The book is intended to get you to ask your own questions, not take our word as gospel truth. One of the reasons that the world is in a mess is because people have tried to impose their views on others by telling them that their interpretation is the only truth. This is our interpretation. It may not necessarily be yours!

The Holiday from Hell

Contents

	Introduction	9
	The Beginning	21
1.	In the beginning there was spirit	23
2.	In the beginning there was science	47
3.	In the beginning there was religion	63
4.	In the beginning there was politics	79
	The Middle	103
5.	In the middle there was spirit	109
6.	In the middle there was politics	123
7.	In the middle there was religion	145
8.	In the middle there was science	159
9.	Questions and Answers about mediums	175
10.	General Questions and Answers	187
	The End	211
11.	Coming Home – Our Science	215
12.	Coming Home – Our Religion	227

13.	Coming Home – Our Politics	241
14.	Coming Home – Spiritually	259
15.	Conclusion	269
	Appendix 1	283
	Appendix 2	297
	Inspiration & Acknowledgements	299
	About Us	301
	The Re-Enlightenment	303

'We don't receive wisdom; we must discover it for ourselves after a journey that no one can take for us or spare us.'
Marcel Proust (1871 - 1922)

Introduction

Welcome to our spiritual journey

As with all journeys it is quite a good idea to do some preparation before we set out. If we are going to another country it is particularly important to know about the current political and economic status of our proposed destination. Our spiritual journey is no different. Before we leave the comfort of our spiritual existence we need to have a look at the current state of play on the earth plane. This will give us an idea of the problems that we will be facing and help us choose which gifts we should bring with us. As we explained in the previous book our gifts are the emotions, abilities, instincts etc that influence the way we think, speak and act and the way we view the world around us. These and other aspects of our personalities are known collectively as our spiritual gifts.

We all have free will and one of the ways we express our free will is to do with how we use these spiritual gifts. All our spiritual gifts can be used for good or bad. We can also allow them to control us or we can control them. Learning to use these gifts for the benefit of all is part of the process that helps us to evolve spiritually. But, perhaps even more importantly, because the world is the sum of the individuals within it, the way we use them will also affect the evolution of the whole world.

So let us begin by taking a brief critical look at how things are in our world at the time of writing (Autumn 2008).

All the worlds systems are now working at full stretch with very little capacity left for unforeseen emergencies. The financial systems that were relying on credit to keep them buoyant and on hedge funds that provided large profits have proved themselves to be inherently unstable. Similar things have happened in the past where large unsustainable investments have cause instability and collapse. The most notable of these include the South Sea Bubble in the 18th Century and more recently the collapse of Enron where only the intervention of the US government prevented the world's money markets collapsing in a scene reminiscent of the Wall Street Crash of the 1920's.

But in the last few months, on an unprecedented scale, the governments of all the worlds' richest nations have had to step in to prop up the banks and guarantee savings and investments. Shares on the stock market have lost billions of pounds in a relative short time and many countries, including Britain, are now in or on the verge of recession and depression. Despite billions of pounds of tax payers money – our money - being given to the banks to ease lending between them and free up some credit, the banks have done very little to comply.

Lack of consumer confidence is fuelled by the dire predictions from most of the major media who seem to revel in the doom and gloom indicated by the poor economic statistics. Unfortunately this does little to help and actually makes everything worse because it reinforces the fear and leaves people even more reluctant to spend what little money they do have. Repeated calls for the Bank of England to reduce interest rates received little response until last month (November 2008) when they finally reduced them by an unprecedented one and half percent followed by another one percent in December. Unfortunately many banks and building societies have still not bothered to pass them on, preferring to use the opportunity to make a quick profit.

The whole situation is exacerbated by continually rising energy prices. The world's resources are under pressure. The oil that the world's economies depend on is set to run out some time in the next 20 years at current rates of consumption although if this increases, which seems likely, it will happen sooner. The demand for oil has soared over the last couple of years as countries new to capitalism undertook massive building and expansion projects. Oil producers eventually bowed to international pressure and increased production after the price of a barrel of oil hit a record high in the summer leading to rocketing energy and fuel prices. But as the world wide economic slow down has reduced consumption and energy prices have begun to fall back to realistic prices they have now cut back production again to protect their enormous profit margins.

The high price of energy has also led to a scramble to find alternative sources of energy and reignited the debate about nuclear fuel and whether need outweighs any safety concerns. The increase in energy prices has also added to the price of food in two ways. First, rather than being nationally self sufficient in food, much of it is transported round the world so any increase in energy prices mean increased costs for suppliers and transporters.

Secondly, the increase in energy prices has led to an increase in fertile land being used to grow fuel for cars rather than us. This has led to shortages of basic foods especially rice which is the staple food of many poor countries. Despite the promises of our politicians and the best efforts of our charities, one third of the world's population still have two thirds of the world's resources whilst one third still continue to live in abject poverty with not enough to eat or drink.

Even our eco systems seem to be on the verge of collapse as we lurch from shortages of water to floods on a scale never previously seen. Add to this the poor harvests because of adverse weather conditions over the past couple of years and we could be forgiven for thinking that our world is on the brink of catastrophe.

The world's political institutions are also becoming increasingly unstable. Many counties are returning to the dictatorships of the past and those countries that claim to be democratic are constantly under threat from those who would undermine their stability and freedoms. This has resulted in many democracies bringing in policies that are undemocratic and that undermine the basic principles of their own democracy. The indigenous populations of those democracies seem unwilling or unable to see what is happening. Governments are elected on minority votes whilst the majority of the population are unrepresented. The media of these nations pumps out a constant diatribe of what, to paraphrase Marx, could be described as 'opium for the masses'. Whilst the populations of these countries are busy watching trivia, changes are happening under their nose that they are not even aware of.

The world's social systems are straining to cope with the results of the growing number of dictatorships as their citizens seek freedom in other countries whose governments are liberal and democratic in nature. But many of these new citizens do not understand democracy and have no understanding of the duties and responsibilities that go hand in hand with the rights that they expect. Others find their new countries lacking in spiritual resources even though they may appear to be rich in material success. Coming from a variety of illiberal cultures they find it hard to adjust their lives to fully assimilate into the culture of their adopted country. Many do not wish to fully assimilate because they see the unlimited freedoms of speech, clothes, ways of life and female equality as alien. This coupled with the lack of parental/familial respect adds to their feelings of alienation.

Many of these cultural groups have a religious basis. Because many of the religious institutions of the world are also becoming less secure with falling congregations and constant media scepticism, those who feel their beliefs are under attack resort to fundamentalism. This takes many forms but is essentially another form of fascism, albeit with a religious basis. All faiths have their extremists although they operate in different ways.

So is there any answer to these problems or like other civilisations before us, are we doomed to fade into obscurity?

The earth is rather like our playground. It is here that we come to learn our lessons and it is these lessons that will help us to progress spiritually. One of the most basic lessons we learn as we are growing up is how to behave. We learn what is considered acceptable behaviour and what isn't. This is something we would normally learn from our role models. Our role models are primarily those who are most involved with bringing us up. This is usually but not always, our parents. But it is not just parents who are role models. Every adult in society is a potential role model for our children. Children learn by example. Therefore, everything we do impacts on them and it is from us that they learn what is and isn't acceptable.

It is important for all of us, particularly our children, that someone sets the boundaries and limits of what is and is not appropriate. Codes of satisfactory behaviour are decided by the society within which we live and are reflected in its legislation and criminal justice system. They often have their roots in religious teachings and are constantly updated as we reassess how we view certain types of behaviour. Some things that were considered unacceptable in the past have now become a normal part of our lives. Other things that were considered normal behaviour are now outlawed or viewed with disfavour.

However, like children left too long unsupervised in the playground, we seem to have not only forgotten why we are really here, but also how to set these boundaries. Think about what happens if you have a dog and you allow it to run wild with no set rules. It will become aggressive, unruly and a danger to itself and everyone it comes into contact with. It could be argued that we have now reached the point in our society where our boundaries need to be reassessed and redrawn. This is not to say that there should be even more legislation, nor should we return to fundamentalist politics and dictatorships of either the past or those that exist in other less democratic countries. But it is now time we all grew up and started to take responsibility for our world. It is time we all worked together to decide exactly what kind of world we really want to live in and what kind of world we really want to leave to our children. As we have said, we all have free will, but with any form of freedom there comes responsibility. The more freedom we have, the more responsibility we have to ensure we use our freedom wisely.

It is now time to look at the chaos and damage around us and decide what we are going to do about it. After all, if you leave your children to run wild in your home sooner or later you will need to take charge, clean up the mess and sort it all out. This is no different. The earth is our home and we have been allowed to run wild and make a mess. Now it is time to start the big clean up. And where better to start than with our thoughts, words and actions. It is now time to grow up spiritually and remember why we are really here.

In the Re Enlightenment we argued for a new identity, one that could override all the social, cultural, political and religious identities that divide us at present. We called this our spiritual identity. But what exactly is this and how could it possibly take the place of all the other identities that coexist uneasily in our world today? The answer to the second question is simply that it can't because it is not meant to. It has no need to replace other forms of identity because it will stand along side them and when differences arise it is our spiritual identity that will reconcile the tensions between them.

Of course this sounds like an impossible task and we agree that it is not easy. But nothing that is worth having is easy. If it was we would not appreciate it. If you have to save up to buy something you enjoy it much more than if you just go straight out and buy it. If you have to fight for something because you are in danger of losing it, it becomes even more precious. Our occupation of the earth goes back several centuries and the logical progression would be for us to be advancing both scientifically, politically, and spiritually from those earliest civilisations. But this does not appear to be the case. If anything we appear to have regressed considerably and are only now making up some of the ground that we have lost over the past three or four centuries.

The same appears to be true of ourselves. Although we seem to have advanced from those ancient civilisations that we look back on is this really the case? Progress seems to be extremely slow and painful and we often seem to be repeating the same mistakes and having the same experiences over and over again. But we are not just individuals. We are all part of our communities and our communities are part of our country and our country is part of the world. Like our personal spiritual journeys, the countries of the world also seem to be undertaking their own spiritual journeys. And like us they seem doomed to keep repeating the same mistakes and experiences, some of them again and again, albeit in slightly different forms.

To discover the reasons for this we need to go back to the beginning and rediscover our roots. Not just our spiritual roots, but our physical, social, political and religious roots. This means opening our minds, stepping outside our physical selves and the stories that we have been told and listening to our spiritual selves. In other words, we need to see things from another perspective – a spiritual perspective.

Both our physical and spiritual evolutions are part of our spiritual journey and as with all journeys ours starts at the beginning. But before we start on our journey it is important to reiterate that we do not have all the answers. We are not historians or theologians in the wider academic sense. However, we, like you, have access to books, libraries, the internet and our spirit guides. We do not expect you to agree with everything in this book. We would be extremely worried if you did. The book is intended to spark debate and to encourage you to open your minds and ask your own questions. One of the hardest things about writing these books was to avoid falling into the trap so many philosophers fall into – that of stating that one theory is true and everything else is wrong. These books are our interpretation of the message we have been given to share with you. Interpretation is highly personal and comes from our own experiences of life. Our experiences of life will be totally different from someone else's experience of life. Thus our interpretation will be different from someone else's interpretation. This does not mean that one is better than another or even that one has more validity than another.

We would not presume to tell you how to think. We only

presume to ask you to think for yourself, to ask questions of yourself and others and find the truth that you are happy with. We only ask that you do not let others dictate how you should think. Allowing someone else to impose their particular interpretation of the spiritual message has led to centuries of war and misery. That was fine when we were spiritual children. As children we accept the interpretation of life that we are given by our elders until we are old enough to make up our own minds. However, once we become teenagers we begin to think for ourselves and to seek our own identity. We have been children long enough. We need to now embrace our spiritual teenage years and to do what all teenagers do.

Teenagers rebel against the systems around them because they can see the problems, the inconsistencies, the hypocrisy that we have learnt to live with. They are seeing the world with fresh eyes and they have fresh ideas as to how things can be changed. It's rather like when you start a new job and you are full of enthusiasm and innovation. We do not have to continue to live the way that we have lived for the last few thousand years. There is a better way, but it is not for us to tell you what that way is. We hope that reading this book will cause you to question the world you live in. We hope that you will begin to take an interest in the way the world is because if you do not understand it you cannot suggest ways to change things. But most importantly of all we ask that you look beyond the physical and think with your spiritual self. Think what changes your spiritual self would like to see. Think what kind of world your spiritual self would like to come back to in the future. As we said in The Re-Enlightenment, if we don't resolve the problems now we will have to come back at a later time and sort them out then. By then the problems could be much worse and take far longer to resolve.

Solving the planet's problems is something that will need all of us to work together, it cannot be done solely by individuals working alone. Although we are individuals we have to also remember that we are part of a whole. We should not impose our solutions or our interpretations on others because it is the experiences of the whole that will provide the solutions. Debate stimulates others to think and encourages others to come up with solutions. Although the final result may be totally different from the original proposal it has still evolved from the original idea and without that original idea it would never have happened. Debate also encourages others to participate which gives people confidence in the solution because it is a solution they have helped reach. We invariably listen to all perspectives and consider the effects on all those concerned before making major individual decisions. We need to do the same when making collective decisions.

We can never completely understand another's perspective because of the differences in our experiences. This is because we are all individuals with our own pathway to follow. Our paths will cross the paths of others and we will share experiences but although these experiences may be similar, they will never be identical. There are many reasons for this but one of the reasons our experiences will never be entirely identical is because we are starting from different places. A good example of this is when we leave home. Our experience of leaving home is not only influenced by where we are going and what we are going to do, it is also influenced by where we have come from, by our own unique experience of home.

Home

What does the word 'home' mean to you? What picture comes into your head when you think about coming home? At the end of any holiday or any journey, however, long, however protracted, we either come back to our original home or we arrive at a new home. So what is 'home'?

'Home' does not just mean the roof over your head. That is just your house/flat/dwelling – a physical building. We do not talk about the houseless – we talk about the homeless. This is because home is so much more that a physical place. At home we learn our first steps, we speak our first words, we are introduced to the world and we learn to follow the examples of our parents and guardians. We learn to interpret the world and to accept the interpretation we are given by our guardians. The meaning of 'home' is much more important than just its physical sense because it has an emotional meaning too. The word 'home' conjures up images. Home is somewhere we close the door on the world. Home is somewhere we are safe and secure. Home is somewhere we are loved and where those we love are. Home is where the heart is. All these things and more come to mind when we speak of home.

However, 'home' is also an ideological concept in that our image of home is also entwined with other images. It can be part of our image of our community or our town, or it can be part of our image of our culture and it can also be part of our image of our country/nation. Thus our ideal of home is also part of our identity. It is part of what defines us a person – a physical being. For a recent example of this we only have to look at WW2 films made in America and hear them talking of 'moms apple pie'.

Another example could be those who have moved to another country and may have lived there many years but still refer to their previous country as 'home'. These images of home are rich in symbolism and hidden meanings. They imply a sense of belonging, a sense of shared culture and experience, a shared history and something that is found within a geographical border – in fact all the things that can be identified as part of our sense of national identity.

But if home is part of our identity what about those whose homes are not a place of safety? What about those for whom the word home conjures up feelings of fear, terror, failure – who feel threatened by the very idea of 'home'? What about those who have no home, have lost their home or have never had anywhere they can call home? What effect does this have on their sense of identity?

We will look at these questions in more detail later but now its time to begin our journey. When we start on a journey we often start from our home and in The Re-Enlightenment we talked about our home in a spiritual sense and how heaven/nirvana is the home of our spiritual selves. From our spiritual home we travel to our physical home and in The Re-Enlightenment we explained that our bodies are our home whilst we are in a physical form. However, several things must happen before we can take a physical form. One of the most obvious is that our physical form has to have somewhere to go to, somewhere that it can physically exist. In the case of our physical bodies the place that we call home is the earth. We will begin looking at that in more detail in Chapter 2. But, equally important, our spirit must make several decisions before we take a physical form and it is this process we will begin looking at in Chapter 1.

'You are a child of the Universe, no less than the moon and the stars; you have a right to be here. And whether or not it is clear to you, no doubt the Universe is unfolding as it should.'
Max Ehrmann

In the beginning.......

The following chapters, in particular 2, 3 and 4 have quite a lot of information in them and although we have tried to keep this to a minimum you may find some of it a bit complicated and perhaps not what you were expecting. But life does not always give us what we expect or even what we think we deserve and sometimes it is the things we don't plan for, the things that we don't expect, that turn out to be the most rewarding.

It is not particularly important for you to remember everything, rather that you are aware that these mysteries exist. We have included them to provide some background and to support the theories we are explaining. We hope that you will find it interesting and that it will encourage you to explore further. However, if you do find it difficult we would rather you skipped bits and read the rest of the book, than gave up in the first section. You can always go back and read the rest later.

The best way to think about it is to consider that it's a bit like when we were children and we were given lots and lots of information and not all of it was easy to understand. Although some of it was quite straightforward, some of it made no sense at all, other bits went in one ear and out of the other and some of it only came in useful when we were older. Just imagine that we are like spiritual children and this is the beginning of our spiritual journey. The world is an exciting place with all sorts of mysteries and ideas that we can't always grasp easily. But, like children, our enthusiasm to arrive will carry us through to the next stage. So take your time and enjoy. Although we share our journey with others it is an individual journey and it is important that we travel at our own pace.

Our holiday begins, as all holidays usually begin, at home. We have now reached a point in our spiritual development where we need to spread our wings a little and put into practice some of the things we have learnt. Preparing for our holiday on earth is no different from arranging our holidays when we are here. We need to choose our destination, the time we are going, what we need to take with us, what we are going to do when we are there and, most importantly, we need to choose our travelling companions.

" Well, I WAS (verbal emphasis on "was") dead, but then I was in the waiting room to be made well again. When I was a baby again, a man with spiky hair (she loves anyone with spiky hair at the moment) sat me on his lap and showed me into several rooms with different mummies in them. When I saw you, I just said " I want her to be my Mummy because she looks lovely – you are so pretty Mummy".[1]

*When you were born, you cried and the world rejoiced; live your life so that when you die, the world cries and you rejoice.---
Cherokee Saying*

Chapter 1

..........there was spirit

According to the Kabbalah, before time began, there was an infinite source of energy. It was the only reality and it stretched into infinity, beyond time and space. The essence of this energy was all giving, all sharing, endless fulfilment and enlightenment and limitless joy. Within it there was everything human kind has ever wanted from personal fulfilment from peace of mind and happiness to health. The kabbalah calls this energy the First Cause.

---

[1] This was sent to us by a friend who was happy for it to be included in this book. 'As promised I am writing to tell you about a conversation I had with my 5 year old daughter Amy a couple of weeks ago. We were actually in the car at the time, I was driving. Suddenly, out of the blue, Amy said "Do you know why I chose you to be my Mummy?" Thinking this to be one of those childlike questions that go absolutely nowhere I rather dismissively said, "No Darling, why did you choose me?". I was stunned by the following reply. She continued with: ' You know my beliefs on this subject but, with her at the tender age of 5, I have never discussed them with Amy, nor in front of her. I cannot even begin to imagine why she used the term "waiting room", never mind in relation to a place to be made well again'.

But the energy needed something to give this endless enlightenment and joy to. So it created the Vessel. The Vessel consisted of an infinite desire to receive. This meant there was now infinite energy and infinite desire. All the souls, past and present, were in the vessel. This energy has been known as God and Divine Creator, but the ancient Kabbalists referred to it by its Hebrew name of *Or*. *Or* means 'the light'. The light contains all the colours of the rainbow and illuminates eternity. Everything we do is actually in pursuit of the light because it is the light that is true happiness. The light is not God but comes from God's positive attributes and spiritual energy.

The infinite Vessel consisted of a female and male energy. These two energies were one and are known by the code name of Adam and Eve. Kabbalists believe that the entire Bible is a code and like any complex code requires deciphering. The creation of the vessel is the only creation that has ever happened and it happened before the origin of the universe. The unity between the two – the energy and the vessel - was called the endless world. But there was a problem. The vessel had inherited the genes of its creator – the energy. This left it with a desire to create not only its own fulfilment but also its own happiness. It had also inherited the energy's desire to share this fulfilment and happiness and to control its own affairs. So when the energy gave the Vessel its infinite desire the Vessel felt cheated because it had not earned its reward. It refused to accept the light and this caused a big spiritual explosion that created the world, as we now know it. It is this spiritual explosion that scientists call the Big Bang.

In the 16th century Rabbi Isaac Luria described the birth of the universe:

The universe was created out of nothingness from a single point of light. This nothingness is called the Endless World. The Endless World was filled with infinite light. The light was then contracted to a single point, creating primordial space. Beyond this point nothing is known. Therefore the point is called the beginning. After the contraction the Endless World issued forth a ray of light. This ray of light then expanded rapidly. All matter emanated from that point.

Science describes the universe as beginning in a single point from nothingness. Although it had no depth, width or length it contained the whole of space, time and matter.

The light then gave the vessel time and space to create and evolve into its own divine nature. But just what is our divine nature and furthermore, how do we create it and evolve into it?

Just as we evolve physically we also evolve spiritually and one of the first things to remember is that our earthly ideas of progress and evolution are not necessarily the same as those of Spirit. As we explained before, to evolve spiritually we have to take physical form.

The beginning of our spiritual journey starts long before we come to the earth plane and as we said in the introduction, we are starting from different places. As spirit we are still continuing out spiritual evolution. This can take many forms but as here we have free will and a choice as to the direction we wish to go. For instance, if we wish to become teachers of healing all our choices, both in spirit and on the earth plane will reflect that. If we wish to be teachers of philosophy, although we will still need to experience the full range of emotions and experiences, our path will take a different direction and the emphasis will be different.

If we have chosen to be a healer trainer we will work initially in the Halls of Healing. There we will learn to cleanse and heal those returning from the earthplane. The time this healing takes varies and depends on the level of development of the returning spirit and the amount of healing they received before returning to spirit. As spirits this not only allows us to develop our healing powers, it also allows us to learn how the energies of the earth plane affect the spirit. We are then able to put this knowledge and these experiences to good use when we are channelling healing through those on the earth plane. We will also watch and learn from those on higher levels and when we are ready, in conjunction with our healing in spirit, we will begin to work with healers on the earthplane. This will already have been agreed before those spirits return to the earthplane. We will be matched with healers whose energy works in harmony with our own. The personality that the healer has chosen will also be taken into account as it is important that both healer in spirit and the healer on the earth plane are totally in tune with each other. Then, when they have reached the appointed time we will begin work with them.

For a spirit just learning to work with healers on the earth plane it can take a while to adjust to the energy of the earth and to the energy of the healer. Even though we may have been on the earth plane quite recently, once we have returned to Spirit, it is still quite hard to remember the feel of the energy and the vibration that exists there. We also have to remember that the earth healer will have been affected by the energy and vibrations of the earth plane. This means their energy is not as pure as it was whilst they were in Spirit. We also have to wait for them to reach the time that has been agreed and to learn that we cannot work with them whenever it would seem to be necessary. It can seem to the healer in spirit that they have been waiting quite a long time for their healer to be ready. The results of this can sometimes causes the healer to shake quite violently as the healer in spirit comes through too forcefully. But this is easily remedied and both healer in spirit and the healer on the earth plane soon adjust to each other. As we work with the earth plane healer we are continually learning. We process the dis-ease within the physical body of the patient and channel the healing energy back through the healer to the patient. If there is something we are not sure of we will ask our own teachers for guidance. This is done in an instant as we pass the ailment to our teachers and they channel the healing energy back through us and the healer to the patient.

Just as spiritual healers on the earth plane have several guides, so we work with several spiritual healers on the earthplane and as we progress we move on to other spiritual healers. The spiritual healer on the earthplane also progresses and they have new guides coming in to replace their original guides. It is an ongoing process of continuing development that only finishes when the healer in spirit is ready to return to the earthplane. This normally happens because the healer in spirit has reached the limit of their development without gaining some more experience on the earthplane.

However, this does not mean that all spirits come to the earthplane. Some choose never to come here and others only come once or twice. This is similar to those professors who live their entire life studying theories of life but rarely venture out from their secluded cloisters of their university to experience actual life. They are chosen to be specialists in their field but they do not have the broad overview of other spirits. They are irreplaceable as fonts of absolute knowledge and it is to them that we, as spirits, always go for advice if specialist advice is needed. There are also other very ancient spirits who have progressed so far that they are able to come to earth briefly whenever they choose to affect certain changes. Because they are so highly developed they usually pass unnoticed and when they return to spirit they do not need to go through the Halls of Healing but go straight through to their own level. But we will explain more about this in the next book.

If we have decided that we wish to specialise in philosophy then we will work in the Halls of Learning and the Great Library. It is here that all the answers to all our questions lie. It is also here that all the pathways with all their intricacies are stored. Those who wish to specialise in philosophy must understand how everything works and how everything fits together. It is here that we go to choose our next life.

We choose to take another life because we have decided that to progress further we must take a physical form. This is because it is through our experiences within the physical body that we evolve quicker and also it is our time in the physical that allows us to practice the things we have learnt whilst in spirit. Much of our learning in spirit is theoretical. We can experience emotions in an abstract theoretical way and we can predict to a certain extent the reactions that we will have to those events and actions that happen on the earth plane. But without exposure to the vibrations of the earth plane and the distractions there it is very difficult for us to truly experience the full range of emotions.

Long before our spirit decides to take another life the spirits in the Halls of learning and the Great Library will begin the search for several lives that will be interlocking and that provide the types of development needed. They will select a considerable number for the spirit to choose from. This is a very complicated process. Not only must the lives contain the necessary tools and gifts, at the right stage of development, they must also fit with all the other lives of those who will be returning with you. It is very much like writing a book where all the strands must come together to produce the desired finished result, except that there are billions of lives to design, many of which touch in ways that may never be obvious but are always significant.

Furthermore, although the lives are designed to touch there is also the added element of free will as the returning spirits are distracted and tempted to use their gifts in ways that may change the overall direction of their pathway. Like our spiritual journey as outlined in this book, our journey through life is in three sections – The Beginning, The Middle and The End. At each of these points, and at many others, there may be special pointers embedded within these lives to enable the spirit to change direction. Alternatively, other spirits may be directed into the pathway of a spirit to give them the opportunity to change direction. However, the spirit still has that free choice. They can ignore the pointers and carry on down the same route. There is no element of force.

Having decided that it is time to put into practice the things we have studied spiritually, we go to the halls of learning and we ask the scribes to find us a life that fits with our studies and that also takes account of the previous experiences we have had. There is little point repeating experiences unless there is another aspect we wish to learn so we will look to take a life that takes account of this. You have to remember that all our lives are interconnected and all the experiences within those lives are interconnected in the sense that they all contained the different spiritual objectives that we will have undertaken throughout many existences. Thus the role that we take has to be exactly right for our current spiritual development and also for the other spirits who are going to play their part in our evolution. Because their lives will interconnect with ours their lives must also be chosen at the same time. There are exceptions to this and these exceptions will also include the types of intervention by the ancient spirits that we mentioned earlier.

We also have to choose the appropriate time frame on the earth that will allow us to achieve our spiritual objectives. For some lives the exact time may not be the most important consideration. If your main spiritual task is to experience or overcome a particular emotion, then it is the people you interact with and the way you relate to them that will be your priority when choosing your life. However, if you have elected to do something that is specifically related to a particular time frame or your experiences are intended to relate to some particular episode, then that timing must take precedence. Otherwise you would not be able to achieve that goal.

Finally we need to choose the country we wish to be born in. This, together with the time frame, is potentially one of the most important decisions our spirits will make. It does not take much imagination to see how different our lives would be if we had been born in another country, under a different political or religious regime.

With all these aspects to take into consideration it can be difficult to know where to begin so our first task is to decide exactly what it is that we wish to achieve spiritually in the life that we choose. What is the best way to achieve these spiritual goals? Is it through the experience of great wealth or great poverty? Would these aims be achieved best through the experience of fame and power or through anonymity?

All lives will have some happiness, some joy, some pain and some sorrow, although they may not be in equal measure. We will need to look at how we used our gifts in previous lives and see whether we need to have the same gifts or whether we are ready to go on to the next stage and experience things in a different way. We might still bring with us the same gifts but we may be learning to use them in different ways this time. Our choice of life hinges entirely on the following question: What is it that we need at that time spiritually to progress? Whilst we are all sitting here thinking how nice it would be to experience great wealth and a long happy pain free life in which to enjoy it, we have to remember that in spirit this would not be a consideration! The only consideration would be our spiritual evolution and to that end we as spirits may choose a life that our earthly rational selves would not even consider let alone choose.

The scribes in the Halls of Learning will give us a choice of lives and it is up to our spiritual selves to decide which is the most appropriate. Fortunately we do not have to make this decision by ourselves. There is plenty of advice and help available and the advice and help available is genuine because unlike on the earth plane, the other spirits that we consult only have our best spiritual interests at heart. We also need this help because it is important that the life that we choose fits with the lives that other spirits choose. This is because they will all intertwine and interconnect with each other. It is also part of our spiritual development that we are able to make decisions about our earthly lives using the spiritual experience and knowledge that we have gained in both our earthly and spiritual evolutions. As on the earth plane it is this experience and knowledge that guides us to make the choices that are right for us.

One of the things we could find quite hard when we come to the earth plane would be to distance ourselves from the other spirits we have been studying with. In spirit the concept of oneness is an automatic, unconscious reality. This can be particularly so if their role appears to be one of hindering our spiritual progression on the earth plane rather than helping. We use the word 'appears' because to learn certain lessons it may be that the spirit that is giving us that experience is causing us great distress. They may have chosen that life purely to give us that experience because it is that experience that helps us evolve quicker than we would have done so had they not been there. This is another reason why we should not judge another persons' spiritual pathway. As physical beings we have no real comprehension of their role in our life, other than the one that presents itself to us whilst we are here. They too may have no comprehension of their true role in our lives otherwise it would hinder their ability to play their part. It is not until we return to Spirit that the truth is revealed to us.

To help us with this, one of the aspects of the lives that we choose is the absence of any real memory of our spiritual existence. But this is not always the case as we will have other lives that do allow us to remember this oneness, this concept of oneness with other spirits that are here. Often our earthly lives will contain a stronger element of spiritual identity once we reach a certain level. But this is not to say that all those who preach this oneness are more evolved than those who find it hard to grasp this concept. The negative vibrations of the earth can often affect those who are more spiritually evolved purely because they are more receptive to it. That is why it is always important to remember to use the white light of protection whenever you are communicating with spirit. (If you have not read the Re-Enlightenment please see appendix 2). Any unprotected communication can lead to an invitation to negative entities to come through and this, in turn, can cause those who are aware of their spiritual identity to become unduly influenced by earthly considerations and forget their true path. There are also those who do not remember this oneness or do not believe it, but see it as a way of making money or gaining power over others.

It may also be that one's spiritual pathway is for understanding to be difficult. After all, the more difficult this pathway the more likely we are to progress if we can achieve the tasks that we have set ourselves. But as we said earlier, we only know our own pathway and that is buried deep within our soul. We are therefore not in a position to judge another's pathway. And nor should we. The only thing that should concern us in this sense is whether we are achieving our own spiritual objectives. We will all evolve eventually – it is not a race so there is no need to feel jealous or envious of others. Remember the analogy in the first book about travelling to Scotland from Cornwall. We all start at different places and take different routes but we will all get there eventually. This life is only one small part of the journey. We have to remember that we have an infinite number of lives in which to evolve. We always progress at a pace that is right for us and when we are ready we will finish this part of our spiritual journey. Rather like the holiday where you didn't get to see all the historic castles or visit all the clubs; if we haven't managed to achieve all our spiritual goals there is always next time.

Of course it may be that jealousy is one of the gifts we have chosen to overcome in this physical existence. If that is the case it is even more important that we do not allow ourselves to follow this negative pathway. Jealousy is a very negative emotion in that it leads to many other negative emotions and often sets up a chain of events that will cause considerable pain to a great number of people including the person who is jealous. Invariably they are the person who suffers the most because they waste so much of their life feeling sorry for themselves, trying to out do the person they are jealous of or to cause them harm. Because the person they are jealous of is often totally unaware of their feelings they are busy living and enjoying their life. The jealous person, however, is wasting their own life and their own emotional energy. If they used that energy in a positive way just think how much light they could bring into the world.

And of course this is one of our tasks - to bring light into the world and to help others whose pathways seem dark and troubled. By helping others to remember their true purpose here we can all bring healing and light to our troubled world. Every time we send out a healing thought or a positive thought we are adding to the light in the world. You can join with many others doing just that. Every Saturday spend 5 minutes sending white light and healing to the world. Five minutes a week is no time at all to us but if we all do this consider the difference we can make. (For more information see Appendix 2). Conversely, each time we send out a negative thought we are adding to the darkness in the world. Given the choice, which would you rather do? This is within the capabilities of all of us, whatever our level of spiritual evolution. As we said in the first book healers are not special. We are all healers and the ability to heal is in all pathways. We just have to make that choice and look into our souls and remember our true spiritual purpose.

Once we have chosen our life and we have worked out the pathway and the broad outline of the direction that life will take, we then need to choose the gifts that we will bring with us. There are so many to choose from and it is important that the gifts we choose give us the greatest chance of achieving our spiritual goals. It is very difficult for us in our physical form subject to all the earthly vibrations to understand the choices that our spiritual selves have made, but if we change our perceptions of our purpose here it becomes easier to understand. Remember the choices we make are to help us evolve, not to make us rich or powerful unless that is part of the experience we need to have to achieve our spiritual objectives. Our choices are also, in part, influenced by the choices that we have made before. We may have not completely resolved some of the issues that we have had with certain gifts in our previous incarnations.

Phobias

We have all heard the theory that some of the phobias we have not only stem from things that may have happened in our childhood or early years but also from our previous incarnations. This is partly true. A phobia is essentially an irrational fear of something that in many cases other people would not normally experience.

Like most things our phobias are something that not only affect our mind, body and spirit, but also stem from an emotional (mind), physical (body) and spiritual (spirit) cause. From an emotional standpoint we may fear something because we have seen a film or some other image, or read something that has triggered something in our minds that has then fed our imagination and has then grown out of all proportion. We may also mentally associate that thing with something that happened in our life at that time that changed our lives in some sense. It may have been an unpleasant event so any trigger of this makes us fearful. But it does not have to have been an unpleasant experience, it may have been for the better or to put us on a new course but at the time it was seen as a threat to the stability of our current life. Therefore we associate it with something bad.

From a physical standpoint our fear may stem from the fact that it does not look, feel or even sound nice. Alternatively its physical presence may just seem threatening in some way even if it actually has a really small physical presence.

From a spiritual standpoint it may well be a residue that is left from a previous life, a memory that has not been completely erased. But if this is the case it is not an accident or a coincidence. This is something you will have chosen to be there so that you can learn to exert your willpower and overcome your fear. It is just another, albeit different, form of the gift of fear. Thus it is one of the gifts you have chosen to bring with you as you aim to put another tick on your list of spiritual targets.

The gift of fear, like all gifts, has positive and negative aspects. The positive aspects are when it warns you not to jump off a high building or jump in front of a train. When you feel fear your body also reacts and goes into fight or flee mode. Your brain, which is your computer, assimilates all the relevant information and makes the decision as to which you should do. But your mind assimilates and processes all your emotional responses so if it decides they are more relevant than the logical information your brain is processing it will err in favour of those. Thus you will flee from something that may be totally harmless from a physical pint of view. It is getting in touch with your own spiritual instincts that will help you tell the difference.

Once we have decided which gifts we will bring with us, and our spiritual soul mates have also decided, we will choose a time to return. Everything is planned to the last detail. We will not only be watching the physical, political and religious activity on the earth plane, we will also be watching as our 'parents' are born and as they meet and as we are conceived. We will watch with growing interest and excitement as the moment approaches for us to return. We will already feel an attachment to the people who will be our parents and our family. This attachment can remain even if there is a 'sudden' change of plan.

Occasionally something will happen that will mean we are unable to take that life. This does not mean it is 'unexpected' because Spirit is omnipotent and therefore nothing happens that is not known or expected. In these case the 'unexpected' happens as an experience for both parents and family and also as part of our spiritual experience and development in spirit. Even though we do not take that life the attachment is still there. It is this attachment that the mother, in particular, feels towards her unborn child even though the spirit that would have taken that form when it is born has not yet done so. Although there is no spirit around the baby because it is in the mother's womb and is thus surrounded and enclosed by the mother's spirit, the baby is still a physical part of the mother because the foetus is a live physical being. It is at the moment of birth that spirit enters and surrounds the baby. Even babies who only take a few breaths will have their own spirit because this is still an experience for that spirit and as such is part of that spirit's development.

Arrival on the earth plane

Once we have arrived here in our earthly body the process of spiritually evolving begins in earnest. We can now experience physical emotions and discomforts. The first of these is usually fear and that is why we cry when we are born. Remember our spirit is unable to feel cold, heat, pain or any other physical feeling. Imagine the shock to our system when we realise that we are back here again! Even though we may not be able to articulate this feeling in any way it is still there. We now have a physical body and although at first we are still aware of our spiritual identity our spirit knows that this comfort will soon be gone as we begin our journey. We are also suddenly aware that we are a separate being. Not only are we separate in a physical sense but we are now a **separated** spirit. We are not a **separate** spirit because the concept of separateness is entirely physical. As spirit we could not even contemplate, let alone experience or understand this concept of separateness. It is this concept of separateness that is the most important thing that we have to overcome here because it is the concept of **one ness** that is the foundation of our spiritual identity.

So, we have now arrived on the earthplane and our spiritual journey in this body is about to begin.

According to a recent scientific study although knowledge seems to accumulate as people grow up, many abilities actually decline. There are many cases of child prodigies who grow up to become 'average' adults. This is because during the process of learning they also acquire experiences and it is these experiences that influence their growth more than the knowledge that they can gain. This also applies to the spiritual gifts we bring with us. Many of these gifts are influenced by these experiences and are bought into play by these experiences and unconsciously we begin to allow them to control our responses to the world. The more deep rooted these experiences become the harder it is to dislodge them and the harder it is to see beyond them to the original spirit that we were when we first came here.

Imagine the new spirit as a pure white cloth. The more that cloth is used the dirtier it becomes until, however many times it is washed it becomes impossible to restore it to its original purity. Along with this purity goes our spiritual wisdom, and our sense of spiritual identity. Instead we embrace new forms of physical identity and we allow these to override our spiritual identity. The further we travel down the road of our spiritual journey, the further we travel from our spiritual identity.

As children we take our identity from our parents and guardians. Although we eventually find a more individual physical identity within us this does not really find expression until we reach our teenage years. As small children the way we think, act and speak comes from watching and copying the example set to us by the adults and other members of the family we grow up in. If we are shown love and affection we grow up being able to show love and affection to others. If we are treated badly or abused we learn that this is the way to behave.

The word 'abuse' means anything that causes someone else harm and includes, emotional, physical or sexual abuse. Nearly all forms of abuse involve some kind of emotional abuse. The Wikipedia definition is as follows: *Abuse is a general term for the misuse of a person or thing, causing harm to the person or thing, to the abuser, or to someone else. Abuse can be something as simple as damaging a piece of equipment through using it the wrong way, or as serious as severe maltreatment of a person. Abuse may be direct and overt, or may be disguised and covert.*

If we see one parent hitting the other or hitting us we assume this is the right way to behave. If we are ignored, neglected, belittled or humiliated it is not only our physical development that is affected. It is also our emotional, psychological and spiritual development as well. It is here as children that we begin to develop our personalities and part of this process concerns the developing of our coping strategies. If we suffer abuse it can not only encourage the development of personality disorders it can also set the conditions for mental health problems in the future.

Then we go to school. At school the way we are treated affects how we learn. If we are continually shouted at and made to feel stupid we will not learn because we will associate learning with something unpleasant.

If we have fun we will learn so much more and we will also associate learning with fun. If our family reads a lot of books or are continually discussing world events then we will grow up with a love of reading and an interest in what is happening in the world. The same is true of the opposite. If we did not have a good time at school and hate learning and books we will influence how our children see books and education. Being unable to read or write properly in a world where it is so important excludes people unnecessarily. It also perpetuates bullying because children, like adults, will always strive to fit in with their peers.

This also works in the opposite way. If the most vocal group in a child's class despises education they too will feel uncomfortable about learning because it marks them out as an outsider. It is often not considered cool to be good at your lessons. This is because those who are often most vocal and therefore set these parameters often come from chaotic backgrounds where education is something to be sneered at. These children are influenced by their own family who in turn were influenced by their family and their background and so on.

Children who come from chaotic backgrounds also suffer in other ways. They often lack a sense of who they are because a sense of identity begins at home. This can lead them into even more traumatic situations whilst they look for an identity. Becoming the local gang leader will give a young person a sense of importance, but also a sense of identity. Because of their position other youngsters will look up to them, will give them the love and respect that is lacking in their home. Although this respect may, in fact, be based on fear, someone from a disadvantaged background may not be able to distinguish between love and fear because of the way they have been bought up.

It will also give them the family that is missing in their life. Sometimes, those who lack a sense of family identity will join the armed forces. This too will provide them with a sense of family, a sense of belonging and most importantly a sense of identity. But this only lasts as long as the military career does. Unless there is something else in that young persons' life, they are only deferring the problems until they leave the forces. When that happens the problems are often exacerbated. Before they joined up they knew something was missing from their life but were not completely sure what it was. Once they leave the armed forces they have experienced a family. They have experienced belonging. They now know what they are missing. If they have no where to go and no family to go back to, this feeling is magnified many times over.

The problem can be made worse if they are returning from fighting a war that is controversial. When World War 2 was finished everybody was in a similar situation so there was a general sense of empathy. The armed forces were held in high esteem. This is not the case now. The Gulf wars and the war in Afghanistan have divided the country and many people are unable to distinguish between those who make the decision to go to war - the government – and those who are employed to carry out those orders. Many of those who leave before 6 years receive limited resettlement advice and if they leave with a pension they are expected to live on that so are not given any welfare benefits whilst looking for civilian employment. If they need medical treatment because of mental and physical injuries sustained whilst fighting for the fellow citizens of their country, they have to join the waiting lists with civilians. They are not given any special treatment and in some cases are even asked to remove their uniforms in case they offend people. Some high profile department stores have even stated that uniformed personnel are not allowed in their store because they are likely to have people ask them where the toilet is. Even if you are a secure confident person from a secure background this kind of treatment is likely to have far reaching effects.

Historically, the armed forces have always been treated badly by governments and this has not changed in recent years. It is this lack of respect and recognition that led to the birth of charities whose remit is to help ex service personnel. The veterans of the two world wars have been treated pretty badly by all governments since the end of the wars and especially as they have got older. But they grew up in a generation that accepted the way they were treated and 'knew their place'. The veterans from the Falklands conflict have come from a different generation and are less likely to put up the same kind of treatment as their previous generation.

But the veterans from the Gulf wars and Afghanistan are from a generation that is even further removed from those veterans of the First and Second World Wars. They are not used to being told no or being ignored. Because of retention problems they are recruiting in ever increasing numbers. This means there is now an increasing number of young people who are trained to kill and act as a unified body. It might be useful for politicians to remember this because if they do ever become seriously disgruntled and organised the country could face serious problems.

As with members of the ex-Services, politicians seem quite content to leave it to charities to look after the really vulnerable members of society. Whilst local authority children's homes had serious flaws, are foster homes doing any better when many of the children in care are moved from home to home, on average, every 18 months? This reinforces their lack of identity and feelings of low self esteem and these feeling increase the likelihood of them becoming even more excluded as they grow up.

Low self-esteem can manifest itself in different ways. The person may turn their lack of respect outwards towards others. This can manifest itself as insecurity and be used to control others: emotionally, physically or sexually. Another way is to turn that pain inwards. This can result in the more obvious and visible instances of self-harm, like cutting oneself. Or it can take many other forms. The anorexic or the bulimic both have low self-esteem. The alcoholic or drug addict also has low self-esteem. The person who goes from one abusive relationship to another also has low self-esteem. They are punishing themselves because think they do not deserve any better. This could be because of things that they think they have done or things that have been done to them. Victims of abuse invariably feel that they are responsible for what has happened to them. They think that in some way they deserve what has happened.

One of the things that should be made clear at this point is that victims of abuse do not deserve what has happened to them. First of all, although our spirit may choose to have an experience of abuse it does not choose to experience a specific type of abuse. As we have seen abuse is a general term that is used to describe a variety of different degrees and types of cruelty. All lives will have a degree of suffering and although we choose to have an experience of suffering we do not specify exactly what that experience will be. Again suffering is a general term used to describe many different degrees of pain. If we knew the exact nature of the experience we would probably know it was coming so we would avoid it or the circumstances that preceded it. Once we have learnt from an experience we may then be able to avoid repeating it if that is in the pathway we have chosen.

As adults we have the choice and we are able to avoid certain situations or certain people. But as children we do not always have the ability to avoid a certain person or situation and this is where our guardians come in. They are meant to be there to protect us and to use their experiences to help us. But we are only human and we may not have any idea that our children are in danger from those closest to them. Neither the guardians of the child or the child are responsible for abuse. It is the perpetrator who is responsible and no one else.

He or she has also made a spiritual choice. He or she has made that spiritual choice to carry out some kind of abuse. As children we normally see the world as a good place. We do not expect to have pain and suffering, nor do we expect to encounter anybody who does not treat us well. The same applies to us as physical beings. We find it hard to grasp the fact of evil. We expect goodness as a matter of course and even though we know that logically everything has an opposite, therefore if there is good there must also be evil, we still find it hard to accept. If someone starts to talk about spirits that do not work on the vibrations of light, then they are either considered to be mad or a religious fanatic.

If you accept the concept that we as spirits choose our physical bodies and the lives that go with them, then the idea that those who work on darker vibrations do the same, should not be too difficult to understand. But it is. Even writing about it we find ourselves questioning it. But we know evil does exist, we only have to look around us to see that. Furthermore, just as there are degrees of light so there are degrees of darkness. If one person sends out light to the world and uses their life for the good of others it will impact on individual lives. If that one person finds themselves in a position of power where they can use their light to help all those within their sphere of influence think how good that would be for the world. This is because that person will be teaching others by example that there is another way. If the thousands or millions of people that are influenced by them also follow that example, then that light will be magnified a million fold.

Conversely, if one person does something evil it affects those closest to them and also affects those who hear about it. If that person becomes powerful think of the damage and havoc they can wreak on the lives of those who fall within their sphere of influence. History is littered with examples of paranoid megalomaniac dictators. If we look at their backgrounds they are all similar in that they suffered something that caused them pain and they were unable to deal with it. The results were wars and atrocities and persecution, either of their own people or those from other countries.

Sometimes these lives were taken by spirits whose intention was to wreak exactly the type of havoc that they subsequently cause. But as with spirits of the light, they also had free will. If the course of their childhood had been different perhaps they would have chosen a different way. Nobody is past redemption but you do have to choose it. Although your life's pathway is set out to a certain extent, you still have the free will to choose something else. Furthermore, just because you have had a traumatic childhood it does not mean that you have to grow up to wreak havoc on the lives of others. We all have a choice and it is in the processing of choosing that we evolve spiritually.

At other times these lives will be taken by spirits from the light who are spiritually immature and are not yet ready to understand that what they are doing is wrong or that although their intentions are right they are going about it in entirely the wrong way. Although this is part of their spiritual pathway, this does not mean they should not be helped to seek a different direction or different pathway. By changing their direction and thus evolving faster they will negate the need to keep returning here, they will be helping to improve the energy of the earth plane and they will also be helping to improve the lives of those around them.

However, you cannot help someone who does not want to be helped, because they will revert back to the previous life if they are not totally committed to change. We all know that you cannot give up smoking unless you choose to. All the adverts, health campaigns and legislation in the world will not make any difference if you do not have the will to do it. It is only when you find your own reason to stop that you will succeed.

Secondly, there is a difference between what we spiritually choose and what happens to our physical bodies once we have taken a physical life. Perpetrators of abuse cannot use the excuse that their victims chose the abuse so it is therefore their fault. The victim's spirit may have chosen the experience of abuse to help their development in some way that we do not understand. They may have also chosen the experience of abuse to help the perpetrator develop in some way that we are unaware of. This does not make it any less wrong or any less devastating for the victim. It is very difficult to separate our physical being from our spiritual being – still less see things from a spiritual point of view when we are suffering.

Victims of abuse often find it impossible to really get over the trauma they have suffered. But it is one of many spiritual experiences that help us all develop and evolve. We also have to accept that we do not see the whole 'picture'. We only see things from our earthly perspective and we do not always understand or appreciate the value of some of these experiences or their effects on others. It is not until we return to spirit that things become clear. Until then we have to try and accept that abuse, like wars, hatred and other atrocities, are something that we will continue to experience until we do something about it. Perhaps it will be our collective abhorrence that will finally signal an end to these things for it is only when we all take responsibility for preventing these things that they will stop. However, until we change the way our children are brought up and educated this is unlikely to happen.

We are always taught that our families are the most important things in our lives. It is through our family that we are introduced to the world. It is our families that teach us how to fit into the society in which we are born. Our family provides us with a refuge from the outside world, it is a place of safety, a place we feel secure. It is a place where we can be ourselves without pressure and where we can grow up without fear. Our family also provides us with a support network. They are the one group of people that we can always rely on to help us physically and emotionally. It is to our families that we turn in times of crisis and our families to whom we turn when there is no where else to go.

But this is not always the case. As we have seen, for many people home is not a safe and secure place and the 'family' is not a refuge from the outside world. In some cases the outside world is less threatening than being at home. For others the family is restrictive and repressive and the word family is used as a means of control. But for many of us our childhood is a happy experience and through the support and love of our families we grow up to become independent free thinking people who pass on this way of life to our own children. The challenge is to make sure this applies to ALL our children.

However, even those who had few problems growing up may suddenly find that, as adults, they actually don't like their families very much. This can apply to both adults and children.

They may suddenly find that they have very little in common with each other anymore. This can leave people feeling guilty because we are all taught that we should love our families.

But we do not need to feel guilty. We chose our immediate family to allow us to tick some boxes on our spiritual to do list. Our physical family is there to introduce us to the world and to allow us to begin our spiritual journey. Once we reach adulthood we are independent and it is up to us to follow our own pathway. Our parents or guardians have fulfilled their role and it is time for us all to move on. From there we meet other people who become our friends and who sometimes become more like a 'family'. It is our spiritual journey that is important not our physical journey and on our spiritual journey we have a spiritual family. It is this spiritual family that helps us on our spiritual journey and because we are all one it is the world that is our spiritual family.

If we all extend our understanding of the word family to include the whole world then we no longer need to feel guilty if we do not understand our immediate family. Like other members of our extended spiritual family, we can just accept them as other spirits who are on their own spiritual pathway with their own spiritual to do list. This change of perception will free us of guilt and the need to control and allow us to move on and continue on our spiritual pathway. This will also allow us to bring up our children in a different way because we will see the world in a different way. Once we see the world differently our priorities will change and when this happens our behaviour will also change.

Setting a different example to our children would be a good place to start. Young minds are extremely impressionable and easily corrupted. Spartans used to bring up their children to experience horrific violence so that they made good warriors. They were taken to schools at the age of 7 and regularly beaten in a group to see who survived the longest without crying out. Their rite of passage was to strangle someone. The only proviso was that they didn't get caught doing it.

For many children around the world this would still be quite a normal experience. Children bought up with generations of hatred poured into them, children bought up in violent abusive households, children bought up by political and religious cults, sects and societies that poison their minds. These children grow up into the next generation, the generation that has the power. These are the future of our world. Would you rather they grew up as peace envoys, scientists and doctors or as dictators, cult leaders and religious fanatics?

The choice is ours. But to understand how we can change direction we first need to understand why the world we currently live in is as it is now. How have we reached this point? The world we have now is a result of the history of our planet and its populations. Religion and politics have historically always been very closely entwined and responsible for the majority of conflicts. To change direction we need to begin by stepping back into the past and looking at the origins of these conflicts.

'Only two things are infinite, the universe and human stupidity, and I'm not sure about the former'.
Albert Einstein

'Science may set limits to knowledge, but should not set limits to imagination'.
Bertrand Russell (1872 - 1970)

Chapter 2

In the beginning there was science……..

For a long time it was believed that the universe was infinite. This meant it had no beginning and would have no end. Scientists no longer believe this. Because of recent discoveries in astronomy it seems to now be universally agreed that the universe did have a beginning. There was a single moment of creation where the universe sprang into existence as a 'singularity' around 13.7 billion years ago. Singularities are zones that are thought to exist at the core of black holes, which are areas of intense gravitational pressure. After appearing it expanded and then cooled going from extremely small and hot to the present temperature and size of the universe today. It is continuing to expand and cool and we are inside it.

There are several misconceptions about the Big Bang theory, not least that there was a giant explosion. Experts deny that there was an explosion and say that it was more an expansion, rather like the way a small balloon would expand. Nor did it appear in space as space did not exist. Instead it was space that appeared inside the universe. Time and space had a finite beginning that corresponded to the origin of energy and matter. The singularity didn't appear in space as there was no space – rather space began inside of the singularity. What the singularity appeared in is still a mystery!

Scientists in Geneva have built a Large Hadron Collider

(LHC) which they hope will help them unlock the secrets of how the universe began. The LHC is a scientific instrument called a particle accelerator, built in an underground tunnel that spans the borders of Switzerland and France. The idea is for two beams of subatomic particles (either protons or lead ions) to travel in opposite directions round the accelerator gaining energy with each circuit. They will then try to recreate the 'big bang' by causing these particles to collide head on. They will then analyse the results. This is not just one experiment but a series of experiments set to run over the next 4 years with the most important one happening in 2012. There are many theories as to what will happen not least that they run the danger of creating a black whole that will end the universe. However, the European Organisation for Nuclear Research considers these fears to be groundless. If you would like to read more information about this including the safety aspects then please visit their website at http://public.web.cern.ch/public

However, in the real beginning, as far as we know there were no scientists! Because the creation of the universe was an event that is not within the normal realm of events it has to be seen as supernatural event. As it was a creation it begs the question, who created it? Furthermore, advances in molecular biology have revealed that there are vast amounts of information encoded in each and every living cell. Molecular biologists have also discovered thousands upon thousands of exquisitely designed machines at the molecular level. It takes intelligence to create that type of molecular engineering and the information contained within these cells. It also requires a designer.

The idea of evolution is comparatively new. It was in the 19th Century that people like Alfred Russel Wallace and Darwin developed their theories of evolution and natural selection. Before this, the wonders of the world were just seen as evidence of the existence of a creator. If people thought about the creation at all they accepted the version written in the Bible. This stated that God had created everything in 6 days and then rested on the seventh. All the species on the earth were created within this time and were fixed. This just means that they stayed the same and did not change throughout time. In other words they didn't evolve. Most studies of nature did not include humans and those that did always saw humans as the top of the evolutionary scale even though they did not consciously think about the idea of evolution.

By the 18th century some scholars began to argue about the role of God in the world. They began by rejecting the idea that God periodically interfered and that everything in the world had been created in just six days. This theory restricted God to just the role of creator. The world itself was seen as a vast machine that was governed by strict scientific laws. This meant God did not need to be involved in the day to day running of the planet once he had created it, because the world ran itself. However, other scholars disputed this viewpoint. They saw these scientific laws as just more evidence of the way God worked.

Scholars also began arguing about the age of the earth. Because all previous knowledge of the creation was based on the biblical account of creation, the prevailing school of thought was that the earth was created in 4004BC. This figure had been calculated by adding together the ages of the patriarchs in the Bible. But by 1656 naturalist John Ray began to question how mountain ranges could possible have formed in such a short time. If the earth was formed slowly, which seemed much more likely, it had to be much older than previously thought. The only realistic alternative was that it had gone through a series of violent events such as earthquakes, meteor showers etc. These 'Time versus Catastrophe' theories guided much of the work on evolution in the 18th and 19th centuries and both these theories finished with the great flood. This was assumed to have wiped out everything and because of this God had replaced all the previous species with new ones. This would explain the existence of fossils that were found of species that no longer existed.

It was the new study of geology that really proved that the earth was much older that had been previously thought. Geology is the study of rocks and the layers tell the earth's geological history. The rocks are found in layers that are fixed with the oldest rocks at the bottom. Each part of the earth's history can be found by examining the layers of rock. This caused problems for the church as it contradicted Genesis [the Bible] which stated the world had been created in 6 days. In an attempt to counter this many theories were put forward as to how these six days should be interpreted. These included the suggestion that the opening verse of genesis "in the beginning…" covered all the years the earth was forming.

Despite the church's opposition it was finally accepted by most scholars that the earth had taken a long time to reach its present condition and was therefore much older than the age stated by the Church. But this didn't stop the debate on catastrophes. These actually intensified until 1830 when Charles Lyell stated that the earth had been shaped by no more than the same forces that were in existence today. This meant that the earth had definitely formed slowly over a considerable period of time and the last catastrophe to have had a significant effect was the great flood.

Alongside this new acceptance as to the age of the earth, new theories had also begun to emerge that saw the earth as an organism. This was a ground breaking theory because identifying the earth as an organism meant it was a living entity that, like other living beings, could also grow and evolve. Although ideas about evolution had yet to really materialise, the fact that the earth was accepted as a living organism meant that when ideas of evolution did appear they would include the earth.

Eventually, in 1809, Lamarck suggested that animals had also changed over time as a response to changes in their habitat and their environment in much the same way as we adapt to changes in our temperature and location. In other words, when it is hot or we are in a country that is hot, we take off some clothes to help us cool down. Conversely, when it is cold or we are somewhere it is cold, we put on more clothes to help us warm up.

The major flaw with this theory was that Lamarck thought these changes happened within a lifetime and were then passed on to the next generation. We now know that this does not happen. But although this point was contentious enough it was his other main point that was even more controversial. He maintained that within each species there was a continuous striving for improvement or evolution. This also applied to the human species as could be seen by its constant search to understand and adapt its environment and its constant ability to theorise and to revise theories about its origins and its reason d'être (reason to be).

This idea of evolution and change was extremely worrying to the class conscious Victorians who did not want any changes to the way their society worked. This was exacerbated by the fact that Lamarck was also French and the French had just had a revolution that had changed the way their society worked. This did nothing to endear him to English philosophers. The debate finally went full circle with George Cuvier who reinstated the belief of fixed species. He divided nature into four categories based on their nervous systems and then stated that all nature fitted in to these four categories. His main emphasis was on design and he argued that animals were designed to fit their environments. This meant that if this design changed they would be unable to exist. In other words if you took two wheels off a car it would not become a motorbike but an unstable car. Thus species were once again seen to be rigid.

So, despite having read various theories of evolution, when Charles Darwin set out on his voyage of discovery, he believed as firmly as everyone else in idea of fixed species. But although Darwin set off on his voyage fully in tune with the thinking of the time, he took with him a copy of Lyell's "Principles of Geology" to read on the voyage. It was this that opened his mind to the ideas of natural causes and endless time and although Lyell had dismissed these in favour of a theory of endless migration, the ideas continued to intrigue Darwin.

There was not one specific moment when Darwin suddenly took on board the whole idea of evolution as we know it today. It was much more of a gradual process. It started with the abundance of nature that he found and the difficulty he had in determining where one species ended and another one began. Questions began to intrigue him. Were, for instance, the finches on the Galapagos Islands a different species created by God or were all finches members of the same species with minor variations? The way these finches had adapted to the differing conditions on the different islands also gave him food for thought. On some islands they ate seeds and on others they ate insects and yet in each case their beaks were adapted for these different needs.

Once he had let go of the idea of fixed species he was open to the idea that if the environment changed slowly, nature could also adapt and survive. Because of his background in geology, Darwin understood that mountains could change if there was enough time. If this was the case then there was no reason why animals could not also change given enough time. Those that didn't adapt would not survive. Furthermore, competition for meagre resources would result in only the "fittest" surviving. Thus the genetic characteristics of the "fittest" would be passed on to the next generation. Darwin then realised that if the changes gave an advantage to the animal, however small, and the changes happen over a long period of time, this would eventually lead to the birth of a new species.

This theory of the 'Survival of the fittest' however, did not just mean that only the most ruthless survived. It also encompassed the idea that competition for food and light would also play its part and influence a species' ability to survive. Farmers and gardeners will know that if they grow their seeds too close together they will compete for the available light and food and only the strongest will survive.

Another way of ensuring this survival concerns the amount of offspring a species has. Some species have many offspring but only a few will survive whilst others have a limited number of offspring and they nearly all survive. This was just another way of controlling population numbers. Darwin understood that this also applied to the human species. If there are too many people competing for limited resources and space one or two things can happen: either the birth rate falls or the death rate will increase or there is a combination of both. Alongside this the species will also expand to increase the amount of space and so give itself access to more resources, often at the expense of other species. This was what Darwin called "natural selection".

However, the most controversial point Darwin made on the subject of evolution, as far as the church was concerned, was that humans had evolved from apes. This left the established church with some problems. If humans had evolved from "beasts" then how could they be expected to behave any differently from the beasts? Furthermore, where did God fit in to all this?

Although the church saw the idea of "natural law" as a threat, Darwin and others saw God behind these "natural laws". Rather than just he who created once, they saw God as the one who had given species the ability to evolve and change throughout time. Although the church was unable to see it, this was actually a much more positive picture of God as it saw his hand in every aspect of development on the planet.

The one thing Darwin did not have an answer to was why there were not more fossils of the intermediate species, those that had limited existence because they were not well adapted enough to survive. Whole species appeared to have suddenly disappeared and others had appeared virtually over night.

The answer to this was not to appear for sometime. In the intervening years Darwin's theory began to be also seen as symbolic. It was interpreted as the struggle of humans to free themselves from the oppression of the state and the church. In Germany, in particular, it was seen as a tool that would eventually lead to an overthrow of current political and social structures

Karl Marx also used this theory effectively. He suggested that eventually oppression would end and the "workers" of the world would "win" in their battle to improve their own lives and those of their families. Later, others took this theory and used it to justify human intervention in the natural selection process. The idea of a "super race" was just one way that Darwin's theory was deliberately misinterpreted. It was used to justify genocide by those who considered themselves superior. They used it as an excuse to remove those whose existence they considered to be a threat to the evolution of humankind.

Thus the real danger of Darwin's theory for the Church was not the idea of evolution itself, but the idea that God was no longer involved in the day to day running of the planet.

Eventually it came to be understood that evolution progressed slowly but every now and again dramatic changes would occur. Unable to adapt to such dramatic, almost instant changes, species were completely wiped out and new species emerged to take their place. This is why the fossil record does not show every stage of evolution. A good example of this is the extinction of the dinosaurs. In a very brief span of time, dinosaurs went from being the dominant form of life to total extinction.

However, although Darwinism has a lot to offer when explaining the evolution of other species he does not appear to offer an adequate explanation as to the evolution of humankind. The main problem concerns the time frame. Given enough time natural selection can be used to explain everything. But did man really descend from the apes?

It would take a significant number of evolutionary steps to jump from an ape to a human. Geneticists agree that mutation is the answer to evolutionary change. But mutation must happen very slowly because of the big changes it brings to a species. If it happens too quickly the species would be unable to breed and would become extinct. Religion has raised several questions in relation to these evolutionary theories about how such complex things such as the brain and eye have evolved and then, unable to find an answer that satisfies both religion and science, have retreated back to the idea that God created man.

Furthermore, if evolution is supposed to be a slow process and it is impossible for us to have become intelligent over night, we should be able to find evidence of this slow evolution. Some kind of evidence of mans first attempts at primitive writing etc. But there is nothing so far.

Many theorists argue, that it would therefore appear, that after millions of years with no apparent changes, humans suddenly appeared about 200,000 years ago with a 50% increase in cranial capacity, a modern anatomy and the ability to speak. They further argue that it would seem there are still no scientific explanations for this. Biochemists and mathematicians have calculated that the odds against life arising from non-life naturally via unintelligent processes are astronomical. In fact, scientists aren't even sure if life could have evolved naturally via unintelligent processes. In which case, if life did not arise by chance, how did it arise?

Other questions also come to mind. Why do we not have hair all over our bodies? Neanderthal man who lived in Europe needed the protection of hair to keep him warm and Neanderthals are usually depicted as having dark skins[2] whilst Homo sapiens are considered to have paler skins. Evidence has now emerged of another civilisation of people who are believed to have migrated to Europe from Africa. But if, as believed, we have evolved from this civilisation, would Homo sapiens not have had dark skins especially if they came from Africa? Furthermore why is human skin so fragile compared to our primitive relatives? Surely evolution would not have removed such protection?

It was once believed that 'original' Neanderthal man had disappeared by the time modern man appeared on the scene. But this "fact" is now disputed with the discovery of the skeleton of a child. This skeleton carries the characteristics of both Neanderthal man and modern man. It is dated 3000 years after Neanderthal man was supposed to have died out. Is this one of the hybrids? Or is there another explanation?

Furthermore, where did this modern man come from? One minute there was Neanderthal man who does not progress at all

---

[2] Scientists now seem to believe that Neanderthal man may have been a redhead. (October 2007). This has come from research into the DNA of a Neanderthal scull.

for millions of years and then suddenly we have modern man. Neanderthal man was much better equipped to survive his environment. But modern man had the ingenuity to adapt his environment to suit him rather than the other way round. Where did this sudden ingenuity come from? Where is the evidence to support this evolution and where are the "missing links"?

Several explanations have been put forward to explain this but the one inescapable conclusion seems to be that man evolved slowly and peacefully. Unlike the rest of species for whom procreation is a necessary biological impetus, for mankind procreation is only part of the process. Sexual activity for human kind is also designed to be a pleasurable experience. Unlike other species, the human female is always "on heat" but is only fertile for a few days each month. Other questions come to mind such as why do we take 6 seconds to swallow our food in contrast to other species who swallow instantly? Again this points to a long and peaceful evolution. But this is not the only puzzle to arise when we are looking at our physical history.

Let's examine another mystery and take a look at the first recorded civilisation that we can prove existed. These were the Sumerians. They were an ancient civilisation dating from around 4000 BCE and it is from them that the zodiac originates although it was not used in the same way that we use it today. It was originally used to divide the heavens and to place the stars in "houses". But why did the Sumerians need to watch the stars? Their mathematical system was so advanced it allowed them to record a heavenly cycle that took 25,920 years to complete yet the Sumerians were only around for 2000 years. Why were they so obsessed with the stars? This is not unique to the Sumerians. All the ancient civilisations studied the stars. But the further in time they were from the Sumerians the less accurate were their methods.

Experts at Cardiff University have led an international team in unravelling the secrets of a 2,000-year-old computer which could transform the way we think about the ancient world.

The Antikythera Mechanism is a clock like astronomical

calculator dating from the second century BCE. Detailed work on the gears in the mechanism showed it was able to track astronomical movements with remarkable precision. The calculator was able to follow the movements of the moon and the sun through the Zodiac, predict eclipses and even recreate the irregular orbit of the moon. The team believes it may also have predicted the positions of the planets. This suggests that Greek technology was far more advanced than previously thought. No other civilisation is known to have created anything as complicated for another thousand years.

This would seem to prove that instead of progressing, the more recent cultures have actually gone backwards. The technical knowledge of these ancient civilisations seems to have gradually receded to be replaced by more primitive things. This can also be seen when studying the pyramids. The constructions of the oldest pyramids are far superior to those of the more recent ones.

So, rather than subsequent generations progressing and advancing and continually evolving, they seem to have regressed and it is only more recently that civilisation has reached the levels attained by the Sumerians. Another anomaly is that the Sumerians seem to have appeared suddenly 6,000 years ago with incredible technological and scientific knowledge even though there is no evidence of their evolution and no evidence of where this knowledge came from.

One theory suggests a possible answer to this puzzle. It suggests that there was an even more ancient civilisation than the Sumerians and it was from there that the Sumerians obtained their knowledge and ability. This ancient civilisation was called Atlantis.

However, there is still no physical proof that Atlantis existed. Plato talked about Atlantis more than 2,300 years ago in an imaginary conversation between Socrates and three friends. He described it as an enormous civilisation that covered a large area, bigger than Libya and Asia combined. The citizens of Atlantis had apparently attacked Athens from their base in the

Atlantic and been defeated. After this there had been cataclysmic floods and earthquakes and the island of Atlantis had disappeared. The origins of Atlantis were described as descendants of Poseidon and the island was described as fertile and rich in minerals, timber, elephants and other species. Their palaces had hot and cold springs and hot and cold pools to which all had access even though there were separate arrangements for each group. But after many generations of civilisation the Atlanteans had degenerated from a noble super race into greedy aggressors.

There is considerable dispute as to whether this was just Plato's way of explaining his political views or whether Atlantis did really exist. There are, however, considerable similarities between many of the ancient civilisations. Many built pyramids, believed in the same gods, (even if they had different names), had similar rituals and built strange monuments that took incredible engineering skills. (We will look at these in more detail in the next chapter). The reasons behind many of these strange structures are still a mystery but these similarities point to the idea that all these civilisations may have originated from the same source.

Let's return to the Sumerians and take a look at their own account of their evolution. The Sumerians believed their gods came from a planet called Nibiru. The "Enuma Elish" is a Babylonian text 4,000 years old that tells the story of the creation in more detail than genesis. In 1976 Zechariah Sitchin suggested that the "Enuma Elish" was a text that described the formation of the solar system 4.6.billion years ago. In it Marduk is interpreted as a planet travelling in a clockwise direction past the other planets that travel in the opposite direction. The combined gravity of the other planets diverted Marduk into the solar system and into a collision course with a watery planet called Tiamat.

> *Tiamat and Marduk, the wisest of the "gods"*
> *Advanced against one another;*
> *They pressed on to single combat,*

They approached for battle.

On the first encounter Marduk's satellite winds smashed in to Tiamat but on the next orbit they did collide. Thus over the course of two collisions both the heavens [the asteroid belt] and the "earth" were formed. This is identical to day one and two in Genesis and in the Koran: *"are the disbelievers unaware that the heavens and the earth were one solid mass which we tore asunder, and that we made every living thing out of water?"*

The interesting thing about this theory is that it, if correct, it would imply that the Sumerians knew how the earth evolved and this knowledge found its way into both the Bible and the Koran.

The planet earth is believed to be 4.6 billion years old but there is no evidence to show that anything existed in the first 600 million years. Scientists also know that earth had a sister planet called Theira. This crashed into the Earth 4.5 billion years ago and increased its density enough to develop an atmosphere. Fossils show one celled creatures appearing 4 billion years ago and within another 500 million years these had evolved into multi celled more complex organisms.

Other theorists have suggested that there have been 5 major catastrophes in earth's history with another 10 smaller ones. These have all led to dramatic changes in climate and thus to the species who existed then. The most recent major catastrophe was the one that wiped out the dinosaurs and this took place 65 million years ago.

It is believed that about 11,000 - 9000 years ago there was the demise of around 50 major species. Before this the extinction rates of species were about 1 every 15,000 years. Thousands of bodies of animals have been found under the ice in Alaska. These were temperate species that died suddenly and for which there have been no explanations. Thus considerable evidence points to sudden climate change and major flooding and this has now been dated to around 13,000 years ago. We know the gravitational pull of the moon affects the tides so could this flood have been caused by the close proximity of the planet Nibiru to the earth?

We began this chapter by looking at the beginning of the universe and stated that as the creation of the universe was as an event outside the realm of normal experience it points to the existence of a creator. We also pointed to how much complexity there is in every living cell within the universe and how it would have needed some kind of intelligence to create this. We would now like to take that a little further.

We often feel that our universe seems to be drifting towards disorder, but how did it become so ordered and complex in the first place? There is perfect order in physics. The law of gravity supports life on earth perfectly. The combinations of all the physical components in the universe are perfect to support life. There could be an infinite number of variable combinations and values that these physical components could be tuned to but they are not. Therefore it would seem that someone set these conditions for life. We can also add to this the fact that human beings also have a sense of morality and a sense of absolute value with which to make comparisons. We also apply natural law and know the values of right and wrong. All these things point to the existence of some outside factor that cannot be explained by just looking at the purely physical aspects of evolution.

To consider this further we need to leave this part of our journey now and take a look at another part of our spiritual journey – that of our religious and political evolution. We have looked briefly at some suggestions about both the origins of the earth and our own physical being. But we are not just physical beings. We also have brains and minds. Our brains are our computers – they sort through all the data and process it. Our minds are the controllers and processors of our emotions. They produce our emotional responses to the stimuli that our brains are processing. We do not exist in a mindless vacuum. We have thoughts and our brains have to have material to process. Our physical presence on the earth is an indisputable fact. But why are we here?

One of the questions we have always pondered is the

reason for our existence and one group of people have always been happy to tell us their reasons. These are the leaders of the major religions. The reasons for our existence have been interpreted and reinterpreted throughout the centuries and this constant reinterpretation has provided humankind with the perfect excuse to kill, maim and destroy each other. It's now time to look at how religion fits into our spiritual journey.

'The stars in the night sky are like the jewels on the cloak of a rich man, many can see them but few can touch them'

'For centuries, theologians have been explaining the unknowable in terms of the-not-worth-knowing.'
H. L. Mencken (1880 - 1956)

Chapter 3

In the beginning there was religion......

In the last chapter we looked at some of the suggestions behind our physical existence on this planet. It's now time to look at some of the theological and philosophical reasons we have been given for our existence. Do not worry if you cannot always understand the point of some of the information in this chapter or where it fits into our spiritual journey. Just as our lives here become clear when we get to the end and return to spirit, you will find that the bits you didn't really understand when you were reading them will become clear at the end. That's not an excuse to skip to the end now! If you do it will not make any sense. It would be a bit like being born and then dying after a very brief time, returning to spirit and evaluating the life that you hadn't lived.

The cosmological argument or First Cause argument is a philosophical argument used to prove the existence of God. It explains that because everything that exists or has occurred has a cause, there must have been a first cause that itself was uncaused. Both Plato and Aristotle used First cause arguments in the 4th and 3rd centuries BCE. Aristotle posited that the first cause was the creator of the universe. Thomas Aquinas followed this by arguing that the cause of the universe is uncaused and the first cause is God. Muslim philosophers in the Middle Ages further developed this theory into the Kalam Cosmological Argument which is based on the following three premises:

- that whatever begins to exist has a cause of existence;
- the universe began to exist;
- therefore the universe has a cause of existence.

Thus the Cosmological argument is consistent with the Bibles account of creation which stated that God created the universe. *"In the beginning God created the heaven and the earth" (Genesis 1:1). "The Lord made the heavens" (1 Chronicles 16:26).*

It also states that God is separate from the universe
". . .the heaven and heaven of heavens cannot contain him". Chronicles 2:6

The Bible teaches that God is the uncaused First Cause who created the universe by willing it into existence. *"the LORD, the everlasting God"* (Genesis 21:33) is eternal and infinite. *"His mighty power rules forever"* (Psalm 66:7).

The Bible goes on to explain that Adam and Eve were the first people. However, most chronological dating processes suggest that the earliest possible date for Adam would be around 5,400 BCE even though science has more or less proved that mankind was around well before the 6th Century BCE. Therefore, a more credible explanation is that Adam and Eve were simply the first people whose names were known and remembered. In other words they were the names mentioned at the beginning of the oral tradition. As there is also considerable archaeological evidence to show that both Neanderthals and Cro-Magnons believed in some kind of life after death, Adam cannot even realistically be described as the first spiritual man. But as the first people to communicate with the God of the Hebrews this makes them the first of the genetic line that led to the birth of Christianity.

David Rohl has identified the Garden of Eden[3] as lying at the source of four rivers – the Pishon, Gihon, Tigris and Euphrates. The Adamites had come from the shores of the Black

---

[3] David Rohl – The Lost Testament

Sea. They had lived there for several centuries until in 5375 BCE the sea level began to rise dramatically. As the Mediterranean broke through the land barrier and flooded the fresh water lake with sea water the villages they had lived in disappeared virtually overnight and the fish died as the waters became brackish. Adam and his people headed south into Eden where they eventually settled in a village at the foot of Mount Sahand. There they came into contact with some people who lived to the south in the Land of Havilah. Eve, the daughter of the chief of the tribe, married Adam and they had three sons and several daughters.

However, there are other theories that also cast doubt about Eve being the first woman. The legend of Lillith suggests a different version. In the Legend of Lillith God was believed to have created Adam and Lillith at the same time, thus making them equal. But Adam wanted to subjugate Lillith who rejected this because she had been created equal. In frustration she is supposed to have called out the 4 letter name for God (**YHVH**) and was then whisked away. Adam demanded the return of his companion, but she refused. It is here that the tale seems to get a little murky. Jewish scribes would often find names in the Bible that they did not know anything about. In an attempt to provide them with a history they would search for other references and if they found some they would use this to create a background history. This practise is called Midrash – to root out. Other ancient texts were also in circulation at the time the Old Testament was being composed and one Babylonian text referred to someone called Lillith who was a demon or evil spirit. Thus any mention of Lillith in the bible refers to her as a demon that causes miscarriages.

Early Jews had always invoked the divine in feminine terms and many believed that Yahweh had a wife and her name was Asherah. An inscription on a piece of pottery, found in 1975/76 at Kuntillet Arjud in the Sinai desert, reads *Berakhti et'khem l'YHVH Shomron ul'Asherato*. This means *"I have blessed you by YHVH of Samaria and His Asherah."*

Goddess worship is referred to throughout history. Modern humans are believed to have originated around 200,000 to 250,000 years ago and until about 8000BCE were hunter gatherers. Because they believed that life was finite they developed primitive religious beliefs in which those who relied on gathering worshiped goddesses, whilst those who relied on hunting worshipped hunting gods. Because the fertility of the crops and animals was essential to their survival, and because its workings were a mystery, the female who gave life became divine. Some Goddess statues dating from 30,000 BCE still survive.

This lasted for tens of thousands of years during which time they generally lived in peace. This can be seen by the lack of fortifications around their hamlets. It can also be seen from their funeral habits that men and women were considered equal. It is believed by many academics that the suppression of this Goddess worship occurred when the Indo-Europeans invaded from the East. They bought with them war and horses and a belief in male Gods. To begin with Goddess worship was gradually combined with the worship of male Gods to produce a variety of polytheistic religions such as the Greeks, Pagans and Celts.

However an even more interesting theory is proposed by Leonard Shlain who suggests that it was the invention of writing that changed things for ever. Because literacy engages the predominately masculine left hemisphere of the brain it overshadowed the holistic feminine right hemisphere. This initiated the disappearance of goddesses, the decline of women's political status and began centuries of misogyny[4] and patriarchy[5].

---

[4] Misogyny is a verb that describes hatred, dislike or distrust of women.
[5] Patriarchy means a form of social organisation in which the father is the supreme authority in the family, clan or tribe and descent is reckoned on the male line with the children belonging to the father's clan or tribe. A patriarchal society is one that is based on this social organisation. As the Jewish line is passed down through the female line this is more evidence that early Jewish tribes were not patriarchal or misogynistic.

As Judaism, Christianity and Islam evolved, the female principle was gradually driven out of religion and women's roles in society became restricted and they came to be considered inferior to men. Although women played a major role in the early Christian church Paul was responsible for restarting the process of suppressing women again. Although a feminine presence was added in the shape of the Virgin Mary, the image was a passive, submissive, pure, virginal image with none of the sexuality of the earlier pagan Goddesses. Despite a certain amount of evidence that suggests Mary Magdalene may have been an important member of Jesus inner circle, the Church has consistently branded her as a prostitute or a fallen woman. This was because the Church did not accept that there was any place within in its hierarchy for women.

Because this subjugation of women was prevalent and accepted when the scriptures of the worlds three biggest religions were written, this attitude towards women has not only persisted throughout the last two centuries, it is actually been encouraged by those texts.

It is now widely accepted that the Old Testament was composed and written between the 11th century BCE and the 2nd century BCE although parts of it such as the Torah and Song of Deborah are probably older. The books of the Old Testament upon which Jesus and his disciples' teachings were based were written long before Jesus' birth.

The first problem with the Old Testament is that it has been translated from its original Hebrew. We are, therefore, at the mercy of the translators. Translation from one language to another inevitably means that there will be subtle changes from the original. First there are variations because sometimes one language will not have the vocabulary that is needed to accurately translate something. Some ancient languages may not have had words to express certain emotions because their lives were spent existing and trying to survive. They did not have time to sit and analyse their emotions or their thoughts. Therefore, the words simply did not exist. Latin was a very abrupt language as opposed to ancient Greek, which was quite a rich language. Translation from Hebrew to Greek and then to Latin would inevitably mean subtle changes to meanings. Secondly, it is virtually impossible for a translator to avoid putting his own interpretation onto his translation. This may not be deliberate but would be almost impossible to avoid.

But the major reason the Bible cannot be taken as literal gospel truth is that it has been continuously edited throughout the centuries. There were originally at least three versions of the Old Testament around – a Palestinian version, a Babylonian version and an Egyptian version. The Egyptian version was the largest and contained about 12 extra texts that did not appear in the others. This version was known as the Septuagint because it was believed to have been put together by 72 scribes – 6 from each of the 12 tribes of Israel. The one in usage now originates from the Palestinian one because the others were not centred around Jerusalem. Texts that were considered unacceptable for whatever reason were left out. There were many reasons texts were considered unacceptable and left out just as there were many reasons why those that were left in were chosen. It would seem that the texts that were finally chosen were those that were religiously acceptable and literarily appealing. They were also the texts that were more likely to provide social cohesion. It is also believed that Jesus may have had access to many of these scriptures that no longer exist.

However, even though it is now an accepted fact that at various periods throughout history the bible has been edited, this does not mean the Bible has no significance. Those who periodically edited it were often focussed on ensuring it complied with the dictates of the day. They, therefore, only removed the sections that were applicable to the circumstances that prevailed at that time. This means that some bits have been left in because they did not understand the significance of them and it is often these that provide the clues to our past. Other bits have been added and deliberately misinterpreted.

All language is ambiguous and we can only interpret it

within the terms of our own frame of reference. This means that when we read things we put our own values on them. Everybody who reads this book will interpret it in a slightly different way even though we have tried hard to make it as unambiguous as possible. This is because we make judgements on what we are reading by relating them to our own experiences. We are a total of our experiences. This sounds complicated but is not really. Everything we think comes from either our own experience or from somebody else. We cannot think like an ancient Egyptian because our society is nothing like the society of ancient Egypt. To take it a step further, if you asked somebody from an ancient culture to describe a harrier jump jet, how would they describe it? Because they would not have our 21st Century vocabulary they would have to use the language and understanding of the day. One theory suggests that is possible that they would describe it like this:

"the lord said "go and stand on the mountain in the presence of the lord, for the lord is about to pass by". Then a great and powerful wind tore the mountains apart and shattered the rocks before the lord, but the lord was not in the wind. After the wind there was an earthquake. After the earthquake came a fire, but the lord was not in the fire. And after the fire came a gentle whisper. When Elijah heard it he pulled his cloak over his face and went out and stood at the mouth of the cave. [Kings I, 19:11-13]

According to this same theory a NASA chief engineer, involved in both the design of the Skylab and space shuttle, has identified the following description as similar to a Gemini or Apollo capsule, yet this is a quote from the Old Testament.

"I looked and saw a windstorm coming out of the north - an immense cloud with flashing lightening and surrounded by brilliant light. The centre of the fire looked like glowing metal, and in the fire was what looked like four living creatures. In appearance their form was that of a man, but each of them had four faces and four wings. Their legs were straight, their feet were like those of a calf and gleamed like burnished bronze.

Under their wings on their four sides they had the hands of a man. All four of them had faces and wings, and their wings touched one another. Each one went straight ahead; they did not turn as they moved.

As I looked at the living creatures, I saw a wheel on the ground beside each creature with its four faces. This was the appearance and structure of the wheels: they sparkled like Chrysolite[6] and all four looked alike. Each appeared to be made like a wheel intersecting a wheel. As they moved, they would go in any of the four directions the creatures faced; the wheels did not turn about as the creatures went. Their rims were high and awesome, and all four rims were full of eyes all round.

When the living creatures moved, the wheels beside them moved; and when the living creatures rose from the ground, the wheels also rose. Wherever the spirit would go, they would go, and the wheels would rise along with them, because the spirit of the living creatures was in the wheels"
Ezekiel 1:4-21.

Because of our 21st Century culture, understanding and values, we often assume that the people of ancient civilisations must have been savages. Because their way of life was different to ours and is outside of our experience we have trouble understanding or emphasising with it. But was this early civilisation as primitive as we have always thought?

As we said in the previous chapter, the Sumerian civilisation is now believed to have dated from around 5500BCE to 2390BCE. It is also believed to be the first culture that could be described as a civilisation although there are those who believe that this civilisation was preceded by another. Some think that this previous civilisation was called Atlantis. However, as also stated previously, whereas there is archaeological evidence to support the existence of the Sumerians, at the time of writing Atlantis has never been found. Some scholars believe that the

---

[6] Chrysolite is a brown or yellowish green, naturally formed, hard glassy crystal, used as a gemstone.

reason it has never been found is because Atlantis was invented by Plato purely to explain his philosophical argument, and never actually existed.

However, Charles Hapgood's classic 1966 book on ancient maps, also argues that there was a more advanced worldwide civilization that existed many thousands of years before ancient Egypt. Hapgood concludes that the Piri Reis Map that shows Antarctica, the Hadji Ahmed map, the Oronteus Finaeus and many other amazing maps were made from even more ancient maps. These maps were originally in various ancient archives around the world that have now been lost. Not only does it appear that these unknown people more advanced in mapmaking than any people prior to the 18th century, it appears that they had mapped all the continents. The Americas were mapped thousands of years before Columbus and Antarctica was mapped when its coasts were free of ice.

But even with this kind of supporting evidence we are still inclined to assume that ancient civilisations were not as "good" or as advanced as us. Yet the Sumerians had a culture and institutions that were very similar to our own. They were not illiterate; they wrote on clay tablets and had the wheel. They had schools similar to our own where they taught a wide range of subjects. They even had a legal system that protected the rights of the poor, the unemployed, the weak and the vulnerable. (Obviously their legal system was considerably more advanced than ours!) Sumerian law also gave 'equal' rights to women. Their medical knowledge was also advanced as was their methods of construction. They are credited with building the world's first boats and were great importers and exporters. They were also experts at smelting, refining, casting and alloying. But it is not so much the fact that they were able to do this as much as the fact that they were able to do this within a few hundred years of first appearing and that there was no evidence to show how they had evolved.

In Sumerian culture the land was God's and they owed their continued existence to his/her procreative power. In the middle of all Sumerian cities, and there were as many as 20, was God's house. All aspects of community development were controlled from this temple. Their early writing appears to have begun at around 3000BCE and our language comes from there. We still use thirty two Sumerian words in the English language. "Alcohol" is an almost pure Sumerian word as is "cane" and "saffron." Furthermore, their precise surveying methods, triangulation and their standard unit of measurement were identical to others used all round the world before 700 CE.

More recently research has traced another group of people who predate the Sumerians. They were known as Anannage to the Sumerians and the Elohim to early settlers in the Middle East. Elohim means Shining Countenanced or Lords of Cultivation and they were believed to have existed in the mountains of Southern Lebanon around 8,750BCE. The seven major cities of the Levant: Kharsag, Jericho (8000BCE), Baalbek, Elba, Catal Huyuk, Olympus and On are believed to have been built by them.

Furthermore, bio-archaeological evidence together with genetic analysis of oral traditions and the earliest writings show that the Elohim played a major part in the development not only of the Sumerians but also the Chinese, Egyptian, Indus, Peruvian and Mexican cultures and language.

In the last chapter we pointed to the similarities between ancient civilisations that did not, as far as we aware, have any contact with each other. It would now seem possible that it was the Elohim who are the common link between them. However, we also stated that there were some strange structures for which there appears no explanation. The following are just a few to give you an idea. There are many more that we have not included.

Baalbek is located at the foot of the Anti-Lebanon Mountains in the Bekaa valley. The Greeks called Baalbek Heliopolis - the city of Helios. Helios was a sun god who travelled the skies in his "chariot" and Baalbek is believed to be the chariots "resting place". Modern warfare and terrorism have meant it is mostly forgotten and is hardly mentioned in some books. But Roman emperors would travel 1500 miles to make offerings to the gods. They built temples here, the most spectacular to their Chief god Jupiter. But it is not the temple but the platform it is built on that is so impressive. Some of the stones in the platform measure 64 feet in length and weigh as much as 800 tons each! These were then fitted together without mortar and with perfect precision. No Roman emperor has ever claimed that he built it, nor is there any evidence to prove the Romans were capable of building it.

Arabic legend attributes it to their god Nimrod who sent a race of giants to build it after the flood. The Bible describes Nimrod as the *'first on earth to become a mighty warrior'* and a *'mighty hunter before the lord'*. Some scholars believe that Nimrod may be Sargon the Great who was the King of Akkad in around 2300BCE. The beginnings of the Sumerian, Babylonia, Akkadian and Assyrian empires can all be traced back to Nimrod. Another tells a tale of Nimrod rebelling against his god and building the tower of Babel. It is also associated with the biblical figure of Cain, the son of Adam, who is supposed to have built it as a refuge from his god Yahweh in the year 133 of "creation" and peopled it with giants who then perished in the great flood. The creation of this platform would be possible with modern technology. But why bother and why not use smaller stones?

On the other side of the world are the ruins of Tiwanaku in Bolivia. Although the blocks are not as big as those at Baalbek, they are set at an altitude of 13,000 feet. The air is so thin here there is a danger from ultraviolet radiation and it is hard to breathe. Tiwanaku emerged around 200CE as a sacred centre. By 500CE it was a thriving empire fuelled by its economic resources. It also had huge agricultural surpluses. This came to an end when the climate changed. The reason they had such large agricultural surpluses was a highly complex and advanced agricultural technology. These methods are considered far superior to modern methods that use extensive fertilisation to achieve high yields. The principal structures of Tiwanaku were believed to be temples but inside one, Akapana, they have found a network of stone water conduits. Similar sophisticated water systems have been found at Puma Punku and at Lukurmata near Lake Titicaca. These water systems had ceased to work by the time of the Tiwanaku.

At Puma Punku, there is a block, several feet high which has a precision cut groove 6 millimetres wide. Inside this groove are holes, with an equal distance between them. This would require 20th century technology. Other stones contain unexplained grooves and niches and bear the indentations of metal clamps. These were made of bronze and are not associated with any these cultures at that time.

2,500 years ago Chavin de Huantar emerged as a sacred site in the Peruvian Andes. Located at 10,500 feet above sea level it is totally remote and well hidden. Why?

The "el Lanzon" monolith is carved from granite and is 15 feet high. It is believed to be the main god of the Chavin region and is a mixture of human and bull features, with serpents flowing from the head. It appears that the temple was built round the statue. The irregular shape of the granite seems to prove that the statue was damaged before the carving was made. The temples have been dated to 500BCE but archaeologists, using radiocarbon dating have dated the site to 1400BCE. The earliest part of the construction is an underground network of stone channels that drew water from a nearby river. The water was carried by means of an advanced hydraulic system. It is a fact that industry relies on water. What industry could there be at this remote location and where did the technology come from to build such an advanced system?

An Inca legend talks of gold, silver and precious stones hidden under the temple. It is entirely possible that this was the location of a gold panning industrial complex. Unfortunately a flood buried the site in 1945. The excavation work stopped at a level dated at around 400-300BCE. So what could lie beneath this?

This is not the only place with such complex engineering works. The Incas are commonly thought to have existed between 1100-1532 CE. Legend has it that the first Inca leader, Manco

Capac disappeared, carried off by the sun god. When he returned he was wearing gold and claimed divine right to start a new line of kings. This dynasty began in 1100CE. The Spanish historian, Fernando Montesinos has discovered that local beliefs record that 62 kings had reigned here for about 2,500 years and 28 kings had reigned for around a 1000 years. This takes us back to around 2,400BCE. The original Manco Capac was told to build a city. He was given a golden wand, a gift from the god Viracocha. This would either sink into the ground or should be used to strike a particular stone and this was where the city should be built.

Thus it seems the Incas were preceded by an unknown, long, unrecorded occupation. In the case of Cuzco this has now been proved. Its origins are now believed to date back to 2200BCE. If the Incas had built all these impressive structures why didn't the Spanish conquerors use the Inca workmen to build for them? Although the buildings erected by the Spanish collapsed in an earthquake, the pre Inca buildings still survive. Like ancient structures all over the world, the engineering does not tally with the time frames when they were supposed to be built. So where did the technology come from?

All the evidence appears to point to the existence of a very advanced people who travelled the world. Many scholars believe that it is these structures that point to the existence of either Atlantis or a similar type of advanced culture. But even if this is the case it does not explain the point of these structures and why were they built of such enormous stones?

Manchu Picchu was supposed to have been built during the last half of the 15th century in less than 100 years. Scholars have now identified this site as that of the legendary Tampu-Tocu. The common theory is that Manchu Picchu and Cuzco, along with Baalbek, Tiwanaku and Chauvin de Huantar are sacred religious sites. But who were these gods who were worshipped at these sites and what is the connection between them?

The Nazca lines are furrows 4-6 inches deep. They cover a strip, 30 miles long, in the Andes and consist of a variety of designs such as a monkey, a spider and a heron with a neck measuring 900feet. Then there are wedge shaped designs with sides more than 2,500 feet long. These are outdone by the Nazca lines themselves which run perfectly straight for up to 5 miles. But the biggest puzzle of all is why they are so big that they can only be viewed from the air from a height of 1000 feet. Like the previous examples, all these sites seem to prove the existence of two cultures. The original culture that built the sites and the later culture that adopted them and preserved the legend of these gods. Was the original culture that of the Elohim and if so why did they build these structures?

Another theory argues that one part of this technology appears to have been aeronautics and that this is supported by the huge platform at Baalbek, the Nazca lines and the legend of the sun god's chariot.

This may not be quite as bizarre as it first seems. In 1969 Egyptologists found something strange in a box of artefacts from the year 200BCE. It had straight wings, a sleek tapered body and a vertical tail fin. It appeared to incorporate modern aircraft design and to be the model of a glider. Two thousand years after it was made this object still sailed neatly through the air. Although it was only seven inches long, experts pointed to how the Egyptians always made scale models the things they built. The Babylonians also talked of flying machines in their ancient text – The Halkatha Records – *'Knowledge of flying is most ancient, a gift of the gods of old for saving lives'*. Another Babylonian work – the Sifr'ala of Chaldea – contains a detailed, if fragmented account of how to build and fly an aeroplane. Dating back over 5000 years it describes the effect of wind resistance on wings and makes specific comments about graphic and copper aeroplane parts. The Mahabharata, an ancient Indian text written about the 4th century BCE, talks about *'an 'aerial chariot, with the sides of iron and clad with wings'*.

But according to some scholars it is not just the existence of these structures that supports this idea. They point to Exodus 33:21-23 *"then the lord said, "there is a place near me, where you may stand on a rock. When my glory passes by, I will put you in a cleft in the rock and cover you with my hand until I have passed by. Then I will remove my hand and you will see my back; but my face must not be seen".*

Moses was then told of the dangers to anyone coming up the mountain and returned with a "radiant" face which frightens the Israelites. Then it gets even more intriguing.

The lord states that he is unable to come with them to the Promised Land but instead will communicate with them through the ark. The ark must be handled by priests equipped with "sacred garments" and with a "shielding curtain". The ark was to be made of gold inside and out with wood between these layers. One theory suggests that this could be an electrical circuit with wood as the insulator. Again this may not be as bizarre as may first appear.

Whilst excavating the ruins of a 2000 year old village in Iraq in 1936, workers discovered a small earthenware vase with a soldered sheet copper tube about one and a half inches long. The bottom of this tube was sealed with a crimped copper disk; an iron rod, seemingly corroded by acid, projected through an asphalt plug at the top. German archaeologist Wilhelm Koenig reached the startling conclusion that if filled with an acidic solution, this could possibly be a simple electric battery. Similar objects had also been found in that area together with thin copper rods that may have been used to link them together. In 1940 an American engineer made a similar device from Koenig's description and generated about half a volt of electricity. In the 1970's a German engineer took it one stage further and filled the tube with grape juice and used the current to electroplate a silver statuette with gold. He was convinced he had confirmed the use of electric batteries over 1800 years before the modern invention of 1799.

So together with the possible previous references to aircraft and space capsules, it now seems we may have a reference to a powerful communications device, operated by a powerful electrical system. Descriptions of such complex technological equipment could not possibly have been dreamt up by the Israelites.

It seems, therefore, that looking into our religious history seems to raise just as many questions as looking into out physical history. Both raised more questions than they answered. But these are not the only questions. In ancient cultures religion and politics were so closely related they were usually one and the same. The next part of our spiritual journey takes a look at our political beginnings.

'Politics is war without bloodshed while war is politics with bloodshed.'
Mao Tse- Tung (1893-1976)

Chapter 4

In the Beginning there was politics...............

We've looked at suggestions about the evolution of our planet and at suggested theories about our religious evolution. It is now time to look at some of the suggested theories about our political evolution. Some of the contents of this chapter may seem to be more religious than political, but, as we said in the last chapter, this is because in the past politics and religion were closely entwined if not, one and the same. Furthermore, one was often used as a means to enforce the other.

Let us therefore begin this chapter by returning to the Bible. The "Enuma Elish", a Babylonian account of the creation, was written nearly 1000 years before genesis and is the acknowledged source of the genesis legend. As we said in the previous chapter, everything the Sumerians achieved was attributed to the gods. Their gods were gods of flesh and blood and appear to be the original gods spoken about in the Old Testament including the God Yahweh who did not appear for several hundred years after the "Enuma Elish" was written. But the "Enuma Elish" does not just give an account of the beginning of the world. According to some theorists it also appears to give an account of the origins of mankind. It would therefore seem possible that the writer of genesis based his story on Sumerian material. He may not have included any references to buildings because the Jews were nomadic and therefore did not know what a city was. But it is not just the bible that has these stories. They are also repeated by other ancient civilisations.

As we also saw in the last chapter the Elohim are believed to have predated the Sumerians and influenced the development of many other ancient cultures including their language. But it was not only language that appeared to be universal. All subsequent common law, philosophy and religion, can trace its origins back to the early teachings of the Elohim around 8,700 BCE. King Hammurabi, ruler of Mesopotamia in 1792 BC, assembled Anu and Enlil's Elohim decrees which comprised of some 282 articles and cast them onto stone pillars. These were erected in public places. This was the origin of The Hammurabi Code. *"Let the oppressed man who has a cause - Come into the presence of my statue - And read carefully my inscribed stele".*

The Hebrew word "Elohim" is actually a plural of "el" the lord. So were the Elohim the gods spoken about by the Sumerians? Were they really gods or were they just so advanced that they were considered to be gods by the peoples of the other civilisations that existed at the same time? In either case, if they were the gods spoken about by the ancient Jewish people why was it that the 'gods' became one god?

As the Enuma Elish was written in cuneiform, an ancient language, there are many interpretations of its true meaning. We have concentrated on just one of these interpretations. We will leave you to follow up on the others! This interpretation begins by explaining that the gods were fed up doing all the work so they decided to create man in their own image to carry out simple tasks. These first humans were sterile but this changed because they needed men to rebuild the cities after a major flood. The gods also got fed up having children so woman was created to bear the children of the gods.

The two main gods who seem to have been instrumental in this were Enlil and Enki. Because Enlil needed a bigger workforce he asked Enki to show him how to clone his workforce. Enki then played a trick on him by impregnating the embryos with sexual awareness and reproductive capabilities. The bible states that Adam and Eve ate the fruit of the forbidden tree. This theory implies that it could be the knowledge of sex.

Once Adam and Eve began to reproduce the scene was set for a population explosion. Adam, who possessed some of the god's longevity, apparently lived to be 93,000 years old and he passed this longevity onto his children. In order to solve the problem, Adam and Eve were sent into "the wilderness "where Enlil hoped they would die but because Enki felt some responsibility for the problem he decided to help mankind survive. Because this was against the wishes of the other gods Enki was later arrested for this. Thus, if we consider the version in the "Enuma Elish" it would seem that the expulsion from Eden came about because humankind discovered sex and this led to a population explosion.

So why was it that the women were blamed for the expulsion? It is now accepted that the Bible that is in use today has been edited many times. At the time this process was happening women were very much dependant on men. The days when women were treated as equals with men had long gone. The early editors of the Bible reflected this in their work. Women were there to be the possessions of men and to fulfil the needs of men including producing the male heir. Sex has long been considered a sin by the church for many reasons. One of these was because it left men reliant on women and this was viewed as a weakness. Rather than accept this need as part of their lives and take responsibility for it they blamed the woman for causing the need in them. In other words the woman was responsible for their sexual need. This led to the myth that women were responsible for the expulsion from 'paradise'. This interpretation has influenced and reinforced the church's uneasy relationship with sex and female sexuality ever since.

Other theories explain the expulsion from Eden as part of man's awakening quest for exploration and knowledge. But as the Bible was based on an Enlilite source it blames Enki for man's expulsion because if Enki hadn't tampered with Enlil's workforce they would not have been expelled.

According to the Bible Adam and Eve had two sons called Cain and Abel. Cain was a farmer and Abel a shepherd and each founded their own tribe. There have been many attempts over the years to find archaeological evidence to support the Bible. Most have failed because of the time lines that are based on the ages of the patriarchs. However, in the Lost Testament David Rohl suggests an alternative way of looking at the time lines which offers a very persuasive account of pre history and which not only supports the Biblical account of history but also offers a realistic interpretation of the Enuma Elish.

After Cain killed Abel the tribe of Cain were exiled and made their way out of An (the Sumerian word for heaven) down to earth (Ki). The local inhabitants, the Kheuba[7], were a wild nomadic people who hunted for food. They wore animal skins and head-dresses with horns which terrified other local tribes. It was the priests and their shamanistic appearance that later became the winged protectors of the entrance to paradise quoted in Genesis. For over four hundred years the dynasty of Cain moved ever southward eventually coming to rest south of the Zagos mountains.

The next major ruler mentioned in the Bible is Enoch after which the Sumerian city Uruk (Unuk in its original Sumerian form) is believed to have been named. Later civilisations raised Enoch and others who followed to the status of gods. They called these gods Anunnaki (sometimes translated as 'the ones from heaven and earth'). In other words: – the ones who had come down from heaven to earth.

The principle title of the god of the Sumerians was en.ki (Lord of the earth) which in fact was the same god known as Eya. This became Aya in the late Bronze Age and finally Yah or Yahweh, by the western Israelites. Yah (Hebrew 'iah' is part of numerous Hebrew names such as Jeremiah (Yah raises up) and words such as halleluiah – exalted is Yah.

Let us now move forward several hundred years and take a look at the flood. Despite the heavy religious editing the bible has received there is still an abbreviated history in there. According to our first theory the "atra-hasis" [the Babylonian story of the flood] tells the story of how the council of the gods knew about the flood because Enki, the scientific god had

---

[7] Akkadian texts call the cherubim or winged creatures of the Bible *kuribu*.

predicted the flood. But they decided not to tell mankind because they could not prevent it and the other gods made Enki swear an oath not to tell humankind. However, Enki, was still friendly to the people he had created, so he decided to break ranks and warn one loyal follower. Detailed instructions were then given to Noah telling him how to build a submersible ship. Once Noah was warned he took genes of all the species with him on his ark.

Our second theory explains that it is now over two thousand years since the expulsion from Eden and the villages of Shinar had now grown into towns and settlements – each with their own temple that worshipped the god of their choice.

Although Enki was still the principal god, each settlement had separate gods. Uruk had An (heaven) and later Inanna (Lady of Heaven); Ur had Sin – the moon god; In the city of Shuruppak the main temple was dedicated to Enlil but the local ruler, a man we know as Noah, was a devotee of Enki.

One day, whilst deep in prayer (or meditation perhaps?), Noah heard a voice telling him to build a boat because Enlil has about to send a rainstorm that would kill everyone. Because Noah was told this by Enki and the rest of the city worshipped Enlil, Noah felt unable to pass on this warning to the rest of the city. Instead he told the elders of the city that his god Enki was in disagreement with their god Enlil. The only way he could reconcile himself to this was to leave Shuruppak and go to where other worshippers of his god Enki were located. It was here he built his boat and here he gathered together the diverse species to protect them from the prophesised flood.

From a spiritual point of view, it would not have been any good for Noah to be told the meteorological reason for the coming flood because he would not have understood it. He would only have been able to interpret what he heard within the context of his own understanding which was related to his own life experiences. The same would have applied to the rest of population of the time hence the explanation in the ancient texts. This was that one of the gods was angry and was intending to send a flood as some kind of punishment. This would have made sense to him because it fitted with the understanding of the time, therefore he would have taken notice of it.

The actual reason for the flood was quite simple. In 3119BCE there was a massive volcanic eruption in the Aleutian Islands. The millions of tons of ash and sulphuric acid released had blocked out the sun causing a mini ice age. The subsequent winters were extremely cold with tons of snow accumulating in the mountains. The summers were not warm enough to melt the ice so it continued to accumulate. Eventually the conditions improved and the ice began to melt. But the Mesopotamian flood plain was extremely flat and criss-crossed with irrigation dykes and canals. These irrigation channels had been dug by the settlers who had successfully grown surplus crops in the years when the weather had been kind. This had kept them going throughout the years of draught when the plains had not flooded but they were fast running out of grain and had resorted to cannibalism which may have been why Noah was praying on that day. When the ice finally melted it flooded the plane destroying everything in its path.

At the same time the heating up of the earth caused an electrical storm and the strong accompanying winds brought storm clouds up from the south. The seas too began to rise and completed the task. Although the translation of Genesis seems to imply the whole of the earth was covered it is now believed that the translation of the word 'earth' is somewhat misleading. The Hebrew word for 'earth' – eretz- can either mean the Earth or the soil and the word 'har' can also mean mound or mountain. It is also assumed that the figure of 15 cubits in reality means 7 metres – enough to cover the cities (mounds) but not the mountains.

After the flood the cities were rebuilt and became even more impressive than before. Cush, the grandson of Noah, set sail for distant continents and Sumer's reputation for trading began. Grain from Sumer was traded for copper, wool and dates from Dilmun and Oman and lapis lazuli from the Indus valley. Eventually they extended their journeys as far as Africa where they brought exotic animal skins, ivory ebony and gold back to

Sumer. The Nile Valley with its riches gradually became the new 'Eden' because it was so much easier to reach then the 'Eden' of the past. This former Eden then became part of the legend of their history, a place from which the gods came down to earth and founded their civilisation.

Whilst Sumer continued to grow another part of the dynasty settled in Egypt and integrated into the existing population.

One of the questions we asked at the beginning of this chapter was if the gods of the Sumerian period became the God Yahweh when did the 'gods' became one God?

One theory is that it was the Jewish people who left Egypt in the time of Moses who bought with them the idea of one God. It was suggested by Sigmund Freud that the Jewish belief in one God came originally form the Pharaoh Akhenaten who had tried, reasonably unsuccessfully, to compel the Egyptians to monotheistic worship of the God Aten in the 14 Century BCE.

They also bought with them the idea of an afterlife which was the basis of the Egyptian religion. The Egyptians were obsessed with an afterlife. This desire was combined with a belief in a perfect age, the first time of creation.

To them death was just the beginning of the journey to the next life that would be lived in the West and was often known as the Kingdom of the West. To prepare for the journey there were elaborate burial rituals and also a detailed account of the reception they would receive when they arrived at their final destination. Once dead they would need a ferryman to row them across the River of Death and they would then face the trials of the twelve gates. It would seem the twelve gates were associated with different goddesses whose character the dead person was supposed to identify. Some would pass through unscathed; others would suffer torment in the Lake of Fire. Once they had arrived 42 assessors read out a list of their sins. They then had to declare their purity and lack of sin. Following this they would be judged in the Hall of Osiris. If they had led a sinful life they would then be destroyed but if they had led a good life they would be given everlasting life in the next world. If we consider the journey taken from the original Eden to Mesopotamia which had taken several centuries we can see where this 'journey to the other world' could have come from. The journey back to the original Eden was fraught with danger through several mountain passes and only those who were most determined would have been able to reach this 'heaven'.

Cush, grandson of Noah, had pushed the boundaries of his empire and his descendants reaped the rewards in terms of the fabulous riches they found in the distant continents. Cush was known by many different names depending on the language spoken. The Sumerians knew him as Meskiagkasher and the Egyptians as Seth.

The main cult of ancient Egyptians was the worship of a female deity. This was the mother goddess who was also "sky". As we saw in the last chapter, this goddess worship has persisted throughout time and had surfaced whenever the official religions of the day lost their grip. It ended with the Isis mysteries of the 2nd and 3rd centuries' CE. The mystery schools that originated in Egypt told of a secret that was said to overturn all previous preconceptions and there is speculation that this secret was that god was in fact a woman. *"I, Isis, am all that has been, that is, or shall be. No mortal man hath ever me unveiled"*.

One of the best known Egyptian legends is that of Osiris and Isis. But is it based on real events? The story is that Osiris is tricked and killed by his brother Seth. Isis was distraught and went in search of Osiris. When she found his dismembered body she bound it together and somehow inseminated herself with the child of her dead husband. Horus later grew up to take revenge on his uncle Seth. Seth was exiled and afterwards became associated with chaos.

These accounts have been linked by some scholars into a sequence of events that describe a fierce war between the rival enlilite and enkite gods. This again seems to stem from the rules of succession. By marrying Isis, Osiris had ensured that it would be his son and not Seth's who controlled the whole of Egypt. It is more likely however, that this is the story of the unification of Upper Egypt. The Horus king Scorpion was busy expanding southwards when his kingdom was attacked by the descendants of Seth. The battle that followed resulted in victory for the Horus king and eventually to the unification of Upper Egypt.

Let's go back to the first theory and see what that has to say about the time after the flood.

After the flood the earth was divided. Enki then arrived in Egypt to undertake the reclamation work. This involved raising the land above the waters. The grandson of Noah, Canaan, decided to leave the lands assigned to him by the gods and strayed in to Lebanon. This caused a full scale war in which the Enkite gods were driven out of Canaan.

In. Anna was the granddaughter of Enlil and was famous for her sexual exploits. Incensed at the death of her husband and the thwarting of her political plans, she plotted to become the sole female god worshipped by the Harappans. This was in marked contrast to the other civilisations that worshipped many gods. In. Anna. returned to visit Enki, apparently got him drunk and tricked him into giving her some divine objects called "me's". No one appears to know what these are but this theory suggests that they were possibly some kind of nuclear warheads. She returned to Uruk and became a very powerful god. It was then she found "Sargon the Great" who founded the Akkadian empire in 2,400 BC. It was then that In. Anna. became more dangerous than ever.

To start with they avoided conflict with the other gods but then Sargon removed something from Babylon that "legitimised" In.Anna.'s city of Agade. This bought the return of Marduk. He built a sophisticated irrigation system that provided the surrounding cities with water for irrigating their crops. But Sargon's successors and Marduk continued to fight and a council of the gods finally persuaded Marduk to leave. This he agreed to do providing no one touched the water supply. However, Nergal, who had been sent to persuade him to leave, then sabotaged the water system. This caused a serious drought for which Nergal was called to account. After Marduk's departure, In. Anna. decided to increase her territory; this time making an alliance with Sargon's grandson. She conquered Jericho, Baalbek, Sinai and finally Egypt.

Whether it was the conquest of Sinai or the Enkite territories that annoyed the gods is unclear, but the council of the gods arrested In. Anna. and removed the source of her power. In retaliation, with Sargon's grandson, she staged a revolt against the council of gods that ended in the destruction of Agade. "The curse of Agade" states that the gods removed all trace of Agade, the Akkadian empire disintegrated and anarchy reigned. Agade collapsed in 2200BCE and has never been found.

The wars continued unabated while Marduk tried to take Sinai. Eventually nuclear weapons were used in an attempt to prop up a failing empire. The Sumerians state the battle for Sumer was fought by Elamite troops against Amorites. In the meantime Sumer disappeared almost as suddenly as it had appeared. Recorded in "Lamentations" the destruction of Sumer was something even the gods could do nothing about. As the Uruk Lament states: *"thus all its gods evacuated Uruk; They kept away from it; They hid in the mountains. They escaped in the distant plains."* Enki and his wife Niinki also left their city of Eridu as can be read in "The Eridu Lament":*"Niinki its great lady, flying like a bird, left her city Father Enki stayed outside the city For the fate of his harmed city he wept with bitter tears."*

According to this theory warfare, something the Sumerians knew all about, was not mentioned. Instead it was described as an "evil wind" a "storm" which accompanied a "ghost". This destroyed several cities and every living being except those gods who escaped.

In fact Sargon ruled for over 50 years and fought and won many battles. The Akkadian language gradually replaced the Sumerian language as the individual Sumerian cities fell under Sargon's control. It was a series of earthquakes that actually heralded the end of Akkadian empire. The earthquakes were followed by plagues and famine as the temperature rose and the rainfall decreased. The land erupted into warfare as rival groups fought over the meagre resources. Eventually a new ruler Ur 111 founded another Sumerian dynasty which survived for a brief time (1900 – 1793BCE) before being overthrown by a new group called the Amorites. The Amorites worshipped the moon god Sin or El as he was also known. El was the Amorite name of the god Eya. Eya was the god of the original Eden.

Sodom and Gomorrah

Abraham is seen as not only the founder of Judaism (Judaism is one of the oldest monotheistic religions and was founded over 3500 years ago in the Middle East), but also one of the 5 universal messengers of Islam. Jewish tradition states that Abraham was born in Ur in Babylonia in about 1800BCE. The son of a merchant who sold idols, Abraham questioned his father's faith and came to believe that the world was the work of a single creator. In an attempt to persuade his father of the truth of his beliefs he smashed all his fathers' idols. When asked why he explained that the idols had got into a fight and the big one had smashed all the other ones. When his father ridiculed this by saying that the idols had no life or power, Abraham asked him why then did he worship them?

Abraham was then asked by God to leave his home and God would give him a great nation and bless him. Thus the birthright or covenant was formed. (Genesis 12). This idea of a birthright is fundamental to traditional Judaism and defines the rights and obligations between God and his people. The birthright also includes giving the Jews their homeland. Thus Jews believe that God appointed the Jews to be his chosen people in order to set an example of holiness and ethical behaviour to the world and gave them Israel. Abraham, who was a city dweller, then adopted a nomadic lifestyle, travelling through what is now Israel, for many years.

Abram and his family journeyed from Harran to the

Egyptian border. Because the area was in the grip of a severe famine they were unable to settle anywhere for long. To cut a long story short, after several years and a brief visit to Egypt, the nomadic tribes of the Northern Amorites were attacked by Amar-Sin, the ruler of the Ur 111 empire. The kings of Sodom and Gomorrah were defeated in bloody battle by the Dead Sea. Lot was taken captive and later rescued by Abram. He decided to settle in Sodom which was then a prosperous settlement on the western shore of the Dead Sea. Even through the height of the droughts Sodom had survived thanks to the En-Gedi spring. In the summer of 1830BCE earth tremors began to shake the city. Although ignored by many of the inhabitants, Lot decided to take his followers back to the hills and escape. The ensuing earthquake was followed by fire and flood, completely destroying Sodom and sinking it beneath the waves of the Dead Sea.

There are other theories which offer alternative versions about the destruction of Sodom. One suggests that there was some kind of battle for supremacy between the gods and quotes the Bible to support it. Genesis 18-19 describes a god who *"carried out a premeditated attack and did not bother to differentiate between the people and the vegetation of the plain".* This refers to the destruction of Sodom and Gomorrah being carried out by a god that destroyed those who pleased him along with those who did not please him. As the peoples of this time did not have the same understanding of geology and fault lines as we do it is not in the least surprising that they would have considered any natural disaster to be the result of the gods.

Other theorists dispute whether the destruction did really happen. Because the location of these places is still disputed its hard to prove either that the destruction did happen or if it did, what caused it. Geologists looking at the geological history of the Dead Sea area point out that there is no evidence of any volcanic activity in the past 4000 years there but there may have been an earthquake along one of the fault lines near the Dead Sea. Other theorists who insist that the story of Sodom and Gomorrah was a true story claim that to destroy everything so thoroughly would have needed a power equivalent to the nuclear weapons used in Hiroshima and Nagasaki.

As bizarre as this may sound there are also many people who now believe that there was an ancient nuclear war. The Mahabharata, an ancient Indian saga that is at least five thousand years old, speaks of flying machines called Vimanas that were used to launch a powerful weapon of destruction:

" ... (it was) a single projectile,
Charged with all the power of the Universe".
"The Earth shook, scorched by the terrible heat of this weapon.
Elephants burst into flames and ran to and fro in a frenzy,
 seeking a protection from terror.
Over a vast area other animals crumpled to the ground and died.
The waters boiled, and the creatures residing therein also died.
From all points of the compass the arrows of the flame rained continuously!
An incandescent column of smoke and flame,
As bright as the thousand suns
Rose in all its splendour...

...it was an unknown weapon,
An iron thunderbolt,
A gigantic messenger of death,
Which reduced to ashes
The entire race of the Vrishnis and the Andhakas.

...The corpses were so burned
As to be unrecognizable.
The hair and nails fell out;
Pottery broke without apparent cause,
And the birds turned white.

After a few hours
All foodstuffs were infected...
....to escape from this fire

The soldiers threw themselves in streams
To wash themselves and their equipment.

But it is not just the Mahabharata that describes such things. Similar accounts of great destruction are also found in the Tibetan Stanzas of Dzyan, the beliefs of the Hopi Indians, and, as we have seen, even in the Bible

In Rajasthan, India, scientists have found of a heavy layer of radio active dust. They have also unearthed an ancient city where the evidence appears to show that there was an atomic blast about 8,000-12,000 years ago that destroyed most of the buildings and up to half a million people. Proponents of this theory quote the following as part of their supporting evidence.

The French obtain their uranium from Oklo in the Gabon Republic in Africa. In 1972 they apparently discovered that the feed uranium was depleted as if it had already been used. When scientists investigated they found that the uranium had indeed already been used. The French also found traces of fission products and fuel wastes at various locations in the mine. Natural uranium can only go critical under special circumstances and needs either the presence of graphite or heavy water as a moderator.

The half-life of uranium 235 is $7.13E8$ years. (This is just a way of measuring and apparently equates to something in the range of 15000 – 300000 years. It can be used to measure millions of years. Suffice to say it is a long time ago and you don't need to remember it!) This is considerably shorter than the half-life of uranium 238 at $4.51E9$ years. Since the original formation of the earth, more of the Uranium 235 had decayed than the Uranium 238. This means that the natural uranium ore had a much higher uranium concentration many years ago than it does today. This would mean that 3 billion years ago the Uranium 235 concentration was high enough to reach critical point and thus cause a chain reaction in the ordinary local water. This would seem to point to the presence of a large nuclear reactor in the area. Yet its impact on the surrounding environment was limited to 40 metres on all sides because of the surrounding geology. Is this a 'naturally occurring' nuclear reactor or a relic from a prehistoric civilisation? If it was a prehistoric civilisation it would have to have been a more technically advanced civilisation than ours is today. Compared to this 'natural' nuclear reactor ours are singularly unimpressive.

But let's now return once more to Sodom and Gomorrah. Other texts that predate the bible give more background information. They claim there was a heated argument concerning the right of the god, Marduk, Enki's son, to return to his city of Babylon. Enki defended his son but the other gods were in disagreement. The gods asked An to resolve the conflict and he agreed to the use of 7 powerful weapons. But one of Marduk's brothers warned him and he escaped. Another brother suggested that the weapons be used against Sodom and Gomorrah because he believed Marduk and his son to be hiding there. According to the "Erra epic" it was this that also created the Dead Sea.

As we said earlier, it is believed that Sodom and Gomorrah are beneath the Dead Sea although the actual location of is still disputed. To this day unusual levels of radiation are found in the water on the edge of the southern edges of the Dead Sea. There is also an enormous geological scar and in the eastern Sinai millions of blackened stones strewn over miles have been found.

Abram

In the meantime Abram is now getting old and he still had no children. His wife Sarai was beyond child bearing years so she offered her maidservant Hagar as a wife to Abraham. This was common practise in the region at the time. Hagar was descended from a Pharaoh and bore a son, Ishmael who, according to both Muslim and Jewish tradition is the ancestor of the Arabs. Abram was then 83 years old.

According to certain scholars the following passage implies that someone told God about the plan of the kings of Sodom and Gomorrah to try and take Sinai and that this person was Abraham. The bible states *"then the lord said: "the outcry against Sodom and Gomorrah is so great and their sin so grievous that I will go down and see if what they have done is as bad as the outcry that has reached me"* Genesis 18: 20-21.

As we have seen Abraham moved around a lot after he left Ur. This movement has been woven into a theory which suggests the following: Abram went to Harran by means of Canaan just before Marduk was due to arrive. He then went to the Negev and from there to Egypt. He was in Egypt between 2048BCE and 2043BCE consulting with the northern pharaohs who were fighting Marduk's supporters in the south. Abraham was in a good position to report troop movements as he had a good relationship with the Canaanite kings. He arrived in Canaan in 2042 BCE a year before the Canaanite kings rebelled against *sin*. After the battle of the kings he took 318 Amorite soldiers and rescued Lot from the east. Abraham returned to Canaan as the kings were getting ready to march on Sinai in 2041BCE. It has been suggested that the "altar" Abraham built to "call on the name of the lord" could have been his way of talking to *sin*. It was then that God promised the land to Abraham's descendants and offered them prosperity.

When Abraham was 100 God promised him a son by Sarai, changed his name to Abraham from Abram (this means father of many) and changed Sarai's name to Sarah (princess). In 2024BCE, when he was 99 and the same year Sodom and Gomorrah were destroyed, Sarah became pregnant. Sarah had a son called Isaac who is the ancestor of the Jewish people. Although Issac was the second son of Abraham because he was the son of Abraham's wife he took precedence over Ishmael who was born out of wedlock. This caused considerable animosity between the two women which eventually culminated in Sarah demanding that Hagar and Ishmael be banished from the camp.

Hagar and Ishmael went south to Egypt where Ishmael married an Egyptian and had 12 sons who founded the Arabian nation. In exactly the same way Issac also had 12 sons who founded the Israeli nation. As both Arabs and Jews are related by birth and as both are descended from Abraham they are both entitled to the birthright as chosen people and to the homeland of Israel. Thus the current political problems in the Middle East appear to have their origins in something that goes back about 4000 years and was essentially a dispute between two women over the inheritance rights of their sons.

Myths, Legends and Politics

Let's finish this section by returning to the Bible and examining some of the "myths" of the church. "Myths" can be defined as "a story about superhuman beings of an earlier age taken by preliterate society to be a true account, usually of how natural phenomena like social customs came into existence".

Interestingly enough there is now a theory that the monsters and giants beloved of Greek mythology may have been based on the fossils they found of prehistoric mammals such as the mammoths, smilodons (sabre toothed cat) and mastodons. Because the fossils were damaged they were unable to see how they really fitted together and because they had no concept of these kinds of animals they assumed they must belong to some kind of giant human or monster.

One of the problems for the church is that the "virgin" birth predates Christianity. Another "virgin" birth myth is that of the Buddha who was born of the virgin Maya around 600BCE. The cult of Mithra is particularly difficult for the church to explain. It comes from the Persian cult of Zoroaster and appeared in the Roman Empire about 67BCE. It also includes baptism, a sacramental meal, as saviour god who died and rose again to act as a mediator between man and god, a resurrection, a last judgement and heaven and hell. Interestingly candles, incense and bells are also used in its ceremonies. Followers of Zoroaster were perfectly happy to live peacefully alongside the many other flourishing cults within the Roman Empire until their "myth" was absorbed by the less tolerant Christians. As we explained in The Re-Enlightenment the Roman Emperor Constantine incorporated these pagan rituals into the Christian religion in order to cement the society together.

The name "Jesus Christ" is actually a later Greek title. It is believed he was known during his life as Yehoshua. This means "Yahweh delivers". While "Jesus" is simply a translation of the Hebrew, where did "Christ" come from? It is a Greek translation of the Jewish "messiah", a person who will become the rightful king of the Jews. It means a king to be or a king in waiting. Although only used twice in the authorised version of the Old Testament and completely unmentioned in the New Testament it was in common usage in the time of Jesus, when the Jews were looking forward to governing themselves and freeing themselves from the Roman occupation.

The Old Testament is used to underpin Christian beliefs, beliefs that are an amalgam of different myths, legends and truths and half truths. For instance: the story of Moses seems to have been derived from the story of Sargon the Great who was believed to be the son of a gardener. His mother's origins seem even more obscure. It is suggested she may have been a prostitute or a priestess of Ishtar or In. Anna.

One legend related of Sargon in neo-Assyrian times says that *"My mother was a changeling (?), my father I knew not. The brothers of my father loved the hills. My city is Azurpiranu (the wilderness herb fields), which is situated on the banks of the Euphrates. My changeling mother conceived me, in secret she bore me. She set me in a basket of rushes, with bitumen she sealed my lid. She cast me into the river which rose not over me. The river bore me up and carried me to Akki, the drawer of water. Akki, the drawer of water, took me as his son and reared me. Akki the drawer of water, appointed me as his gardener. While I was gardener Ishtar granted me her love, and for four and (fifty?) ... years I exercised kingship."*[8]

Sargon, throughout his long life, showed special deference to the Sumerian deities, particularly In. Anna, his patroness, and Zababa, the warrior god of Kish (Cush). He called

---

[8] Roux, Georges (1982) "Ancient Iraq" (Penguin, Harmondsworth)

himself *"The anointed priest of* Anu" and *"the great ensi of* Enlil".

The editing of the Old Testament was begun as early as 2CE. At the beginning Christians saw themselves as Jews. But as the number of gentiles [non Jews] increased they no longer considered themselves to be Jews. Thus was begun a long tradition of anti - Semitism that has its roots back in the 2nd century and still exists today. Christians added new passages and whole new chapters then accused the Jews of doctoring the Old Testament. The 22 books of Holy Scriptures of the Old Testament were increased to ensure there were plenty of references to the "saviour". They then proceeded to produce the entire New Testament.

Jesus

Modern democracies have, for the most part, separated religion from the state. However, in many countries this is still not the case and, as we have said, in the past religion and politics were one and the same. In Judea and Galilee the political struggle was synonymous to their relationship with God. Nowhere in the Old Testament did it prophesize the coming of a world saviour. The Jews were expecting an earthly king who would deliver them from Roman rule and give them autonomy. Jesus could not be a messiah because he never became the undisputed king of Israel.

Let's now move on to the crucifixion. The name of the murderer released in preference to Jesus was Barabas. But Barabas was not a name it was a title. It means "son of god". Early manuscripts of Matthew 27: 16 use the man's full name: Jesus Barabas.

So according to the gospels the man who was released was Jesus the son of god. The first name was deleted from later manuscripts in an attempt to make the facts fit the myth. The gospels further state that Barabas was a Jewish terrorist, facing a similar accusation as to the one bought against Jesus.

The plot thickens! We now have two men of the same

name with the same claim and both accused of the same crime. So how do we know which one was released? Many of the world's oldest sects do not believe Jesus died because another died for him. Muslims consider Jesus to be a prophet who was ordered to be crucified but that another had taken his place. This myth is central to Christianity but so many people do not believe it. Why? The only evidence to support the Christian version comes from the New Testament which was written by the Church.

So if we accept that Christianity is just an amalgam of different myths and superstitions, perhaps we need to also look into this idea that there were two men called Jesus. This is not as strange as it may appear. It is now believed that the myth of "Robin Hood" was based on the lives of several noblemen who lived outside the rule of the Norman rulers and not just on the life of one man. There is also mention, in other documents that have survived, of several other healers and prophets who were active around the same time as Jesus. It is possible that the life of Jesus was actually based on the lives of several healers/preachers/prophets who were active at around the same time and have been subsequently airbrushed from history.

There was also a tradition of two messiahs working hand in hand to free the Jewish people. One was a kingly messiah from the tribe of Judah, the royal line of David. The other would be a priestly king from the tribe of Levi. Both were caught in a round up of "trouble makers" and accused of inciting a revolution. Feeling the ugly mood of the crowd Herod decided to release one of the men in the hope it would quell trouble. The Jesus from the royal line of David thus died while the priestly Jesus went free. So which was which? The gospels have done such a good job of combining the two it is very difficult to decide.

The Jesus born to Mary could not be the kingly messiah because his ancestry, according to the gospels, was through Joseph, Mary's husband. However, Joseph was not Jesus' father the gospels tell us. If this Jesus was the Son of God, he could not be the royal messiah, but he could be the priestly messiah. He was related to John the Baptist, who was a Levite and would therefore have had Levi blood. Thus it may not have been this Jesus who died.

There is a gap of 10 to 15 years between the writings of Paul and the other ones of Mark etc. The country was a mess. Taxation was unfair, officials were increasingly corrupt, privateers had their own protection rackets and unrest grew daily at the unfairness of it all. (Sounds familiar?) Not only did the Romans make life difficult but the ruling families made things worse.

This finally led to outright war between the Romans and Jewish people. The Jewish people waited in vain for Yahweh to save them but it was not the right time. Eventually all that remained was a religion for which they have been persecuted ever since. One of the reasons for this is that history is always written by the victors and is always biased towards the victors. Eventually what is written becomes "fact" because the "losers" do not have the means to put the truth across. Instead they resort to hiding it for a time in the future when it is the right time to release it to the population as a whole. Is this what happened to the truth about our beginnings?

For centuries the pagans have been vilified because the Roman Christians needed to remove all traces of their history and culture. It is only recently that historians have begun to unearth the other side of the story and as time goes on more and more will be uncovered. But perhaps more importantly, the Romans were also responsible for replacing the enlightenment, free thinking and tolerance that prevailed among the pre Christian civilisations including the Celts and the many tribes in what is now Europe, with their own barbarism and with a totalitarian regime.

In fact, if we look through history, we can see that periods of enlightenment, freedom of thought and new ideas are invariably followed by periods of totalitarianism and fascism in one form or another. It would seem that we have lost huge amounts of spiritual knowledge in the past because of these totalitarian regimes who often destroyed considerable amounts of knowledge in their attempts to control their populations and to stifle protest and freedom of thought. It has been suggested that when the library at Alexandria was destroyed some time after 400CE we lost at least 532,000 documents. One of the first things totalitarian regimes often do is destroy knowledge but why is this?

Knowledge is power

There is a saying that knowledge is power and if you think about it this is very true. If you own the means of information and knowledge you can become very powerful because you can control the answers. Much of the power the Catholic Church had in the past stemmed from the fact that their monks and priests were able to read whilst the rest of the population couldn't. This enabled them to edit the bible and to ensure that their version of events became the established and accepted version. By destroying opposing views and opposing texts power became concentrated into the hands of a few. It was this concentration of power that enabled the church to control the populations of the post Jesus era.

But this is as true today as it was then. The Nazis destroyed millions of books and restricted the reading of Germans in the 1930s. As recently as the 1980s the Mullahs in Iran wanted to destroy a book – The Satanic Verses- as they considered it to be insulting to their beliefs and even issued a fatwa against the author. Numerous other petty dictators have ordered restrictions on the information that they want their populations to have access to.

But it is not just dictatorships and religious groups that restrict the freedom of information. Modern liberal democracies are often not as free with their information as they would have us believe. One way of ensuring that the information you possess is restricted from general distribution is to clothe it in language that makes it totally inaccessible to most of the population. By using acronyms and special language the general population are often excluded from accessing information until the language used is assimilated into modern usage. But this can take time. And this is not the only way of restricting the flow of information.

There are many 'historical' films. However, because of artistic license, they are not truly historical. Instead they are 'based on' historical events. This is not a problem if this is made quite clear and if the world's populations are reasonably well educated and know the truth. If they are not, the truth becomes the version shown in the film. In some films the story is distorted to such an extent that it bears no reality to the truth. This is exacerbated by the need for filmmakers to make huge sums of money to cover their costs. To do this the film needs to appeal to the American audience. Unfortunately the filmmakers seem to think that if the hero or heroine is not American, the American people will not bother to go and see the film. This is extremely insulting to the population of the US, as well as citizens of other countries who have had their history hijacked. There have even been some war films made that totally exclude the main participants, replacing them with soldiers of a country that was either not there at all or that played a minor role in the conflict. Whilst this is this an insult to those who fought and died in that conflict, it also shows how easy it is for the truth to disappear beneath myth and legend.

Another way that is popular with modern liberal democracies is to bombard people with so much useless information that anything that is relevant gets lost. We are sure you can all remember the publicity over the leaking of information that was done on September 11th 2001 by civil servants who considered it to be a good day to release news that reflected badly on the government.

It would therefore seem that just as we, on our own personal spiritual journey, are destined to repeat many of our experiences and mistakes, the world is also on its own spiritual journey and as such is also destined to keep repeating the same experiences and mistakes. Furthermore, it would seem that like us, the world, is also unable to leave the past behind and move on, with the same disastrous consequences. To find out why this is we need to take a deeper look at why we are here and why it is that we need to evolve.

'Politics is supposed to be the second oldest profession. I have come to realize that it bears a very close resemblance to the first.'
Ronald Reagan (1911 - 2004)

'Many forms of Government have been tried, and will be tried in this world of sin and woe. No one pretends that democracy is perfect or all-wise. Indeed, it has been said that democracy is the worst form of government except all those other forms that have been tried from time to time.'
Sir Winston Churchill (1874 - 1965), Hansard, November 11, 1947

The Middle

We have now arrived at the most important part of our journey. We have progressed through our spiritual childhood and adolescence and are now ready to take our place in the adult world. Like most children and teenagers we cannot wait to grow up and become adults, to take responsibility for ourselves and to have control over our own lives without having someone else tell us what to do. But is adulthood really like that?

There are still rules that we have to abide by and boundaries and limits that we have to stay within. We may be living with another adult who has grown up with a different outlook and a different set of boundaries. If we are to have successful relationships with others we have to learn to compromise and to sometimes put other people's wishes before our own. Conversely, we also have to learn to listen to ourselves and not to be influenced by others if we do not agree with them. In other words we have to find out who we are, accept ourselves as we are and find security in that knowledge. We also have to learn that all actions have consequences and that the ultimate responsibility for our actions rests with us. We may also now have responsibility for a child and if we have then it is us they rely on for all their material needs, not to mention our example that they follow. We sometimes have to make difficult decisions and things do not always work out as we planned. But this is all part of life and our life is our spiritual pathway, the pathway that we chose when we were in spirit. But for the majority of people the time in spirit is now long forgotten.

However, there are those whose pathway means they remain close to spirit as they spend much of their life in meditation, secluded from the outside world. Sometimes these are older spirits who have chosen this pathway so they can spend their earthly life sending powerful healing thoughts out to the world. But the majority of us find ourselves so busy that moments of quiet reflection are few and far between. Think for a moment about how difficult it is to find true silence now. Even if you turn off your radio or television and switch off the phone, there is still noise. You will still be able to hear traffic, generators humming, electrical equipment and other noises in the distance. Even if you go out into the country it is still hard to find total silence. Most background noise is so much a part of our lives that we do not really notice it any more.

As we grow older it becomes vitally important that we find some time in our lives to sit quietly and enjoy the solitude that being in our own company brings. It is this time that allows us to reconnect to our spiritual self and to listen to our inner voice and understand our true spiritual pathway. Taking a break from the turmoil of our thoughts gives us an opportunity to relax and recharge our batteries. Whilst our primary aim is to experience life we are also here to learn to listen to our spiritual voice and we can only do this when we are able to still our earthly thoughts. The easiest way to do this is to sit quietly and meditate. As with everything in our lives, we need to find balance and harmony and this also applies to whether our lives are noisy or quiet, and whether we spend our lives in crowds or in solitude. For a balanced life we need to experience both.

As children we were close to spirit and we could often remember being in spirit. As we grow older we forget. Those who had happy childhoods saw life through the eyes of a child with trust and belief that things were always good and that if they weren't our parents could always make them better. That certainty and faith begins to go as we travel through our adolescence. The first time we realise that our parents do not have all the answers can be quite devastating, but we do learn to adjust. It is this that spurs us through our teenage years as we begin to question and find our own answers. We can even become quite arrogant as we assume we have all the answers about life and our parents know very little. This is all a perfectly normal part of our physical journey through life and the same is also true of our spiritual journey.

The following section is about our spiritual adolescence and our emergence into spiritual adulthood. For the planet, our spiritual adolescence could be loosely described as the last 5000 years. We covered the first 3000 of those in the last section – the period after the emergence of masculine gods and war up until the birth of the Common Era, as it is now known. This section roughly reflects the last 2000 years from the birth of the Common Era.

Our physical lives here are totally dependant on the politics and religion of the societies in which we live. Even if you think you have no interest in politics or religion, it affects every aspect of your life. From the minute you get up in the morning until you go to bed at night, someone somewhere is making decisions either on your behalf or that will affect you in some way. One of the responsibilities of being an adult is to participate in the society in which you live. If you do not, others will make decisions for you that you might not agree with.

Spiritually, we also have a responsibility to participate in the decision making process in our community. At present, decisions are made by those whose motives are physical, earthly and materialistic. Evolution and development are only seen in these terms. This will only change when we allow our spiritual selves to again become the dominant force of our existence. In Chapter 2 we saw how the world lived in comparative peace and real gender equality until the Indo-Europeans invaded and bought with them the idea of conquest, subjugation and the worship of their male gods. We also considered Leonard Shlain's theory that explained how literacy engages the masculine half of the brain and it was this that changed how the world behaved. As spiritual children we lived here in spiritual harmony. The feminine peaceful and gentle side of our spiritual selves was able to express itself freely. There was no need for gender inequality because the feminine side of our physical selves did not understand insecurity or jealousy. This is not a feminist statement because we each have a left and right side of the brain. The left is predominantly masculine and the right is predominantly feminine. Again this is not a feminist statement. Masculine and feminine in this sense is not really a gender difference more an interpretation.

This interpretation has arisen from the generally accepted description of the gentle peaceful side of us as feminine and the strong, aggressive, forceful side of us as masculine. This is because when these categories were decided the world was dominated by men who saw strength, aggression and might as the virtues and gentleness and peace as weaknesses. The Bible talks of a left and right side of God, referring to the left side as 'bad' and the right side as 'good'. Is it possible that this refers to the left and right sides of our brains?

During puberty our bodies, brains and minds undergo several changes. During our spiritual puberty the same thing happened and we began to engage the left hand side of our brain in a much more forceful way. This left us with several thousand years of chaos. It also left us with several conflicting views as to the best way to live as, like all teenagers, we thought we had all the answers and we thought we knew best. Unfortunately the only thing all these answers had in common was a need to impose them on every body else. We challenged all the spiritual wisdom of the ancients and gradually removed spirituality from our lives. It was rather like letting children loose in a sweet shop and then wondering why they made themselves sick!

It is impossible to consider our spiritual journey without looking at the politics and religion of the last couple of thousands of years. The following section does look at religion and politics in quite a lot of detail. As with the first section you do not need to remember all the details, just be aware of them. Just as when we get physically older the things we learn become progressively more difficult, we are now travelling through our spiritual adolescence so the things we are learning also have to become more involved. But just as when we get older we find more difficult things easier to understand, we will find the next section less complicated because much of it is already common knowledge, just explained in a different way. As with the first section, it is perfectly acceptable to skim read over some of the detail. You can always come back and read it in more detail after you have finished the book.

'The weak can never forgive. Forgiveness is the attribute of the strong'.
Mahatma Gandhi (1869 - 1948)

Chapter 5

In the middle……there is spirit

Change is inevitable. Without change we would not be alive in any sense. However, how we react to change is crucial. How we react to change is one of our gifts and how we use it, like all our other gifts, is up to us. We can react violently against change or we can embrace it and see it as the quickest way to achieving our spiritual goals. It is, after all, the reason that we have taken our earthly form. Disliking change and reacting against it are negative reactions and they normally stem from fear. The fear of the unknown is a very normal emotion but whereas overcoming fear can be very rewarding, allowing it to rule you can be very restricting, not only individually but collectively, as we have seen. But it is not only restricting whilst we are on the earth plane, it can also have an effect on your spiritual development after your physical death. Let's take an example.

When we meditate or open ourselves spiritually we need to use protection otherwise we have no control over who connects to us. Not only are there spirits who work exclusively on the vibrations of love, light and healing, there are those who work on exactly the opposite vibration and then there are those who are through fear have not gone to the light when it was time. The majority of these are people who allowed their fear to stop them doing something they were meant to do. This did not just happen when it was time for them to go but they were like this throughout their lives. Their outlook was always negative. They always assumed things would go wrong and so they did. Thus when it came for them to go to the light they wouldn't go. Even though they were not happy here it was a case of the devil you know. So they stay, but because they are no longer alive they find themselves at a loss. They wander about aimlessly for variable amounts of time and then find someone to attach themselves to.

People who are very negative often behave like this when they are alive. They attach themselves to people and do not let go. This is not because they are evil but because they are scared to strike out on their own, scared to take decisions in case they go wrong and just scared, in general, of anything that is slightly different because it represents a threat to what they know and are used to.

Because they allowed this negative attitude to control their life they are no longer able to overcome that and because they are not able to overcome it they are stuck in a form of limbo. If a negative spirit attaches itself to you it will do its best to live its negative life through you and the first thing that will happen is that you will fall out with anyone that is likely to be able to help you get rid of it.

After that you are likely to become very negative in your outlook on life. As our thoughts are very powerful you then begin to think that everything you do is likely to go wrong and so you start to send out the message that you want everything you do to go wrong and so it does. When you feel negative about something you subconsciously don't really put everything into trying so it is less likely to work. The more things don't work out the more you believe they are going to go wrong and so on. It becomes a sort of self full filling prophecy.

You also start to distance yourself from people and the more you shut yourself away the more likely you are to have negative thoughts because you have no one to bring you out of it and make you laugh. But you do not have to just sit and accept this. Once you have recognised that this is happening you can make a conscious decision to change your pathway.

The first thing you need to do is to use your white light. This is your connection to your spirit and it is this white light that is also your spiritual protection. It is very easy to protect yourself. All you need to do is visualise a white light in the centre of your chest. Visualise this white light getting bigger and brighter until it covers your whole body and you are cocooned in a pyramid or egg of white light so bright that it can be seen for miles! You can then cover this white light with a blue light. While the white light covers you from top to toe and nothing can penetrate it, the blue acts as camouflage so when you stop concentrating on the light your protection remains in place. Ask in your head for protection and that's it. You can do this at any time. Not just when you are going to meditate. Do this when you feel miserable. Do it when you are angry. Do this when you are depressed. Just concentrate really hard on that white light and it will be there. You will find that when you are sad or angry it will be harder to find but it is there.

You may find that when you first try to use your white light you will hear lots and lots of really negative stuff in your head telling you it is a waste of time and a load of rubbish. You have to completely ignore this and concentrate on that white light and replace those negative thoughts with lots of positive thoughts about all the great things you are going to do in the future once it is gone and how you will be able to use this experience to help others. You should then seek someone who is used to sending spirits to the light. Again this is not difficult to do but you do need to know what you are doing so you should not attempt to this yourself. However, once the spirit that has been attached to you has gone it is not completely finished. It's now your turn and this can be the really hard bit! You will also have to do something to overcome the negative feelings that you may still experience.

Because this has been around you for a while you are going to find it quite hard to shake off the pessimism and negative thoughts. They have become a part of you. But you have to try. You need to make a big effort and every time you find yourself thinking something negative, stop and change it to something positive. When you get out of bed in the morning tell yourself what a great day it is going to be and continue telling yourself that all day. If you get out of bed and tell yourself its going to be a horrible day it will be because that is what you are asking for. Because you are in that frame of mind, you will continue to see the day in that light even if it is not really that bad. You can always see something positive if you try hard enough.

For instance insurance companies never pay you what the car is insured for so, if you have an accident, even though it may be no fault of your own, you now have to find extra money to get another car. It is possible to see this differently. You can decide that you have traded in the car and upgraded it for a newer one so of course you have had to put extra money to it. Ok it was something you would have preferred not to do now but it's happened so you will make the best of it. It may be that the new car will be more fuel efficient or that you would not have had the money to change it later in the year. You might have been stuck with an older model that might have started to deteriorate and needed lots of work which would have cost you more money. You have now turned something negative into something positive. This will allow you to move on and turn your attention to something else instead of fretting about something you can't change. It's just a matter of changing your perceptions.

Alternatively you can use your experiences to try and change things so that other people do not have the same problem. Either way, you are using that experience in a positive way and the simple act of taking control of the situation will make you feel much better. You can do this with anything if you put your mind to it. Every experience, whether good or bad is an opportunity for you to put this into practise. In this sense there is no good and bad, all experiences are really just opportunities for you to evolve and develop along your chosen pathway.

Whatever has been around you may have stopped you doing things, in your physical opinion, but it may be that you were being guided in a particular direction so that you could do something else, something you wouldn't have considered if other things had worked out how you intended. You will also be able to use your experiences to help others which may not have been the case if you had followed a different path.

Spirit will always help you to resolve your problems if you ask for help, but it is a partnership. You have to meet them half way. This means that you have to do things to help yourself as well. By making the effort to help yourself you will become automatically more positive in your outlook because you will begin to feel that you are back in control of your life. Ok, you may have times when not everything goes to plan, but that is what life is all about. The trick is to change something that seems negative into something positive. That's what changing your perception really means. You are taking control and seeing that negative event as giving you an opportunity that otherwise would not have been there. If you see change as a positive force in your life and a vehicle towards your progression it becomes less threatening.

But thoughts do not just have a negative effect on our immediate lives. Every time we think something negative, every time we send out a thought that is filled with hate or violence we are adding to the negative energy on the planet. Our thoughts join with all the other negative thoughts of every one else and become the black clouds of hate that engulf so much of our world. Sounds far fetched? Well if you accept that thoughts are energy then like all other forms of energy then you would also accept that there must be positive and negative elements within that energy. That is because everything must have an opposite. If you are continually thinking negative thoughts you become depressed and those around you are affected by your negative energy to one degree or another. If thousands or millions of people are thinking negative thoughts think of the massive wave of negative energy this is sending out.

If you take this one step further consider the effect on the atmosphere of all this negative energy. If you go into a room and some people are having an argument – you can feel it. It is like a physical presence in the room. If there is a war going on in a country this is releasing continuous waves of negative energy into the atmosphere of that country. This atmosphere soaks into the energy of the individuals within that country and they get caught up in a maelstrom of negative energy. The same thing applies to places where ley lines are. Ley lines are considered to be the earth's energy lines. Don't forget the earth is also a living entity and the earth is also a part of the universe.

We have energy centres within us called chakras and these can be energised by us. They can also be opened and closed to regulate the flow of positive energy throughout our bodies. The ley lines fulfil the same function on the earth. They energise the earth with positive energy and the places where they meet are supposed to be very strong conductors of positive energy. Much of the positive healing energy of the earth is completely untapped, because we have yet to learn how to harness and use it properly. But the lines are still there and do not just remain dormant. They will be energised by whatever comes into contact with them, whether it is positive or negative. Ancient civilisations knew the power of these energy centres but were unable to harness the power because the knowledge had been lost. Those who had the knowledge encoded it and hid it for fear that it would be misused because the civilisations of the time were not considered to be sufficiently evolved enough to be trusted with it. In an attempt to access the power, the energy lines became corrupted. This did not stop them working because if they are corrupted with negative energy they will fulfil exactly the same function they were originally intended to do only with negative energy.

There are two ways these lines could have become corrupted. The first is deliberately and the second is unconsciously. We will return to the second in a minute.

Much as it seems hard to accept there is an evil, dark energy that also exists. As we said in The Re- Enlightenment, if you accept there is light then you must also accept there is dark. It is simple physics that everything has an opposite. Research in America has shown that 75% of the population believe in demons. But what are demons?

There are those on the earth plane now, and there have been through out history, who are here solely to promote evil.

These are spirits who have chosen this pathway deliberately. Just as the rest of us evolve towards the light, these spirits evolve further down the path of darkness. Just as the rest of us encourage only the highest and best spirits of the light to be our guides, they will encourage the opposite. Whether these evil spirits take the form of imps and devils may be open to question, but if we accept that there are angels then presumably the opposite of angels must also exist. But even if we don't accept that they take the form of imps and devils we must still accept that evil, in whatever physical form, does exist. We do not really have to look far to find examples of evil anymore than we do not have to look too far to see examples of good. Furthermore, just as there are many ways of ensuring that light, love and truth, are perpetuated on the earth plane so there are several ways of ensuring that the opposite is perpetuated on the earthplane.

One way is to ensure that it is passed down through families. Not through the bloodline, but simply that those who have attracted evil spirits to them, perhaps through Ouja boards, through the misuse of perception altering drugs or excessive alcohol, or simply through the pain of their physical lives, will ensure that their children will also be affected. Although this may be unconscious or conscious, they may cause such pain to those around them that their close relatives live in a state of permanent negativity. This negativity permeates outwards and attracts more negativity, which in turn may attract negative attachments.

Historically, the way of promoting evil was to harness the power of the earth's energy lines. To this end sacrifices were made to the gods and various other rituals were carried out on these sites which desecrated them, much as carrying out black rituals in sacred places does now. This left them corrupted.

Thus by carrying out atrocities and deliberately inviting spirits who are not of the light into the areas where energy lines are situated they have succeeded in reversing the polarity of the energy. Yes we know this sounds really far fetched but lets try to put it another way. If you can energise your own positive energy with the white light, as explained above, then you can do the same to the energy lines of the earth. If you can do this it must be able to work the other way. There are many people who believe that most of the energy lines of the earth are now pulsating negative energy around the earth instead of the positive energy they should be circulating.

But it is not just the deliberate targeting of this negative energy that is causing problems. It is the addition of all the unconscious negative energy we are sending out that is increasing this negativity. So how can we stop doing this? To stop increasing these waves of negative energy we have to first understand some of the ways that we are adding to them.

One way that we all add to this energy without even realising it is when we fail to forgive both others and ourselves. Forgiveness is one the most beautiful words we have because by forgiving we free both ourselves and the person that was responsible for the problem. However, for some reason we find it is much easier to forgive others than it is to forgive ourselves. We forget that we are too are human so we too have faults. We all make mistakes – if we did not make mistakes we would not learn and if we do not need to learn we would not need to be here in the first place. But why do we find it so much harder to forgive our own mistakes than to forgive the mistakes of others? If forgiving others allows us to move on then it stands to reason that if we do not forgive ourselves we cannot be free and if we are not free then we cannot progress and move on.

There is nothing so bad that you cannot be forgiven if you are genuinely contrite. To not forgive is to judge and to judge is a purely human negative emotion. Judging is something that allows you to have a measure of control over others. We are not here to judge others' pathways or learning curves. Nor are we here to judge our own pathways and learning curves.

When we go back to spirit we will have the opportunity to evaluate our lives and the decisions and choices we made and how they affected others. But the key word here is *'evaluate'* not judge. Evaluate means looking dispassionately at a situation - assessing a situation rationally without recourse to an emotional response. Judging involves an *emotional* assessment. This is not a rational assessment because your emotions will automatically colour your response to a situation. The closer you are to a situation the less able you are to evaluate dispassionately and the more likely you are to use your emotions. This will result in a judgement. Once you start to judge you lose your ability to see things rationally. Things become magnified and completely out of proportion.

Spirit does not judge so why do we judge ourselves so harshly? It is because forgiveness, like guilt, is one of our spiritual gifts. And like all our spiritual gifts in can be used positively or negatively. Guilt in its positive sense is what stops us hurting others but in its negative sense it becomes a luxury that you cannot afford in that it allows others to control your destiny.

Many people only apologise because it allows them to control others. If you are genuinely sorry you will do your utmost not to repeat that mistake, that action. Saying sorry is not a 'get out clause' that allows you to keep doing and saying the same things that hurt others, nor should it be a way of making others feel sorry for you.

It is often those who are least likely to take responsibility for their actions that make the most apologies but actually do not mean them. Paradoxically, it is these people who often need the most self -forgiveness. They cannot accept that others will love them if they appear less than perfect. Furthermore, it is usually those people who judge themselves as less than perfect who expect others to be perfect. This sets up a conflict that they find difficult to resolve. On the one hand they need the person they are with to be perfect as this allows them to lean on that person. On the other hand they are constantly looking to destroy that person's confidence because their 'perfection' is a threat – 'if they are perfect they will not love me because I am not so they will leave me etc'.

None of us are perfect, we all have our faults, foibles, oddities, eccentricities and we all make mistakes. If we were perfect we would not be human nor would we need to be here, there would be no need. Our 'mistakes' are our learning curves. But we have to accept this. We can work on our faults, we can constantly strive to improve but when we fail, as we will from time to time, we have to learn from that, let it go and move on. That is self- forgiveness and self- acceptance. Apologise to yourself and take back control of your life. Only by taking control of your life can you become the person you wish to be. Do not hang onto your guilt or your fear – these will just hold you back. Do not use them as an excuse for not moving on or for not changing things.

Playing on some ones emotions is exercising just as much control as using violence to prevent some one in your life doing something that you do not want them to do. Emotional abuse is probably even more common than physical abuse and much harder to see. It also nearly always accompanies other forms of abuse. With physical abuse there are usually physical signs like bruises, cuts, abrasions, burns etc. With emotional abuse there are very few visible signs. The person who is suffering the abuse may not even be consciously aware of it to start with. Those who use emotional abuse to control their partners, children, friends etc do it for the reasons we have already mentioned. They are terrified that their partner, child, friend is going to leave them because they consider that they are not good enough for the person they are trying to control. Eventually they spend their whole time trying to control the emotional responses of that person because it is the only way that they feel in control. Unfortunately, this usually results in the person they are trying to control, leaving them anyway. This happens, not only because their actions have driven them away, but their constant worry has sent out powerful thought messages saying that this is what they want to happen.

Many of those who use physical or emotional abuse as a means of control also use sexual abuse to control their victim. Even though the motivation is control and not sexual this is one of the most devastating forms of abuse. All forms of abuse leave the victim wondering if it was their fault, even if they know logically that it wasn't. But sexual abuse not only leaves the victim feeling dirty and unclean on a physical level it also leaves them feeling dirty and unclean on an emotional level. Whereas a person may eventually be able to move on after physical or emotional abuse, many of those who have endured sexual abuse find it almost impossible, however strong they are and however much help and support they receive. This because the abuse is in the deep recesses of their minds and can be triggered by the slightest thing. It is further exacerbated because the way women and men experience the after effects of sexual abuse is different

For women, sexual stimulation begins in the mind. For men sexual stimulation is a more visual experience. In other words women get turned on by what is happening in their minds more than by what they can see. For men it is the opposite. Because female sexual stimulation is more cerebral it can be much harder for a woman to be able to override the mental images of abuse than for a man. But for a man it is equally traumatic because men are taught that they should be strong and in control. Therefore, for men, the feeling that they should've been able to prevent it adds to their feelings of inadequacy. Part of the recovery process involves being able to accept that it was not your fault – that you are not responsible for the actions of someone else. Recognising this is the beginning of the process of forgiving yourself for being a victim. This may sound totally ridiculous. Those who have never been victims will find this difficult to understand, after all, why on earth should you feel guilty for being a victim?

Unfortunately, all victims feel guilty to some degree or another and victims of abuse are no different. This is because all victims feel that they should have been in control of their own destiny. Because they weren't they feel guilty. It is this guilt that is a negative emotion and it is this guilt that allows those who have abused you to continue to do so. However, understanding and accepting this in a logical sense and understanding and accepting it on a deep psychological level are two different things. It is only when this point has been reached that you are able to finally move on and leave the past and your abuser behind. It is then that you will rediscover your inner peace.

Our aim here is to find happiness but to find happiness we first need to understand what that is. If asked to define what the most important things in our life were, how many of us would say our car or our designer shoes? Bombarded by adverts telling us that we cannot live without things that we have managed perfectly well without for years, it is easy to forget that the things that are important to us are often the things that we cannot see.

If you were told that you were going somewhere tomorrow and you could only take three things what would they be? I am sure that given time for reflection, most of us would say our family (whatever form that family takes), our health and the health of our family (we'll cheat and include this as one item!) and happiness. Not one of those things can be seen or bought, at least not in the conventional sense of the word.

Of all of these it is the last that is the hardest to define. We can have all the possessions in the world but they are not guaranteed to bring us happiness. We can have all the money in the world, but again this is not guaranteed to bring us happiness. Most people with money and possessions spend a lot of time trying to hang onto those possessions and worrying that other people will take them away. We can have all the celebrity and fame in the world but again this is not guaranteed to bring us happiness. Many famous people spend their time trying worrying that someone else will be more famous or popular than them. The strain of trying to hang onto their celebrity at all costs is certainly not guaranteed to bring inner peace. We can have all the power in the world but that too is unlikely to bring a lasting happiness. It may bring fleeting satisfaction but with immense power comes immense responsibility. Many people who start off seeking power with the best of intentions get caught up in the sense of their own importance and forget why they wanted the power in the first place.

Happiness is not found in someone else either. People who are constantly looking for the perfect relationship that is going to 'make them happy' will not find it because happiness starts within and is actually a state of mind.

Happiness is therefore probably best defined as peace of mind. If you have peace of mind then you have no worries or cares because your mind is at peace. The same applies to our spirit. If we have spiritual peace we cannot help but have happiness.

But what is spiritual peace? Spiritual peace is when we know that we are living the life we are meant to be living. Spiritual peace is when we are listening to the spiritual voice within us and following the pathway that we, as spirits, have chosen to live.

This is not as complicated as it may seem. As spirits we have not only chosen the direction our lives will take here, we have also chosen the spiritual destination that we are intending to reach by the end of our time here. Our spiritual destination can be reached however we choose to reach it. We can take the direct route on the motorway or we can meander through the country lanes, stopping to admire the scenery and deviating to look at places of interest. It doesn't matter which way we go because we will all get there in the end. It doesn't matter how many stops we have on the way, or how many times we get lost.

It also doesn't matter which route others take on their spiritual journey because we are all part of the whole and as such have all agreed our spiritual pathway together. This means that there is no reason to be jealous of someone else's life because you are all on your spiritual journey together. Letting go of jealousy and envy is one step towards achieving happiness and happiness is just one of the many free gifts that you can give yourself. Although your paths will cross those of other peoples, all journeys are of equal importance and all journeys will achieve the spiritual aims of the spirit who has chosen them, however many deviations and rest stops they take.

It is not just as individuals that we agree our spiritual journeys. We are also members of our communities so the spiritual choices that we have made also impact on the journeys that our countries are making. The next chapter looks at the importance of identity, change and control in the political evolution of our communities and countries.

'The universe is change; our life is what our thoughts make it'.
Marcus Aurelius Antoninus (121 AD - 180 AD), Meditations

Chapter 6

In the middle there is …..politics

We finished Chapter 4 by asking what would happen if we did not evolve into a higher consciousness and why it is so important that we do. From a physical point of view that is not a particularly difficult question to answer. We only have to look around us to see that the world, like us, seems to be continually repeating its mistakes, albeit in a slightly different form. Why is this?

All living matter is in a constant state of flux- it just happens at different rates. Species evolve into other species over enormous time frames as we discussed in the first chapter. Physically, in the body that we have chosen, we age. As we age we experience many changes within our physiology. We progress from childhood to adulthood and from there to old age. Our culture at present glorifies youth and vilifies old age but is this the way it should be? As children and young adults we make many mistakes - hence the saying that 'you cannot put an old head on young shoulders'! Yes we know that we continue to make mistakes as we grow older but in the main, it is our childhood and young adulthood that is the time for us to make mistakes and to learn from these. This is also true spiritually. It was us, as young spirits, who populated the earth throughout the past centuries. It was us, as young spirits, who slowly began to understand that certain behaviours are unacceptable. But, not only do we experience change physically, we also experience change politically and spiritually. As we said at the end of Chapter 5, it is not only our physical and spiritual beings that evolve and progress. We live in communities and they too evolve and progress.

We have seen, in the previous chapters how civilisations have come and gone. After the fall of the Roman Empire, Europe degenerated into the Dark Ages. Cities and large communities disappeared and the people went back to living in small groups. The emphasis was on survival, not only against the elements but also against other groups and cultures. As we evolved spiritually we learnt to live in bigger groups. These became communities, then small states. These small states joined together to become nations and it is the nation state that is the way we have chosen to live in the last few centuries. But as with the continual fighting of the dark ages, the formation of nation states has not put a stop to war, it has just put it on a bigger scale. One of the reasons we are still fighting is our fear of change. Anything or anybody that threatens to change our way of life causes fear and when we are frightened we hit out.

Why do we dislike change?

One of the most important gifts we all bring to our physical bodies is the gift of change. Like all our gifts it has its positive and negative aspects and it is the way we view and deal with change that governs much of our life on the earth plane. As we, as individuals, came to change our understanding and perceptions of life, our political systems also changed and evolved to incorporate this new social and cultural understanding. However, just as it follows that not everyone evolves at the same rate or in the same way, neither do communities. Political, social and cultural change does not happen overnight and just as we, as individuals, dislike change so did many of the individuals within these communities. One of the reasons we dislike change so much is that change invariably brings instability. Although this may not be a bad thing, because it is taking us outside of our comfort zone, we fear it. Often everything we have known and relied on for our stability has changed or is changing. This makes us fearful and when we become afraid we often become angry.

The early 20th Century was a time when many of the countries that could not accept the changes that were happening turned to backwards' looking doctrines for their stability. By trying to stop the changes that they considered to be undermining the stability of the world that they knew, were comfortable in and where they had a role to play, they hoped to take back some control. We all like to feel useful and productive and the speed of modernisation made many people uncomfortable because they no longer knew where they fitted in. If you also add to this, those whose power was waning, it becomes very clear why the 20th Century in particular was so turbulent. People born at the turn of the 19th and 20th centuries have seen incredible changes in their life times, not just to do with work and technology but with culture and customs and the way they view and are viewed by society.

It is the way we view and are viewed by society that forms part of our identity. It was because people's individual identity was being subsumed under such changes that other forms of identity grew to take their place. We all need a sense of identity to feel part of the world. One of the things change does is to make us question the validity of our identity. Modernisation led to many changes in the workplace and one of the places that gives us a part of our identity is the workplace and the role that we have within the workplace. For instance, if you have always been a miner and are part of that community, part of your identity comes from being a miner in a close knit community. If someone tries to take away that part of your identity you start to doubt who you are. This leads to fear and then to anger especially if you do not really understand the reasons given to you for the need to change, or if you believe or are told that those driving the changes have ulterior motives.

The same thing happened with countries. The populations of countries like Germany who had been used to an absolute monarchy suddenly found themselves in a country where all the boundaries had changed and where everything they had been used to was fast disappearing. They saw the chaos and hardship that resulted from the settlement imposed after the First World War as an attack on their collective personal identities. Add to this the high rates of inflation and unemployment and people needed something that they could depend on that would re-establish these boundaries and give them back their personal identity. Thus a political party that promised full employment and a return to order from the chaos and also blamed someone else for the problems was welcomed with open arms. People needed the reassurance that it was not their fault and scapegoating is an extremely important part of any illiberal government's strategies to win over the population. This is because it is an integral part of human nature to absolve ourselves of responsibility and try to blame someone else. What the people failed to realise and what we all fail to realise to a certain extent is that change is inevitable. It is much more important to ensure that all change is in every body's interest and not just for the benefit of a few and to manage change to ensure it becomes a change for the better for all.

In Germany and Italy the response to change was to turn to fascism, in Russia it was to communism. Both were opposite sides of the same coin. Both ideologies gave structure and order and provided their populations with a sense of identity. This identity was nationalist in character because it was centred on the nation state. It provided people with a common identity that stemmed from shared boundaries, a sense of shared (often mythical) history, a sense of shared national characteristics (again often mythical and more about perception than reality), a shared culture and finally, and most damaging, shared race.

To belong to something implies that others do not belong. Thus any form of national identity implies that others do not belong. As we saw in the first chapter the Darwinian idea of evolution into a higher species became misinterpreted and used to justify ethnic cleansing on a horrific scale. We are here to evolve to the highest level that we can but spiritually not physically.

However, even the death of over 6 million Jewish people was not enough to prevent this happening again. Forty years later we saw the same horrors happening in Europe again after the break up of the former Yugoslavia. This time it was the Muslims who were mainly the targets although there seems to have been policies of ethnic cleansing amongst both Christians and Muslims. One of the reasons for the conflict in the Balkans was that the populations of those areas had not progressed politically since the end of World War 2 because the communist regime prevented any change. Once the communist regime crumbled, the populations of these areas continued the fighting that had been going on 40 years earlier. They had not been allowed to evolve beyond 1945 so once the constraints were removed their evolutionary process continued from where it had stopped in 1945.

The same process is ongoing in Africa where attempts to impose democracy have failed in many countries because they are not ready. Like individual evolution, a nation's evolution needs to take place in its own time. In many cases the problems that exist in Africa and other places, do so because outsiders, who did not understand the people, drew boundaries in the wrong places. Rather than draw boundaries on tribal lines, boundaries were drawn on geographical lines (rivers, mountains etc). Whilst this was logical to those drawing them it made no sense to the peoples of those lands. Because they had not been given the opportunity to evolve in their own time tribalism was the only way they knew. Because these tribes may not have known much about the other tribes or had much to do with them they had no idea how to live in harmony with them. In any case there may have been historical issues that needed to be resolved first. By imposing boundaries and systems of government that these tribes were not able to understand, these issues were not able to be resolved. The only reason European and American democracy works is because this system was chosen by the people as the way they wanted to be governed. It was a voluntary choice. It was not imposed.

This doesn't mean, however, that we should sit back and let atrocities happen. As children we learn by example, as well as by a system of rewards and punishments, and this is no different.

Nations too can learn by example. Perhaps we should look at the example that we have set and are setting before we begin judging and imposing our punishments and our solutions.

Democracy is the result of a thousand years of political evolution and social and cultural conflict. One of the reasons it is so hard to impose democracy on other parts of the world without the same political and social history is because having not experienced the same political evolution they are not ready to accept the changes to their political and social culture. If you add to this the very human dislike of not having someone else impose changes on you then it is not difficult to see why many attempts to impose liberal democracy fail and cause conflict.

If you have a country whose political and social culture has not progressed in many ways since the 7th century for whatever reason, it will be virtually impossible to impose a 21st century political and social culture on it. This is because to live and participate in a democracy you have to understand why it is like that, how it became like that and what your role is within that democracy. This understanding comes as part of growing up within that society and within its culture, from its education system and also by participating in that society.

Whilst democracy provides citizens with rights it also imposes a set of duties on those citizens. It is a two way street. If you expect your country to provide you with legal protection against transgressors and a say in how you are governed and the laws that govern you, you have to participate. The law cannot protect you if you do not support it and you cannot complain about the laws that govern you if you make no effort to vote in those who are governing on your behalf.

One of the modern ways we become part of our culture and society is through the mass media. The media represents and promotes the dominant culture within society and is part of the state's way of unifying its citizenry. But the media in liberal democracies is not owned by the state but by individuals and groups. It is their view of the world that we, the population are subject to. It is they that decide what we should be watching.

They in turn argue that they just put on the programmes that we, the public want to watch. So which is it? Presumably if we are not offered a choice we are not aware of the options that could be available. If you can either watch Big Brother or a programme about celebrity lifestyles you do not have a choice to watch a programme about poverty or injustice or something that is educational about your world.

Not only do we as citizens have a personal responsibility to ensure that we control our thoughts words and actions, we as a community have a collective responsibility to ensure that our thoughts, words and actions are in the best interests of our community. The individuals within the media who are responsible for the content of our programmes, films and video games are also members of their community. They may not live in the community in which their product is sold but they are still part of the community of the world. They do not live in an isolated environment where they have no contact with the world. The content of their programmes, film and video games is their responsibility as individuals and as members of the community. They will be as affected by the outcomes of their product as every other member of their society. They have chosen to be a part of an industry that has immense power and influence. But with this power and influence comes an obligation to ensure that it is used in a responsible manner.

Around the world people are dying and suffering. Yet it often seems that priority on the news broadcasts is either given to trivia, like celebrity life styles or is concentrated on very parochial issues. Although these are often examples of other people's mistakes that we could perhaps learn from, are they more important than a hundred people dying in a car bomb in the Middle East or people starving under a brutal regime?

We are here to evolve and to make the world we live in a better place. How are we going to do this if we do not know what is going on in our world? Our news broadcasts are meant to inform us of news which is why they are called news programmes. The media use the excuse that they broadcast what the viewers want to see but should this also apply to news programmes? If we allow children to choose what they want to eat they will eat all the wrong things and be overweight and unfit. If we want to progress on our spiritual pathway we need to participate in life not just watch it from the sidelines. Concentrating on someone else's pathway is doing exactly that – watching. We are here to evolve and we cannot do that if we do not live **our** lives. It's perfectly ok to watch programmes about celebrities and other more trivial issues but on the whole it is entertainment and should be left at that – it is not news. News means things that are happening in the world that it is important for us to know about. Things that might affect our lives and that are certainly affecting other people's lives on a big scale and whilst we do not want to spend hours watching news about wars and killing and atrocities we do need to know that it is going on.

Strangely enough it seems we are quite happy to watch these things when it comes in the guise of entertainment. Maybe it is because we have lost our direction spiritually that we are perfectly happy to watch violence, killing, wars and atrocities when it is not real but object to seeing it on the news when it is real and real people are suffering. The other problem that arises with treating suffering as entertainment is that we become anesthetised to it and we find it hard to empathise with the real victims because they appear no different from the ones we see in the films and video games.

If you deal with violence and bloodshed on a daily basis a part of you shuts down in response. This is to allow you to continue to survive in this situation. Second hand violence and bloodshed, as seen in the guise of entertainment, has the same effect and although it may be slower in taking effect it is also more invasive because most of the time we are unaware it is happening. It is this daily bombardment that we subject our children to. Because the parameters of films and video games are moved slowly we do not realise the changes that have happened. This only becomes apparent when you begin to compare their content to something that was made a generation earlier.

The second problem that arises is that these type of films and video games not only desensitise us to the victims they also de humanise people. The Nazis used images and film to great effect in the 1930's to dehumanise the Jews with the horrifying consequences that are now so familiar. If you dehumanise someone it is so much easier to encourage people to act against them. This is because they have literally had their human personality taken away and it is replaced with either a form of 'nothingness' or with a two dimensional caricature that only depicts the negative qualities. Just because we think that we have gone beyond this type of behaviour does not mean we should not be vigilant. Perhaps we should take a closer look at the images we use on television, film and video games. Sony has apologised to the Church of England over the use of virtual images of a cathedral in one of their more violent games A cathedral is supposed to be a place of peace and love therefore to use it in a violent way is a form of desecration even if it is not real. They have also withdrawn their latest game because it contains verses from the Koran as part of the backdrop of the music. As members of the community we all need to accept collective responsibility for the direction that our media has gone.

Ignoring a problem does not make it go away. It just gets worse. The same applies to ignoring the problems in the world – not only do they get worse but those who have control over events are able to have a free hand because no one is paying attention. It is our world and only we can do something about it. As individuals it is very hard for us to change things but when individuals join together they become a whole and as a whole we are able to change things. Part of our spiritual journey is about re discovering the one- ness of spirit. Working together and seeing the problems of others as your problems, is part of that.

As we have said the reason the media give for prioritising celebrity before real news is that it is what the public wants. But the price of this is not only that we as a nation are becoming less educated about the world in which we live, but our children are also becoming less well informed about issues which will be of

major importance when they grow up. Furthermore, we, all of us, are being prevented from progressing on our spiritual pathway. Participating in life and achieving our spiritual goals is the reason we are here. If we do not know what is happening in the world around us we are unable to do this and we will not progress. Thus as well as allowing our politicians to escape the consequences of their actions by our apathy.
we could be endangering our spiritual evolution by allowing ourselves to be distracted by trivia.

If we want an educated citizenry with people able to participate in their democracy they need to know what is going on in the world. We should be concentrating on how we can make life better for other citizens in our nation and then in our world, not worrying about and judging someone else's earthly and spiritual pathway.

Control

A large part of our time on the earth plane is spent in working. It is important that we like what we are doing – not only because of the time spent but if we don't enjoy it we will not be doing it properly or giving our best. Like everything we do it should be done to the best of our ability and work is no different. Unfortunately many of us are trapped in jobs we hate and we find it hard to find an alternative.

One thing that traps us in employment and that makes us miserable is that we don't like change. However unhappy we are, the thought of change makes us uneasy and many of us stay where we are because it is a case of better the devil you know than the one you don't. But just think of all the opportunities you could be missing. Staying in a job we hate is not only unproductive physically it is also unproductive spiritually. We are not progressing or moving forward, we are stagnating. If you do any job for too long you become comfortable and you no longer look for ways to improve things or ways of challenging the status quo. Often, because you are inside the situation, you are unable to see whether there is a better way of doing things. Because things have always been done that way and you have learnt to work within or around that problem you stop looking for alternatives.

The other problem that arises is that you begin to think you are the only person who can actually do that job properly so you lose the ability to delegate. No one is indispensable. Sooner or later you will move on and if you do not delegate and let go of the control of that organisation all the hard work that you have put in throughout the years will be lost because there is no one able to take over.

Spiritually we are all one and as part of the whole we should be acting in the best interests of all the other parts of that whole. This means ensuring that there is someone ready to take over and continue the good work.

You are also missing opportunities if you do not delegate. Whilst you are continuing 'in control' your time is occupied and you are not able to make the most of other opportunities that may come along.

Think back to when you started your job. You were full of enthusiasm and constantly thinking of ways to improve things. They may not always be feasible but passion and enthusiasm are the driving force of our physical and spiritual existence. It is this passion and enthusiasm that also drives industry and new innovations in the economy and that drives the engine of a country. Just as we are all part of the whole spiritually, we are all part of our country too and the world as a whole. Without drive and enthusiasm many of the biggest inventions, the greatest medical breakthroughs would never have happened. By taking a chance and finding another job who knows what you might be capable of.

However, one of the major physical things that stops us moving on is our home. Do you remember at the beginning we asked what the word home meant to you? Many of us, in Britain at least, are trapped in employment because it is the only way that we can afford to pay for the roof over our head. Much as we might like to move, find a less demanding job, change direction, spend more time with those we love, we are unable to do this because of the high costs of keeping our homes. Even more people are prevented from fulfilling their true potential because of a lack of housing.

Thousands of people in Britain are homeless. Homeless means not having a permanent home. Thousands of others live in substandard accommodation or in accommodation that they could lose because they are unable to afford it. This is not just a problem for Britain, in America there are thousands of people homeless and rough sleeping in New York alone. This is staggering and in the third world the problem is worse.

This lack of sufficient affordable housing is now exacerbated by the recession and by the ugly spectre of negative equity – where people have paid more for their homes than they are now worth and repossessions. It is ridiculous for banks and building societies to re-possess the homes of people who are having trouble meeting repayments in the middle of a recession when house prices are falling anyway. This just makes the whole situation worse because it adds even more properties to the market when those already there are not selling anyway. It makes much more sense financially and socially to allow those people to remain where they are and pay rent until they are in a position to continue to pay for a mortgage.

As physical beings we need food, warmth, light, water and shelter. These are our basic minimum requirements. The world is full of resources. There is sufficient for everybody if the resources were shared. But they are not. It seems that once we get to a certain point on our journey we forget why we started. We forget that we are here to help others evolve. The more we help others to evolve the more we ourselves evolve. We are all part of a whole so it stands to reason that helping someone else evolve helps us as well.

Unfortunately having forgotten why we are here, we resort to listening to our physical instincts instead of our spiritual instincts. Our physical instincts are pre-programmed into us because we are physical beings. They are commonly known as our animal instincts and they tell us that the 'survival of the fittest' is the only way to ensure our physical survival. Thus we are in competition with everyone else and anyone who appears to have more than us or tries to change things or has different beliefs or views becomes a threat. It is in this way that our animal instincts are closely linked with our spiritual gifts especially the gift of insecurity.

Insecurity

It is the spiritual gift of insecurity that causes the majority of the problems on the earth plane. This is because insecurity leads to fear and this in turn leads to hate and then to articulations of that hate like violence and wars etc.

We are here to empower others not control them. The only person we are here to control is ourselves. We need to exercise control over our own thoughts, words and actions not the words thoughts and actions of others. The more we empower others to help themselves the more we empower ourselves because we free ourselves physically, emotionally and spiritually to move forward. It is the ability to move forward that drives our spiritual evolution.

Insecurity permeates every aspect of life and can be seen in the way we treat others from the personal, through to and including religion and the politics of nations.

If we first look at how the governments of Fascist Germany and Communist Russia treated their citizens we can see that the insecurity that governed their relations with other countries also governed how they treated their own populations. Democracy can be seen as a more evolved form of government that gives its citizens rights and equal access to redress when things go wrong and against excessive interference by the state. This form of government is only successful when all its citizens understand the rights and duties involved and also feel confident that they are part of this whole and have protection against threats to their own conception of how to live their own lives without too much state interference. Liberal democracies are by nature, very open societies. But citizens within this form of state have to have reached a certain level of political evolution otherwise things begin to break down. This can happen for a variety of reasons.

Citizens of liberal democracies accept that for their society to be able to offer equal opportunities there has to be some form of welfare provision for those in society who are not as capable. This is also a spiritual requirement as we have a responsibility to help others. But helping others means empowering others, giving them the ability to help themselves and to change their own lives. If we do everything for other people they not only lose the ability to do anything for themselves they also expect everything to be done for them and this prevents them progressing physically and spiritually. This is just as true on a personal level as it is on a national and international scale.

If you have a relationship with someone and you do everything for them they eventually come to assume that you will always do that. When you suddenly say that you are not going to do it they react badly because something that was done originally in the spirit of giving has become something that is taken for granted. By withdrawing that service you are making changes to something people have got used to. As we have said, when you change things, people become uneasy or threatened. By continually doing things for others and not empowering them you are also making them more insecure because they begin to rely on you. This is damaging to both parties in the relationship as it is preventing both of you from progressing in your spiritual and earthly lives.

The same applies nationally and internationally. Taxation is raised, in part, to help provide services to those who need extra help to allow them to participate in the society in which we all live. However, when the levels of taxation, either indirect or direct, rise above a certain percentage of earnings it can make people feel that there is little point going to work. When this happens and it is coupled with a perception that others who do not appear to work as hard are treated better or that there are those who have come into this country more recently are benefiting without having contributed, problems can arise.

Often immigrants to a country have not had a chance to experience the same political evolution in their homeland. They are attracted to what they see as a better, freer more liberal society as well as the economic benefits and opportunities that appear to present themselves. But they may not understand what is expected from them in return and how they can play a full role in the society to which they have emigrated. This is exacerbated if they do not speak the language very well. Translating things from one language to another does not always work very well as we have seen with the Bible. If you add this to cultural differences and a different sense of humour and misunderstandings can easily happen, especially if they have come from a completely different cultural background with totally different values.

If it does not seem like the host nation is particularly welcoming either then it is easy to see how immigrants can become isolated and want to set up enclaves where the neighbours speak their language and understand them. This can happen even if the host nation is welcoming. The problem that then arises is that the host nation begins to feel uneasy about the seeming colonisation of areas within its cities and towns and tensions arise. This is when extremist parties begin to gain political ground because they play on the fears of people who are not well informed. Of course the reason the people are not well informed is normally because the government, the education system and the media have failed in their role of producing an educated, informed citizenry.

Governments can respond in different ways to these problems. Some allow scapegoating of minorities to take place. This allows them to appear blameless and frees them from having to address the real problems. If there is unrest they can use this to allow them to bring in more stringent laws or to increase the amount of surveillance they have on their citizens. The more insecure the government is, the more likely they are to use these methods to ensure that they remain in power. Paradoxically it is the governments that have been in power the longest that are more likely to behave in this way because staying in government too long leads to exactly the same feelings of insecurity that we have seen on a personal level, with exactly the same results. Control on the reigns of power are tightened, there is a belief that you are indispensable and there is a refusal to delegate because of a fear that someone new might actually be better than you. Again we are back to a fear of change.

Change is only really welcomed when people begin to realise that anything is likely to be better than what they have. But often the problems have become so bad that a considerable amount of time is wasted because these have to be resolved before you can progress forward. This applies on a personal level as well as a national level.

Looking forwards

The present, as so many have said, is a gift and as such we should appreciate and enjoy every minute of it. Looking backwards and forwards is another gift and as we saw in The Re-Enlightenment our gifts can be used in a positive or a negative way. Although we should not be continually looking forward or backwards, there are positive and negative aspects to both. It is the positive aspects of both that we should be concentrating on not the negative.

How can looking backwards or forwards be a negative experience?

Those who spend their lives looking backwards are those who fear change the most. They either waste their time reinventing the past so that it conforms with their idea of how the past should have been or they spend their time regretting past actions that they no longer have any way of changing. But, of course, it is much easier to concentrate on things we can't change than on things we can. If something has happened then it is in the past and cannot be altered. If there is something in our lives now that needs changing it requires us to make some effort. Because we do not know what will happen if we do change things we are often frightened to try in case it goes wrong. But making choices and trying things is part of our spiritual progression and learning to listen to the advice our inner voice is giving us is a major part of that. This is the positive aspect of looking forwards.

Making choices helps us to learn to take responsibility for our actions. Although all actions have consequences some of these are unforeseen. But it is finding solutions to these unforeseen circumstances, being able to adjust to whatever life throws at you, that makes you a strong person and helps you to progress spiritually. If we knew everything that was going to happen to us here there would be little point in being here because we would be able to plan our every move and there would be no surprises. Sometimes surprises can be great! Just think how boring it would be if we knew everything and there was nothing that ever surprised us?

This attempt to make sure that we always know what is going to happen when we make decisions has another side effect and this is one of its negative aspects. There are some people who have become dependant on mediums. These are the people who consult a medium at the drop of the hat. This is not the same as those who need a little reassurance at certain times in their lives so consult a medium to hear the advice or guidance from a loved one. These are the people who about to take a holiday so consult a medium as to where to go, or who are going on a first date and want to know whether this is the man they should marry! Mediums are not there to tell you what you should be doing at every step of your life. You are here to live your own lives. That means making your own decisions and listening to your own instincts. If you get it wrong then put it down to experience. If you never make a mistake you will never progress. Taking responsibility for your own decisions is a really important part of our spiritual development. Going to a medium and expecting them to tell you what you are meant to be doing is not living your life because you are abdicating your responsibility to someone else so that if it goes wrong you have someone else to blame.

If there is something you particularly wish to happen you just need to say that you choose it to happen and then make every effort yourself for it to happen. If it is in your pathway it will happen. But remember, all choices have consequences so make sure that your choices are made in the best interests of everyone. By making choices you are in control of your life, not allowing life to make your choices for you. Being in control of yourself and your life, gives you confidence and when you have confidence you can do so much more to improve your life and the lives of those around you.

So how can we use our gift of looking backwards and forwards in a positive way?

Looking back towards happy memories is a great way of using your gift. But we also look back for other positive reasons, like looking back to see where we went wrong so that we can try to avoid the mistakes that we have made in the past. We live in a modern culture where we are no longer taught how to make choices and decisions for ourselves. The state now has so much control of our lives that it is very easy to blame the state when things are not as we would like. However, the state is essentially the people that we, the people, have elected to represent us. Presumably if we do not like what they are doing we should do something about it. It is not good enough to sit back and blame the politicians for everything. We have given them a free hand because we have taken our eyes off the ball.

The same thing happened in the 1930's. Because everyone was terrified of having another war, the rise of the Nazi's was totally ignored by most people. Only a few spoke out and they were vilified. We are now the most watched nation in the world. We have 1% of the world's population and 20% of the worlds CCTV cameras. The average person is now filmed on camera over 300 times a day and we have over 4.2m cameras – that is one for every 14 people. Yet our crime rate does not appear to have decreased. The amount of information now held about us is also staggering and ranges from what we like to eat (the supermarkets) to our internet habits (the search engines). Although the idea of road pricing has now been shelved, its proposals would have meant that everywhere we went in our cars we would have been tracked. It is already possible to track our every movement through our mobile phones. There are also plans by the current government to bring in ID cards for every adult and also plans to put every child in Britain on a database so they can identify those who are being abused. This is despite the regular headlines proclaiming the loss of yet more sensitive personal data. Is this really the direction we want our society to go?

One of the things our parents and grandparents fought WW2 for was to protect the individual from unnecessary state interference. Whilst the state justifies these infringements of our freedoms by stating that it is for our protection it is also gradually eroding our ability to think for ourselves and to take responsibility for our own actions. The world has been here before and the consequences were global conflict. Those protagonists also told their citizens that the state was acting in their interests and for their protection. Then, as a way of unifying their people, they turned their attention to other states, saying that they posed a threat to the security of the nation.

With freedom comes responsibility. This is the responsibility to ensure that we act in ways that do not infringe the freedoms of others. But in order to do this we have to understand how to do this and this is where our education system has a vital role to play.

However, our education system fails a large percentage of our children because it tries to mould them into one ideal. It needs to adapt to encourage individual talents and abilities to ensure that all our children feel a part of the society in which they are living now and will live in the future. The current system concentrates on fulfilling targets. It stifles freedom of expression and does not help educate children in their role as citizens. All the outside activities that we used to enjoy as children are now denied them because of Health and Safety concerns yet their emotional and psychological welfare is largely ignored. This has left a generation of children who are unable to make decisions for themselves, need someone to tell them what to do, need their entertainment organised for them and lack the confidence to aim for the best in their lives. They are bombarded by images in the media that are at best confusing and at worst, dangerous. They have become both victims and scapegoats.

They are victims because we often do not have enough time to give them because we are too busy trying to pay for the roof over our heads, or because we are excluded from society because we live in ghettos of poverty. Because of short sighted housing policies of successive governments, social housing is now so rare it is a luxury that only the most vulnerable in society are able to access. This leads to enclaves of poverty and vulnerability. The children growing up in these areas have decreased life expectancy and reduced opportunities. Children learn by example and one of the things they learn from us is parenting skills. These patterns of deprivation are therefore likely to be continued as people in these ghettos are forced to live in conditions which enforce poverty and low expectations.

The gap between rich and poor is not decreasing. A recent report stated that Britain was the worse place in Europe for children to grow up in. We also have the highest rate of deliberate self harm and suicide in Europe. Someone commits suicide in Britain every 82 minutes. If we do not accept that we have a problem we are unlikely to be able to resolve it. As members of our society we have a collective responsibility to ensure we take control of the situation and look for some solutions. If we do not change the way we view our lives and arrange our societies our children will grow up with the same insecurities, low self esteem and lack of imagination that we as a nation have.

We have lost the ability to use our imagination and it is our imagination that is our driving force here. It is our imagination that allows us to dream and it is our dreams that create our reality. Without our dreams we would still be living in caves. It is our dreams and imagination that provide us with a positive way of using our gift of looking forwards to how the future should be.

Looking back

The problem with looking backwards in a negative way is that it does not just permeate our personal lives but, as we are part of a community, it affects our political and religious views as well. One of the dangers of nationalist politics is that they often refer to a mythical past to present the kind of past that people would want to return to. Adolf Hitler and Joseph Stalin both wanted to retain control over their populations indefinitely and because both had taken power in undemocratic ways assumed that someone else would do the same to them - hence their paranoid behaviour. But in both societies there were people who supported them. These people saw these men as the saviours of their nations.

Germany after WW1 was suffering from a severe identity crisis. Part of the settlement after the war allowed the German soldiers to return home with their weapons. This allowed those in charge to present defeat in such a way that focussed the blame on the internal problems caused by fighting between the emerging communist and fascist factions. The Treaty of Versailles also imposed reparations that the Germans were unable to pay thus fostering bitterness and animosity towards those who were demanding payment. Democracy only seemed to bring more chaos to their society which was already suffering from high unemployment and hyperinflation. By blaming their misfortunes on an international Jewish conspiracy that was not only demanding these reparations but had stirred up trouble within the country and thus had caused Germany to lose the war they began to reinvent their national history.

The aim of this was to give the German people back their sense of identity, their sense of who they were. The Nazis even went as far as using the swastika (a symbol from the ancient world that came from the Sanskrit word meaning well being). The swastika is actually an ancient symbol that is said to depict paradise with the four rivers flowing from it. But merging myths into their history was not enough to provide complete cohesion. In order to belong to something others have to be on the outside. Thus the scapegoating of the Jewish people in Germany began and in this they were silently aided by the rest of the world who did little or nothing to prevent it. To continue this quest for a national identity that gave them a sense of pride they began to turn their attention to the conquest of others. This shows just how easy it is for nationalist identities to be formed as a result of a sense of national insecurity.

But it is not just nationalist identities that cause problems in the world. Religious identities also cause many problems, not least because they too are rooted in the past and in a world that no longer exists.

'Remember it is the message that is important not the guide'.

'God is not dead but alive and well and working on a much less ambitious project.'
Anonymous, *Graffito*

Chapter 7

In the middle there is…..religion

God as a scapegoat

One of the problems religions have is that throughout the centuries they have insisted that only God has the power of life and death. Unfortunately this has led to God being blamed for all the death and destruction within the world.

Recently certain members of the church have stated that God is responsible for all the floods currently afflicting parts of England[9]. This is apparently a judgement from God on our decadent materialistic lives. This implies that first of all God is extremely judgemental. Presumably a god who is omnipotent would be above such an obviously human failing. Secondly, are they saying that the people suffering flooding are solely responsible for the problems facing the planet or is he/she using them as an example?

Surely a God of love and light who is omnipotent would not stoop to anything quite so low as to target a random sector of society to punish in order to set an example to the rest. If he is that petty wouldn't he be better targeting a sector of the world who do actually have some power and control over planetary events like the leaders of the nations of the world? Or maybe he can't tell the difference? Is this not a prime example of certain people making a god in their own image with their own thought patterns, values and perceptions?

---

[9] 2007

Religious Fundamentalism

Religious fundamentalism is now a well accepted part of our 21st century vocabulary. Fundamentalism simply refers to a belief that if you return to the original status of something, things will improve. Religious fundamentalism shares many of the insecurities and characteristics of nationalism. Its advocates invent the past to suit their view of it and to reinforce their sense of identity. They also scapegoat those on the outside as a way of providing cohesion within their religion. They often claim a territory, although they may no longer live there ie: Jerusalem. They may also claim the right to self determination (having their own political power).

Religious fundamentalists also persist in creating a god who has all their own characteristics. By preaching a version of their religion that is full of righteous judgement they claim they are returning to the fundamentals of their religion. However, as we saw in the first section of this book, the gods of the Old Testament were written in times when the people were politically, socially and spiritually immature and therefore the gods they created were in their image. Thus these gods were vengeful and warlike. Because we have evolved politically, socially and spiritually since then we now perceive god as a god of unconditional love. Unconditional love means non judgemental amongst other things. But because these religions are being interpreted narrowly, in the same way they were centuries ago, they are allowing extremists to claim that God is on their side and it is in Gods name that they are carrying out their atrocities.

Although the media concentrates almost exclusively on Muslim extremists, Christian fundamentalists are also extremely active around the globe. Two thousand years of practise and political and cultural evolution have taught them to be much more subtle in their approach. But this does not make them any less dangerous. The most dangerous of these groups is called The End Timers.

For millions of fundamentalist evangelical Christians across the United States, the Bible foretells the end of the world in The Book of Revelations. These End Timers believe that the Book of Revelations is the literal word of God and that come the end of the world only the true believers will survive to be with god. Everyone else will perish. They also believe in The Rapture. This is the belief that their ascent into heaven will be instantaneous and so complete that they will leave no trace behind other then their clothes. This belief is so strong that there are firms in the USA who prepare letters for these people to leave behind for their relatives explaining why it is that they have just disappeared. The "Left Behind" series of books are runaway best sellers, with 40 million books in print and there are numerous website devoted to The Rapture. Taken in isolation this hardly seems like much of a threat but unfortunately these believers are so looking forward to this that they are actively attempting to bring it to fruition.

The Book of Revelations appears to cite certain events that will foretell the end of the world. These include the rebirth of the State of Israel, rebuilding Solomon's Temple on The Mount in Jerusalem on the site of the Dome of the Rock and spreading their narrow version of Christianity to all countries of the world. According to Jewish tradition those living through the End Time will see all Jewish exiles returning to Israel, the defeat of all Israel's enemies, The rebuilding of the Jewish Temple in Jerusalem and the resumption of the sacrificial offerings and Temple service. There will also be a revival of the dead and at some point the Jewish Messiah will become the anointed King of Israel. He will divide the Jews in Israel into their original tribal portions in the land. During this time, Gog, king of Magog, will attack Israel. Who Gog and the Magog nation are is unknown. Magog will fight a great battle, in which many will die on both sides, but God will intervene and save the Jews. This is the battle referred to as Armageddon. God, having vanquished this final enemy once and for all, will accordingly banish all evil from human existence. After the year 6000 (in the Jewish calendar), the seventh millennium will be an era of holiness, tranquillity, spiritual life, and worldwide peace, called the Olam Haba ("Future World"), where all people will know God directly."

The End Timers are encouraging these things to happen to accelerate the process and bring about the end of the world. It is alleged that many of the people in the current administration in the USA, including President Bush, are End Timers or at least sympathetic to their worldview. It is further alleged that the End Timers are always consulted before major policy decisions are taken. From trying to rebuild the Solomon's Temple on The Mount in Jerusalem on the site of the most holy Mosque, to ignoring the effects of global warming, there are some very powerful people actively working to bring about the end of the world. This is so they can go to Heaven and leave the rest of us unbelievers here to suffer.

But they are not the only extremists we have to worry about. Islamic extremists believe that only those who are Muslims will be saved and that those who die in the name of Allah will be taken instantly to paradise and their reward will be to be given 72 virgins. If you go back to the 7th Century, when the Islamic religion started, you might be able to see why it was considered necessary to provide physical incentives to young men to encourage them to fight for their religion. The Muslims were constantly under attack from many sides and it was Jihad that seemed to be giving them victory. However, as we leave our physical bodies here and it is only our spirit that continues we will have little use for the material in the 'next world'.

It is hardly surprising that both Christians and Muslims are concerned about the long term futures of their religions when fundamentalists amongst them both are busy trying to destroy what they see as the opposition. It is both this fear of the 'others' and insecurity about their own faith that drives this extremism. After all, people who are secure and confident in their beliefs have no need to fear outside influences. And in the middle of this epic struggle, both physically and theologically, are the Jewish people.

Why are Christians and Muslims anti Semitic?

The origins of Christian anti Semitism stem quite simply form the accusation that the Jews killed Jesus Christ who is, for Christians, the literal son of God. Therefore all Jewish people will, for time immemorial, bear this terrible responsibility because they are all to blame. However, if as Christians claim, the death of Jesus Christ was preordained in order to save the world should not those accused of killing him be praised rather than condemned? Furthermore it was not all the Jews who were responsible for his death it was only those living in and around Jerusalem who would have been aware of it. Even those in Galilee were more than a day away and at this period during the occupation by the Romans the majority of Jews were living in Diaspora (elsewhere).

Another point to bear in mind was that when the Gospels were written it was some time after the death of Jesus and they were written at the time when Christianity and Judaism were in open conflict. It is only the Gospel of John that describes the Jews, collectively, as the enemy of Jesus and it is now believed unlikely that this gospel was really written by a Galilean fisherman. The other gospels refer to those who were calling for Jesus' death as a small group of rulers, not the entire population.

The scriptures used by Jesus were from the Law of Moses, the Prophets and the Psalms. It seems that he may also have had access to some of the texts from other versions of the Old Testament as well as he is seen to refer to them at certain points. His teachings were simple and practical, ethical in nature without being parochial or arrogant. They often consisted of parables and legends and were often prophetic in nature with frequent references to the Kingdom of God and the end of the world. Although he used the expression 'Son of God' it is now believed this did not mean the literal son of god; more the spiritual relationship everyone has with a god who is a father figure. He was active in the politics and culture of his time and also believed in the spiritual teachings prevalent at the time including possession, evil spirits, exorcism and the fact that the world was a result of God's miraculous intervention in the world.

Much of this has now been lost and the Christianity we now have comes primarily from Paul. The spontaneity of the early Christian religion was replaced by an authoritarian church system with creeds and scriptures. The key to this was its encounter with the philosophy of Greece.

At the time Christianity separated from Judaism, the world was teaming with Greek, Persian, and Egyptian cults. These cults were mystery religions that offered salvation through faith in which they conquered sin and then became one with the saviour. It is not difficult to see how easy it would be for Paul and the other missionaries to unconsciously use the accepted messages of the day and amalgamate them into the newly evolving Christianity. Many of the new converts would have also bought their previous beliefs with them. Thus, as Christianity grew, the moral message of Jesus became subsumed under his importance as a person. This was essentially a hellenisation of Christianity. This just means it took on some of the beliefs of these other mystery cults that were prevalent at the time and of which came from Greece – the birthplace of western philosophy and whose religion had dominated the world for 1000 years.

The more Christianity separated from Judaism the quicker it grew. From the days of Paul there had been hostility from the orthodox Jewish church at Christianity's insistence that the prophet Jesus was God. This hostility was aggravated by the fact that Christianity was now becoming a threat to Judaism because of the speed it was growing.

The Jews refusal to accept Jesus as the Son of God probably stemmed from their disbelief that a prophet was being elevated to the position of a God. This continued refusal to accept Jesus as the messiah in turn angered the early Christian fathers who launched repeated attacks on them. Because Christianity now saw and described itself as 'Israel' it had to discredit the other Israel.

The strongest attacks on Jews and Judaism can be found in the Homilies of Chrysostom (347-407 C.E.) in his Antioch sermons. Known as St. John the Golden Mouthed his sermons resulted from his disapproval that many Christians were on friendly terms with Jews and used to visit their homes and attend their synagogues. Chrysostom said:

"The Jews sacrifice their children to Satan....they are worse than wild beasts. The synagogue is a brothel, a den of scoundrels, the temple of demons devoted to idolatrous cults, a criminal assembly of Jews, a place of meeting for the assassins of Christ, a house of ill fame, a dwelling of iniquity, a gulf and abyss of perdition."

"The Jews have fallen into a condition lower than the vilest animal. Debauchery and drunkenness have brought them to the level of the lusty goat and the pig. They know only one thing: to satisfy their stomachs, to get drunk, to kill, and beat each other up like stage villains and coachmen."

"The synagogue is a curse, obstinate in her error, she refuses to see or hear, she has deliberately perverted her judgment; she has extinguished with herself the light of the Holy Spirit."[10]

Chrysostom further said that the Jews had become a degenerate race because of their *"odious assassination of Christ for which crime there is no expiation possible, no indulgence, no pardon, and for which they will always be a people without a nation, enduring servitude without end."* [11]

The very fact that Christians named him St John the Golden Mouthed shows the appalling intolerance already

---

[10]Quoted in Bratton,83-84. From Chrysostom's eight "Homilies Against the Jews" in Patrologia Graeca (Paris: Garnier, 1857-1866), 843-942.
Ibid.
Ibid.
[11]Ibid.

ingrained in Christianity. It is also a clear indicator of how insecure the early Christians felt themselves to be if they could be threatened by something so common place as friendship between people of different religious beliefs

Thus the changing face of Christianity began with Paul and his exposure to other religions and their beliefs based in saviours and redemption. From this there followed a complete lack of understanding by those converts to Christianity of Jewish law, Jewish life and the way the Jewish people thought. Paul did not actually teach that they shouldn't follow the Torah (the Jewish system of laws). But because he wanted to make the faith accessible to the Gentiles and because they were not Jewish he saw no reason for them to follow the demands of Jewish Law. Converts to Christianity were not required to have male circumcision, and were allowed to continue life very much as before without changing their whole culture. This was the beginning of the amalgamation of pagan and Jewish customs which became institutionalised eventually into Christian customs: Christmas, Easter etc.; Thus, to the Gentiles, some of the stricter customs and laws of the Torah seemed to be wrong. It was this that caused some of the reactionary attitudes of the early Christians. Because these attitudes were anti Judaism, these attitudes later became the attitudes of the Church and led to the rise of Christian anti Semitism.

These seeds of Anti-Semitism were to grow and persevere throughout the centuries with horrendous consequences for millions of people, and its legacy is still with us today.

It was Orthodox Judaism's belief in prophets that was also at the root of their problem with Islam. The common misconception is that before the birth of Christianity the Jews and Muslims actually lived side by side with little difficulty. Although there is some truth in this it is not the complete truth.
The origins of Islamic anti Semitism are disputed and depend entirely on the Islamic Imam who is interpreting them. There are training course available to Imams but many do not have formal

training and many of the Imams that teach in British Mosques have been criticised for not teaching in English.

The training courses available consist of training in the fundamental basics of Islam. Students learn to understand the Qur'an and Hadith and classical Arabic - so that they can use the original sources (and secondary scholarship in the original language). Secondly they are taught an understanding of contemporary European life. This is normally through a course which explores the historical and cultural interaction between Islam and Europe. In addition they can take a course on key aspects of western thought, culture and philosophy and their application in modern European society. However, Islamic Imams do not have to have any training. If they feel they have the knowledge to teach the word of Allah as written in the Qur'an they can claim themselves as Imam and begin to teach.

It is like this because, to a certain extent, this is exactly what Mohammed did. It would seem that Mohammed was initially quite impressed by the Jewish and Christian people who he referred to as the 'People of the Book'. He was impressed that they had this knowledge and messages given to them by God. It wasn't until he started to see himself as a prophet and thus also responsible for writing down the words of God that the problems started. The Jewish people of the day refused to recognise him as a prophet.

As Mohammed was unable to write he was given the words of the verses to recite and memorise. The written books of the Qur'an were put together after the death of Mohammed. Before this they were memorised and recited orally. This is not as difficult as it may seem. Most people then were unable to write so it was normal to commit large amounts of information to memory. They were only written down as the adherents to Mohammed's words realised that the further afield the word spread, the more likely it was that the word would be corrupted and changed. They therefore set to writing all the verses down. They were also very strict about the criteria needed. Any verse submitted for inclusion had to be verified by witnesses that had heard Mohammed speaking them.

Finally, they are not put together in any chronological order. The scholars of the day put the longest verses first (suras) and the shortest verses last with the exception of the very first, a short sura called al-Fatiha, the Opening. The only concession to chronology is in the sub-heading of chapters as 'Meccan' or 'Medinan', referring to the Prophet's residence in Mecca (up to 622 CE) and Medina (to 632, the year of his death). Thus some of the later verses are not anti Semitic and some of the earlier verses are. However, there is a difference in the tone of the writings. Those written after the move to Medina are more concerned with every day living instructions that would have applied to ensuring community cohesion and how the community governed itself.

As he developed his prophetic career he fled to Yathrib in 622 and became influenced by the Arabian Jews and Christians who lived in this city. This was later to become known as the city of the prophet or Medina. Mohammad had now begun to develop monotheism of his own and was very interested in the scriptures possessed by the Jews and Christians. He professed himself to be a prophet to the Arabs who had never previously received divine revelations, but more importantly he professed himself to be the *last* in a long line of prophets beginning with Adam, Noah, Abraham and finally Jesus.

As Mohammad grew in political and military strength he began to resent the Jews and Christians for not recognising him as a prophet. Because they were the People of the Book and because they had been given the scriptures or words of God they had to be protected. However, there began a distinct shift in the verses from accepting the People of the Book as best friends to accusing them of corrupting the scriptures and distorting the words of God. This growing animosity can be seen in both the Qur'anic text and in the expulsion of all Jews (and Christians) from the Arabian Peninsula. Within 2 years of his arrival in Medina (February 624), Mohammad had also changed the direction of formal prayers from the same direction as the Jewish people to the opposite direction towards Mecca and the Ka'ba in its centre.

But the most important part of this brief history is that of his belief and his teaching that he was the **last** in the line of prophets. It is this that is essentially responsible for Islam being unable to change and adapt to an ever evolving social and political word. The Qur'an can not be updated because Muhammad is the one and only prophet. Furthermore according to the Qur'an, Ibrahim (Abraham), all the biblical figures, the prophets before Jesus and Jesus himself were all Muslims prophets who preached Muhammad's message, Islam (i.e. "submission to Allah"). *"Abraham was not a Jew nor a Christian but he was an upright man, a Muslim, and he was not one of the polytheists"* (Sura 3:67).

Thus the prophets of the Old Testament up to and including Jesus are respected as Muslims, not as Jews and this is another source of conflict. Muslims do not accept the Judeo-Christian interpretation of history. They do not see their religion as the third religion but the first. The religion of Adam and Eve is their religion. This is why they do not recognise the historical legitimacy of Israel today. Israel has no roots in the Holy Land because its biblical history is considered to be a Muslim history. David and Solomon were Muslim kings, as were all the Israelite prophets and Jesus. Therefore the Jewish and Christian version of history and the beliefs which underpin them are wrong. The only true version of biblical events is the Qur'anic one. This is different from the Bible because the Qur'an is declared to be verbatim the word of Allah. Thus, the fact the Muhammad is the last of the prophets and the Qur'an is the verbatim word of Allah and cannot be changed, explains some of the reasons for the difficulties Islam faces. Furthermore it is the traditional view that everyone is born a Muslim - *"The mother of every person gives him birth according to his true nature. It is subsequently his parents who make him a Jew or a Christian or a Magian"* (Sahih Muslim, Book 033, Number 6429).

However, it is worth reiterating that although this is the interpretation of Islamists, not all Muslims share this view.

But it is passages such as this that Muslim anti-Semites are able to exploit and use to deny any Jewish origin for their religion. Those who adhere to this view argue that the Christians and Jews have perverted the teachings of the prophet to form the teachings of their religions, and that the real, untwisted teachings of Moses, Jesus, etc., are identical to the teachings of the Qur'an. One of the things both Fundamentalists and mainstream Islamists agree on is that they draw a line between the teachings of the Judaic faith as given by God and the Jews as a people. Thus they can distinguish between the faith which is identical to the teachings of the Qur'an, and its interpretation, claiming that the Jews have corrupted the meaning and subverted the original meaning of Judaism. In other words both Islam and Judaism are essentially one and the same but that Judaism is just a later version of Islam.

Thus, by accusing the Jews of rebelling against God and his prophets, including Muhammad, they can be anti Jewish without compromising Islam's perceived roots in Judaism. Islam does not have to accept the beliefs of other communities given to them by their prophets because these prophets are Muslim anyway. This, together with the points highlighted earlier allows Islamic theology to be used by Fundamentalists against Jews.

But anti Semitism is not a thing of the past. Present fundamentalists share many characteristics with the Nazis. Both have a racist pathological obsession with Jews, which they see as the embodiment of evil. For both, Jews are the focus of hatred, envy and frustration. Both share the same inhumanity and contempt for life, human rights and dignity and both spread lies and defamations that subvert the truth.

Although Nazi anti-Semitism was an amalgamation of fanciful conspiracy theories and racist mythology, Muslim anti-Semitism has a theological basis. But both share a taste for those fanciful conspiracy theories. Muslim anti-Semites today buttress their positions with a great deal of material that the Nazis also used. The notorious forgery about the Jewish plot to rule the world, *The Protocols of the Elders of Zion*, is a prime example. Not only did it circulate widely in Nazi Germany it is also widely circulated in the Muslim world today. *Mein Kampf* also circulates in the Muslim world, and it must be remembered that during World War II, the Grand Mufti of Jerusalem, Haj Amin al-Husseini, met with Hitler to ask for German help in exterminating the Jews of the Muslim world.

Both Nazis and Muslim fundamentalists blame the main problems of their nations on the Jews and claim that the Jews are a world problem. Fundamentalists further argue that Jews have diverted from Judaism and therefore a solution must be found to that problem. *"Allah's curse be on them: how they are deluded away from the Truth!"* (Sura 9:30). Thus they deserve to be cursed and to be punished. The only difference is that under Nazism, the Jews people were to vanish, whilst in the context of the Jihadist ideology, it is the Jewish state that is to vanish.

In the introduction we asked what effect not having a home has on someone's identity. This does not just apply to individuals but to communities as well. Both Islamists and Orthodox Jewry claim the right to Israel because both are descended from Abraham. The same applies to many other countries in the world where borders have been moved over the centuries. But often the claims are not specifically territorial. Often these claims can be met by just allowing different cultures to have their own laws and way of government. It is those who do not want others to have their own laws or government, who do not believe that others have a right to have their own laws and government, who often cause the problems. The reason they are unable to accept the right of someone else to have their own system of laws and government lies in their insecurity. And the basis for this is their lack of security in their own identity and their fear of change.

But it is not just religions that can be fundamentalist. Science can also be dogmatic and blinkered in its approach to anything that it cannot prove scientifically.

The next chapter takes a look at some of the ways in which science does accept spirituality

"He who is plenteously provided for from within, needs but little from without."
Johann Wolfgang von Goethe

Chapter 8

In the middle there is.....science

You are what you eat

One of the things we all normally do on holiday is to over indulge ourselves, either through over eating or drinking too much. One of the choices we have to make on the earth plane is whether to give in to the many temptations that surround us. Some are reasonably harmless; others can be fatal and cut short our spiritual journey before it is time.

There have been several studies done on the causes of addictions but it would appear that like the phobias we looked at in Chapter 4, they too are a spiritual gift. As such they are both influenced by our emotions (mind), genetic make up (body) and spiritual openness (spirit) and also have an affect on our mind, body and spirit.

Life on the earth plane is never easy and it is very easy to turn to something to help us along. The list of possible addictions is enormous but includes tea, coffee, alcohol, cigarettes, chocolate, food, exercise, sex and drugs, both prescription drugs and those that are illegal. These are just some examples of the crutches we use to help prop us up here. But what they have in common is that like love, hate, fear, insecurity etc addiction is a spiritual gift that we have bought with us to learn how to use in a positive way.

It has long been acknowledged that it is not only what we eat and drink and our life styles that can affect our physical bodies. We have all heard the saying 'you are what you eat' but how many of us have ever thought to apply it to our spiritual selves. Our spirit needs nourishing as much, if not more, than our physical selves. If we fill our bodies with chemicals, alcohol and other toxins it affects the way our bodies function. But it also affects the way our spirit functions. We are, first and foremost, spiritual beings and our bodies are our homes whilst we are on the earth plane. Therefore, mistreating our physical selves means also mistreating our spiritual selves. We do this in many ways but one way that we may not have thought about concerns what we put into our bodies.

If we eat too much unhealthy food it not only affects our digestive systems it also affects our ability to function in our every day lives. It makes us feel lethargic and sluggish. When we feel like this we often do not do things that we are meant to do. We might have to take time off work or instead of going out with our friends we stay indoors feeling depressed. When we are prevented from doing things that we would like to do or are meant to be doing our spirits become low. All that negativity acts as a spiritual dampener on our lives and the more negativity we have around us the more we attract.

Food becomes the enemy. We either eat too much or we starve ourselves. We use it to cheer ourselves up or to punish ourselves. We also use it as a way of avoiding facing problems that may be a result of something that happened to us in the past. Victims of sexual abuse may overeat because by over eating they will become fat. This could make them unattractive thus removing the need to deal with the underlying cause which is the abuse. Other victims may under eat as this is a way of punishing themselves for not being in control and letting themselves become a victim.

Food is also used subconsciously by people who wish to control their partner. This applies to both sexes. Insecure people subconsciously encourage their partner to overeat as, theoretically, this will make them less attractive to other people. This reduces the likelihood of them having affairs or finding someone else.

These are all negative emotions that are made worse by the fact that much of the food we are putting in our bodies is slowly poisoning our systems. Because of this our spirit begins to reflect the unhealthy state of our physical bodies and we become ill. When we feel ill we become low spirited and depressed, we hit out at others or we hit out at ourselves. Either way these are yet more negative emotions to add to those already circulating in our systems. One of the best ways of getting over feeling low is to chat with friends and have a good laugh but the one thing we often do when we are surrounded by negativity is to sit indoors and actually avoid seeing or speaking to other people. This adds to our feelings of negativity and then we turn to food or drink to cheer us up and the whole cycle begins again.

Alcohol can be even more harmful to our spiritual selves. Alcohol lowers our defences both spiritually and physically. The more aware we are the more dangerous it can be. Not only do we put our physical selves in danger if we drink too much we also put our spiritual selves in danger. When our defences are lowered we are much more open. This openness is fine when we are conscious of what we are doing and when we are capable of making conscious decisions as to who we wish to communicate with. But if we are not capable of making this decision how can we have any control over who we are inviting in to communicate with us?

There is nothing wrong with having a drink or eating 'unhealthy' food occasionally, but we just need to find the right balance and, if we find it is not just occasionally, look deeper within ourselves to find out why it is that we need to have that extra drink or that extra cake, burger, bar of chocolate. What is missing in our lives that we feel the need to replace it with unnecessary food or drink? What is it that we are trying to forget or run away from? If our spirit is low is it really going to feel better if we eat or drink to excess? We might be better meditating and using our white light for a few minutes and seeing if that makes a difference first. If it is our spirit that needs feeding, feeding our physical selves is not going to help. Although it might help in the short term, in the long term we will probably feel worse.

There is no easy solution, if there was we wouldn't have a problem. But looking at out physical problems from a spiritual angle may be just what we need to change our physical habits for the better. After all, if we don't look after our bodies, where will we live?

Meditation

Scientific evidence now seems to support the idea that meditation can also help in the cure of disorders such as over eating. The theory is that we are all so busy that we pay little attention to what we eat. The following simple technique is based on an ancient Buddhist and Zen philosophy that combines meditation with enhancing greater awareness about the body's natural feeling of fullness.

The idea behind mindful eating is that when we eat we are often not paying attention to what we area eating. The idea of the meditation is that it allows you to focus the mind on overcoming the particular fears or habits that have led to unbalanced eating habits. It is now accepted by most good dieticians, that setting a list of "forbidden foods", can eventually lead to overeating them. At the same time, if you are over anxious about food, it can lead to forced starvation and anorexia.

It is also easy to mistake emotive clues such as anxiety and depression as hunger. So the idea is to work out when your body is hungry and when it is responding to other things. Often when we think we are hungry we are actually thirsty so it is always worth having a drink of water first. Meditation can help you to develop a focus on eating when the body requires it. Try the following exercise:

Try putting a single raisin in your hand, feel the raisin, look at it, and then put it into your mouth, but don't actually swallow it while savouring the flavour and making a meal of the raisin. Sounds ridiculous? Well, apparently not. Scientific research also suggests that it is this lack of mindfulness that often leads to binge eating, which affects millions of people, especially women, around the world.

In the United States alone, over 25 million people are estimated to suffer from the disorder, according to the National Eating Disorders Association. It is also believed that it is more likely to affect perfectionists and over achievers. This is because perfectionists and over achievers impose high standards on themselves. When they feel they don't measure up to these self-imposed standards or they are not in control of situations, they indulge in secretive eating binges.

There has also been recent research that seems to show that meditation can change the physical structure of the brain and also enhance memory. Because neuroscience has now confirmed that adult brain cells can continue to grow (previously they thought this process stopped in the adult brain) and new technology is available that can measure and show changes better, research into the connection between meditation and the physical structure of the brain has increased.

In the early 1990s a Harvard educated researcher measured electrical activity and changes to the brains of Buddhist monks. During the research it was found that electrical activity in the left prefrontal cortex (the area behind the left side of the forehead) increased. Scientists have associated activity in this region with positive emotions, as opposed to the right prefrontal cortex, where increases are associated with negative feelings. Furthermore the research also showed that long term practitioners of meditation (like the Buddhist monks) were able to induce more control over their concentration and emotions than other groups.

As we get older the outer layer or cortex of our brains gets thinner. This is the part thought to be involved in integrating our emotional and cognitive functions. Research by another neuroscientist, using a FMRI (a type of X ray) to take pictures of the brain, has shown that regular meditation seems to delay this process. According to the researcher the findings suggested that meditation can make changes in the areas of the brain used for cognitive and emotional processing and well being and that the pattern of thickening corresponded to how long the person had been practicing meditation. Scientists are not particularly surprised that meditation alters the physiology of the brain as any part of the brain that is used a lot produces the same thickening in the areas that correspond to its use. Musicians and athletes also have thicker brain tissue in the areas that they use most.

It also appears that meditation can help to improve brain function in the same way that sleep can. Using a variety of tests to measure alertness all those tested improved after they had meditated. This even seemed to work when all the subjects were deprived of sleep. Those who had meditated did better than those who hadn't.

Furthermore, meditation has already been shown to be effective as a treatment for anxiety and depression, substance abuse, and the stress associated with physical conditions such as trauma, chronic pain, or cancer. So what are you waiting for!

Thoughts

But it is not only our physical bodies that affect our spirit, our emotional state can also affect our physical bodies. More research has now proved that our thoughts are indeed a powerful energy that can also affect our physical health. Scientists at Princeton University have spent over 25 years investigating the correlation between our thoughts and whether they can affect machines. Their research seems to show that untrained individuals can influence the output of random mechanical and electronic number generators, just by thinking in which direction the numbers should go. These effects also occurred when the individual was thousands of miles away. But our thoughts are even more powerful than this. People who have a positive outlook are usually fitter and healthier than those who are more negative in their approach to life. But it seems that the old adage 'getting wound up' is not good for you is more than just a saying. It seems there have been experiments that also show that the feelings of an individual can help DNA heal itself.

The following are three experiments on DNA taken from the internet. It seems an experiment was done by the Institute Of Heart Math and the paper that wrote up this experiment was called the Local and Non-local Effects of Coherent Heart Frequencies on Conformational Changes of DNA. Yes we know this is a bit of a mouthful but bear with us as we explain the experiment. They were doing some investigations into how anthrax worked on DNA. To this end they placed some human placenta DNA, which is apparently the most pristine form of DNA, into a container. The idea was to measure any changes to the DNA. Twenty-eight vials of the DNA were then given (one each) to 28 trained researchers. Each researcher had been trained how to generate and experience feelings and to harness and experience very strong emotions.

The incredible findings were that apparently the DNA changed its shape according to the feelings of the researcher. When the researchers felt gratitude, love and appreciation, the DNA responded by relaxing and the strands unwound. The DNA became longer. When the researchers felt anger, fear, frustration, or stress, the DNA responded by tightening up. It became shorter and switched off many of our DNA codes! The shut down of the DNA codes was reversed and the codes were switched back on again when feelings of love, joy, gratitude and appreciation were felt by the researchers.

This experiment was later followed up by testing HIV positive patients. They discovered that feelings of love, gratitude and appreciation created 300,000 times the resistance they had without those feelings. So it would seem that even science agrees that the answer to helping you stay well is to hold onto those feelings of joy, love, gratitude and appreciation! These emotional changes went beyond the effects of electro magnetics. Individuals trained in generating feelings of deep love were able to change the shape of their DNA. From the point of view of those who carried out the experiment they felt it 'illustrates a newly recognized form of energy that connects all of creation. This energy appears to be a tightly woven web that connects all matter.

Essentially we're able to influence this web of creation through our vibration'.

We just want to make one brief point about this experiment: the expression 'being wound up' is quite an old expression, certainly much older than our knowledge of the existence of DNA. Of course it may simply be that it was said by someone who was likening tense behaviour to that of a tightly coiled spring. On the other hand it may go back further. If you know we would love to hear from you.

Remember that the law of the Universe is that we attract what we focus on. If you are focused on fearing whatever may come, you are sending a strong message to the Universe to send you whatever you fear. Instead, if you can get yourself into feelings of joy, love, appreciation or gratitude, and focus on bringing more of that into your life, you are going to avoid the negative stuff automatically. Find something to be happy about every day, and every hour if possible, moment-to-moment, even if only for a few minutes.

Another experiment was done by Dr. Vladimir Poponin, a quantum biologist. In this experiment, they first emptied a container to create a vacuum within it. The only things left in it were photons (particles of light). They measured the location of the photons and found that, as expected, they were completely random inside the container. Then some DNA was placed inside the container and the location of the photons was re-measured. This time the photons were lined up in an ordered way and aligned with the DNA. In other words the physical DNA had an effect on the non-physical photons. After that, the DNA was removed from the container, and the distribution of the photons was re-measured again. The photons remained ordered and lined up where the DNA had been. What are the light particles connected to?

It would appear that a new field of energy, a web of energy, is there and the DNA is communicating with the photons through this energy.

The following were experiments apparently carried out by the US military. Leukocytes (white blood cells) were collected for DNA from donors and placed into chambers so they could measure electrical changes. In this experiment, the donor was placed in one room and subjected to "emotional stimulation" consisting of video clips, which generated different emotions in the donor. The DNA was placed in a different room in the same building. Both the donor and his DNA were monitored and as the donor exhibited emotional peaks or valleys (measured by electrical responses), the DNA exhibited identical responses at exactly the same time. There was no lag time, no transmission time. The DNA peaks and valleys exactly matched the peaks and valleys of the donor in time. The military wanted to see how far away they could separate the donor from his DNA and still get this effect. They stopped testing after they separated the DNA and the donor by 50 miles and still had the same result. The DNA and the donor had the same identical responses in time. Thus it would appear that living cells can communicate through time and distance. This is a previously unrecognised form of energy.

The study of universal quantum physics has led scientists to propose the probable existence of an alternative dimension and furthermore that there is the potential that life can exist on an alternative dimension. Could the spirit realm be classed as another dimension?

Spiritual progress?

Science also considers any proposed events with odds greater than 10 to the power of 50 to be scientifically impossible. Yet a simple cell is by no means simple. One requires around 2,000 proteins acting as enzymes to survive. Science considers the odds of this evolving by chance to be in the region of 10 to the power of 40,000. So does this mean that science is now suggesting that there is at least a possibility that God or some kind of omnipotent being does exist?

Digital photography has, and will in the future, transform our view of life and other realms and dimensions as more and more images will be picked up. Professor Klaus Heinemann was one of several experts featured in a daily newspaper that ran a feature on orbs. A researcher at NASA he and his wife began taking digital photographs of orbs at spiritual gatherings. They found that orbs moved at over 500 miles an hour. The world's first conference on orbs was held in Arizona this year where several scientists stated that they believed in the paranormal. A member of the International Theological Commission at the Vatican has even collected over 100,000 pictures of orbs from all over the world. This would seem to prove that it is not an isolated phenomenon or some fake photography. Many of the other mainstream newspapers are now printing pictures of orbs and asking questions and many health care professionals are speaking out about their experiences of caring for the terminally ill. Qualified nurses and doctors have all reported seeing something leaving the body at the time of death, seeing lights round the patients' bed and hearing so many people say that their relatives, long gone, are round their bedside.

Although scientists are still trying to find rational explanations for out of body experiences they are not entirely convincing. They have carried out experiments suggesting that when the connection between the mind and the senses of sight and touch is disrupted, it can create the sensation that the mind has left the body. In the experiment the volunteer was asked to put on goggles that were linked to a video camera trained on his back. Looking through the goggles the volunteer saw an image of his back, from the perspective of a person sitting six feet behind him. He was then prodded with a rod. Because he could not see the person touching him he was left with the sensation that he was sitting in the position of onlooker. However, this does not explain how those who have out of body experiences can see things on top of cupboards, go out into corridors or travel to other places and then accurately describe the things they have seen when they return to their bodies. In an attempt to investigate this properly researchers are now in the process of placing small objects on top of cupboards and other places in hospitals to see if people experiencing 'out of body experiences' can describe them. As the experiment was widely publicised by the national media we can only assume that the results too will be widely publicised. Watch this space – as they say!

We cannot keep ignoring the evidence however much sceptics would wish us to. Don't forget that 'professional' sceptics – bought out every time there is a programme supposedly investigating the truth or otherwise of psychic phenomena - have a vested interest in maintaining their scepticism. They earn their living from being sceptical. If they were to change their minds they would be out of a job.

Scientific Evidence of Telepathy

Most people would accept that some form of telepathy does exist. How often do you know what your partner or friend is thinking and how often do you say things that they are thinking or vice versa? Furthermore, many of the sceptics who refuse to accept that it is possible to speak to those who are in spirit, will argue that the medium is 'picking up on the persons thoughts'. However, when pressed to accept the truth of telepathy would refute that it was possible.

On August 4, 2002, Iain Bruce of the Sunday Herald published a scientific discovery by a Scottish scientist, Paul Stevens, which unveiled the first-ever scientific proof of humanity's ability to communicate by thought. "Our research is not yet complete, but we may have found a significant pattern which we hope will demonstrate psychic ability and the underlying mechanisms responsible for it," said Dr. Stevens, who conducted the experiments at Edinburgh University's world-renowned parapsychology unit.

The study looked at links between people with extremely well developed relationships, such as lovers, friends and relatives. Each couple was split up and the participants labelled as "senders" or "receivers" (of the messages). Those in the first group were shown a series of randomly selected video clips and told to "send" the information to the partner who sat in a sound-proofed room 25 meters away.

Sound signals called "white noise" lulled the "receiving" partners into an ultra-receptive state and they were asked to say what came into their heads while their body was measured for any changes. Many subjects were able to talk about the information being read by their partners.

The Power of the Mind

So let's now return to our thoughts and their power over our physical being. Negative thoughts can make us ill and prevent us from recovering. Positive thoughts can heal not only our bodies but our minds too and this can transform our lives. There is a tremendous body of scientific research that can support these principles. Ancient Chinese medicine and Ayurveda (a traditional Indian medicine) draw links between bodily symptoms and emotions. In Chinese medicine, the lung is the repository for grief, the liver for rage, and the kidney for fear.

Some examples of how our minds can affect our health include the following: positive thinking lowered blood sugar levels in diabetics, lessened asthma attacks, reduced colitis symptoms and improved immune function in HIV-infected individuals. Not only can our thoughts affect our bodies, but also our thoughts can affect others. Numerous studies have demonstrated the clinical efficacy of prayer, most notably the positive effect of prayer on patients in a coronary care unit.

So what else can our minds do? It has been suggested that if you concentrate hard enough you can even make breaks in the clouds to allow the sun to shine through! Again this sounds ridiculous but perhaps that is just because we don't try hard enough or because we don't believe that we can do it. Most people would now accept that Telepathy is at least possible, especially if you are close to the person, so why not telekinesis?

Stanislawa Tomczyk was born in Poland. Under hypnotic state she could levitate small objects when she placed her hands either side of them. Although her hands were carefully examined beforehand, Julien Ochorowicz, watching at very close range, observed something like fine threads emanating from her palms and fingers. And it didn't seem to be a trick. "When the medium separates her hands," Ochorowicz observed, "the thread gets thinner and disappears; it gives the same sensation as a spider's web. If it is cut with scissors, its continuity is immediately restored." In 1910, Tomczyk was tested by a group of scientists at the Physical Laboratory in Warsaw where she produced remarkable physical phenomena under strict test conditions.

One of the most celebrated and most scrutinized psychics to claim psychokinetic powers was Nina Kulagina, a Russian woman who discovered her abilities while attempting to develop other psychic powers. She was reportedly, able to move a wide range of nonmagnetic objects, including matches, bread, large crystal bowls, clock pendulums, a cigar tube and a salt shaker among other things. Some of these demonstrations have been captured on film.

Uri Geller became one of the world's most well known "psychics" after a British radio show in 1973. He demonstrated key bending to the astonishment of the host, and then invited the listening audience to participate. Just minutes later, phone calls began pouring into the radio station from listeners all over the UK reporting that knives, forks, spoons, keys and nails began to bend and twist spontaneously. Watches and clocks that had not run in years began to work. It was an event whose success surprised even Geller and thrust him into the spotlight. Although sceptics have contended that it was just a magic trick, in April, 2001, University of Arizona psychology professor Gary Schwartz conducted a "spoon-bending party" at which about 60 students were able to bend spoons and forks, with varying degrees of success, seemingly with the power of their minds.

There are several theories as to why it could work. Some researchers suspect there might be a connection with quantum physics. Because unpredictable, often bizarre effects have been documented in the world of subatomic particles, and these are ruled by the perplexing laws of quantum mechanics, it has been suggested that our minds might also be capable of directing subatomic particles and energies in a way that results in PK phenomena.

Another theory is that psycho kinesis is the manipulation of the human "magnetic field" which is around the body, (the aura), which can be concentrated in a specific area. For this to work, they say, you must be able to relax completely and focus your attention without distraction.

Others speculate that mediums are able to coalesce sound or heat waves within a room to form coherent energy which can then be directed at an object, such as a table, causing it to move.

There are apparently several ways to do this but you could start by sitting quietly, and focussing your mind on a small light object, perhaps a paperclip or something similar. Then visualise the paperclip in a tunnel connected to you and visualise a wind drawing it towards you. Alternatively you could visualise a thread coming from your hands and attached to the paperclip and then drawing it towards you.

Another way is to sit quietly and focus your mind on the flame of a candle. Gradually visualise the flame growing bigger and then shrinking. You can use either the tunnel or the thread or anything else that works for you.

There are so many things out there that we do not yet understand, but that does not mean they are not there or that these things are not possible. We only have to look at the incredible changes technology has bought to our lives in just the last 100 years. If you had mentioned these things to people a few centuries ago they would have thought you were mad or locked you up as some sort of witch.

We have now reached the end of the middle part of our journey. We have looked at the political, religious, spiritual and scientific aspects of our spiritual teenage years and seen how they have affected the last 2000 years. Even the best holidays can be tiring and as life's journey can hardly be described as the most peaceful of holidays it is sometimes good to take a break. We are

now going to take a break from our Holiday from Hell and look at some questions and answers about meditation, Mediumship, healing and spiritual philosophy in general.
.

'Knowledge becomes wisdom only after it has been put to practical use.'
Anon.

'What is now proved was once only imagined'.
William Blake

Chapter 9

Some questions and answers about mediums

Why do modern mediums seem to develop more quickly than they did in the past?

One thing that has changed over the years is the rate at which those coming into the spiritual movement progress. In the past mediums would take a long time to reach a certain level but this does not seem to be the case now. Whilst it is important that a certain amount of time is spent when studying to be a medium or healer the time span seems to have reduced to years rather than decades. This does not mean that you can become a medium overnight. Like anything it takes time and dedication and most of the reputable spiritual organisations will have certain standards that they expect their mediums to conform to.

In January 2008 we co-founded The Spiritual Workers Association (SWA)[12]. The SWA was originally a response to changes in legislation which affected mediums and healers. Its stated aims are to raise standards, raise awareness, to give spiritual workers a voice and to raise the profile of spiritual workers. It has quickly grown to become an international umbrella group with members of many different faiths and beliefs but who all believe that the world needs some more light. Although originally intended to be for independents, it also has several partnership organisations that all support its aims and objectives.

---

[12] The Spiritual Workers Association – www.theswa.org.uk

It was deliberately called 'Spiritual' rather than 'Spiritualist' because the founders considered that the term 'spiritualist', rather like religion, had quite negative connotations. One of the many things that attracted me originally to spiritualism was its philosophy with its emphasis on individual free choice and SELF control. Whilst other religions often seem to be concerned with controlling others for earthly reasons, Spiritualism was about making our own decisions, being responsible for our own choices and following our own individual pathway. It is this personal responsibility and our willingness to give others the freedom to do the same that will help us evolve and it is this emphasis on SELF control that separates Spiritualism from other religions. Spiritualism has no need to control others because this would prevent us making our own decisions and therefore interfere with our spiritual evolution.

Sadly, Spiritualism has now become almost as divisive as many of the other religion/belief systems. Instead of showing the world a better way and working together to bring love, light and healing to the world, many spiritualist organisations have allowed themselves to be distracted by earthly concerns and seem to have forgotten their true purpose.

By denying people the freedom to choose and the freedom to make their own rules through discussion and consensus they have effectively removed personal responsibility. This not only affects the individuals' earthly existence but also their spiritual development. We decided that there had to be another way. Hence the Spiritual Workers Association is a member led organisation with the **independent** individual members drawing up the guidelines that they will choose to adhere to. We emphasise **independent** because many of our individual members belong to other organisations and as such will adhere to their own organisations' rules.

It was also intended as a body to unite all spiritual workers not just spiritualists. We are all spirit whatever our beliefs so why exclude people who might consider themselves spiritual but not spiritualist. We may define our personal spiritual beliefs in many different ways but these differences in interpretation are irrelevant. It is the shared belief in our individual and collective spiritual identity that transcends all religious boundaries and that has bought us together. As a **spiritual** workers association we are totally inclusive. We can and do welcome members from all other faiths, belief systems and ways of life, and from anywhere in the world: in fact anyone who considers they work in light, love and truth or who is interested in bringing some spiritual light back into our beautiful world.

One of the concerns that has been bought to our attention was that there are some in the spiritualist movement who make a point of being deliberately uncooperative with platform mediums that do not belong to their particular organisation or who do not work in exactly the way prescribed by that particular organisation. They attend the service and when the medium comes to them they refuse to accept any information that is given to them. This is not because they cannot take it but because their group is so wrapped up in the politics of which group should be in charge that unfortunately they seem to have lost their way.

Many mediums start their clairvoyant evening with messages that have come to them before the service starts. They will often throw this open to the gathering as the messages came before they stood up on the platform so they are not always sure where they should go with it. This is a genuine attempt to give out a message to someone whose relative/friend has come through early. They may have done this to ensure that they get a chance to speak as there will inevitably be a rush of spirits wanting to communicate a lot of information in a short space of time. By refusing to accept the message at the time they are missing out on the rest of the information. At the end of the service they will often go up to the medium and inform them that they could take the message but didn't because the medium was not 'with them'!

There is a difference between this and when a medium is 'fishing'. Fishing occurs when a medium throws out a name and very little else to the gathering and then gives a message that is very general and could be accepted by anyone. Many mediums were taught to connect to spirit and then find the person they relate to. But they usually have a lot of information to give out and if no one can take it they will normally go to the person they think they are with. Once with someone they will offer something else in the form of proof to make sure they are with the right person.

Spiritualism should be above this petty politics and those organisations who encourage their members to be like this should take a long look at their motivation. We are not suggesting that you should take anything just to make the medium look good but if you can take the message why pretend you can't? Not only have your relatives and friends wasted their time but any new people to the service will have their doubts reinforced instead of having the proof that they need that there is life after physical death. Furthermore, it is extremely unlikely that the medium will change organisations because it will just reinforce their view of that group.

At the end of the day a good medium is one who provides proof of life after physical life and all mediums work differently. There is no right or wrong way to work on platform. As long as the messages are good, and provide specific evidence to the person who is given it, the medium is doing their job properly. Interestingly enough, we watched a medium who was struggling suddenly change tack completely. She went up to a member of the audience and asked them who they wanted to speak to. When the person gave a name she then linked in with little problem and began describing the person in detail and definitely to the person's satisfaction. The advantages of this were that the member of the audience spoke to the relative she wanted to speak to and didn't have to try and work out who it was! Whether this would work every time remains to be seen, but is worth bearing in mind for other mediums when they find themselves struggling, as does sometimes happen, however good you are.

The public also need to be absolutely sure what it is they want when visiting a medium. If you want to know what your future holds then write down what you wish to happen. Create your own future by listening to the inner voice within you – your spirit. Mediums will not tell you your future, only pass on the guidance from your loved ones in spirit. And you also have to remember that the medium is interpreting that through a distorted vibration. We have already seen what happens when we translate things from one language to another and how misunderstandings can happen. The likelihood of this happening when it is through another vibration is even more likely that is why the other role of a medium is to eventually make himself or herself redundant by teaching you how to do this for yourself.

So let's go back to the original question about why modern mediums seem to be developing at a quicker rate than in previous years.

There are several reasons for this. The world at the moment is in a state of change. It is very important that the world's population wakes up to the dangers that it is facing. For this to happen the populations of the world need to evolve. Thus there is an explosion of interest in spiritualism and its related spiritual fields. There is also a lack of spiritual guidance and morality in the world at the moment which seems to be getting worse. There is intense polarisation now as the darker some areas of the world become the more light is needed to counteract this. To counteract this darkness there needs to be more people who are able to spread the light hence the growth of mediums and those interpreting spiritual messages for people. There is a great sense of urgency as the world hovers unable to decide which way it is going.

Another reason for the speedy development of those who are developing their skills in this field is that those who are choosing this way of life are more evolved and further on their spiritual pathway than others here. There are also many older spirits who have chosen this time to come to the earth plane to spread the light in this most troubled of times.

It is also true that we are a very impatient generation. Unlike our parents and grandparents we want everything immediately. We are not prepared to wait nor are we prepared to develop our skills slowly. We would get bored! Thus those who choose this way of life are extremely motivated and develop very quickly.

However, this does not mean that all those who have come into mediumship will develop at this speed. We are all individual and we all learn and develop at different paces. Developing healing and mediumship skills is no different from learning other things. You would not get in a Boeing 747 and say you were quipped to fly it just because you have got your light aircraft license! Although you may think there is no connection between the two it is very dangerous to mess about with things you do not understand and even more dangerous to teach other people when you, yourself have no idea what you are doing. A little knowledge is a very dangerous thing in mediumship as in everything else. Many of those who come to see mediums are vulnerable. A properly trained medium will never tell someone they are going to die, will never tell someone that they or those around them will get better from life threatening conditions. Spirit's idea of someone being 'fine' could simply be that they will be going home to spirit!

Is it true that your prayers have to be clear and unemotional for them to be heard?

No, of course not. We heard a medium give out this garbled message at a service. She told a member of the congregation that it was their prayers that had helped a child get better, not those of the parents because they were so upset their prayers were incoherent. All prayers are heard and answered even if it is not in the way you were expecting or hoped for.

'You should not shut out your friends and loved ones in spirit'

On the face of it this seems like good advice but the lady that was given that advice had asked her friends and family not to come through for a particular reason. She had attended services regularly and every week was given a message. She decided that it was time others also had messages so she asked that for that particular service they did not come through to allow others to have a chance of a message. She was told by another medium that this would upset her friends and loved ones. In this situation this answer is completely wrong. She was asking for a totally unselfish reason so she was hardly likely to upset anyone.

As your loved ones are with you all the time they would have been perfectly aware of the reasons she asked for them not to come through. They are hardly likely to take it personally! Apart from anything else they will now think like spirits not like the physical being they were on earth so they will not be hampered by all the physical emotional stuff, like hurt feelings, that we, as physical beings have to deal with. They will definitely be much more understanding than the medium!

How can I ensure that I get the best from my reading?

We covered this in quite a lot of detail in The Re-Enlightenment but there are a couple of things we would like to add. First it is really important that you know the type of reading you want. There is no point going to a psychic medium if you want lots of proof or going to a spiritual medium if you want a psychic reading.

Mediums can obviously help by explaining exactly which type of reading you are likely to receive if you come to them. If the client is looking for something different then point them towards another medium who can provide the type of reading they would like. Most mediums would agree that their role is primarily to pass the message that there is life after physical life. This said it is important for the client to receive the type of proof that they need to allow them to accept that live continues after the death of the body. We are all here to work together, it is not a competition. If we do our work properly we should be able to make ourselves redundant. This should be our aim. If everybody understands the basic message and lives their lives accordingly we will have succeeded. But for this to happen we have to ensure the client receives the proof they need.

However, there remain people who are very hard to give readings to. No matter who they go to they still do not receive anything they can take. If they have discounted all the reasons we gave in The Re-Enlightenment then perhaps they should learn how to do it for themselves. They can then talk to their relatives themselves and gain a lot more from the experience.

Maybe mediums should look at giving more general advice about how to meditate, where to go for help with this etc. This does not mean they should use it as a marketing opportunity! If the person lives near and you are holding beginners groups that is fine. But you should also offer them alternatives and point them in the direction of the internet or local library where they can find the information they want without it costing them anything. Websites that offer options are ones like the www.thespiritguides.co.uk or the Spiritual Workers Association www.theswa.org.uk which has a directory of members that is accessible to the public. You could also give them local spiritual magazines which may have listings of groups. If they are meant to come back to you they will. In fact they are more likely to come back to you if they have felt that you were genuinely helpful rather than if they feel that you are just trying to take their money.

Why do mediums sometimes receive lots of information but none of it relates to the client?

This is probably a question many mediums ask themselves. There could be lots of reasons for this, including that the client is mistaken. Again, as we covered this in quite a lot of detail before we do not wish to repeat ourselves but rather to add to the answer.

It is important to make sure that the area where you are giving the reading is cleansed and that there is nothing around you that might also have some spiritual residue attached. If you are at a psychic fair and have just bought some second hand books they may have some residue with them. This would not normally matter because normally you would not be tuning in when you read them. Although this may sound a little strange, if you remember that when you do Pyschometry you are picking up from an article, it makes more sense. Books are no different than any other personal item. How many mediums have asked for some item of jewellery only to give a reading on someone else entirely because the client has forgotten to mention that it belonged to their mother! But this can also apply to something that has been recently given to a client. It may be that the person who gave it to them owned it for a while before giving it to them. It could even be that other people have tried it on and it is this that the medium is picking up on.

Why do some people call themselves mediums and others clairvoyants?

A medium's role is to provide proof of life after physical death by bringing a relative of loved one forward. They will give proof first and them the message. A clairvoyant will often describe your current circumstances and then give you a message but will not necessarily bring forward a relative or give your proof in the same sense as a medium. But both are providing proof in their own way and with the fragmentary nature of our families now sometimes we do not know our relatives, so describing them would not be proof in the sense previously mentioned. But it is not really that important what they call themselves as long as they provide the proof in an acceptable way to the person they are giving the reading to.

If we return to spirits and just become energy then why do mediums describe relatives with such clarity?

If a medium said to you that they had your grandmother with them and she was a wisp of energy you probably wouldn't think this was very good proof! The medium will see the person as they have chosen to project themselves. This will normally be how you are likely to remember them or how you have seen them in a picture. Once this description has been given, they will often revert to the time when they were in their prime. This can be quite disconcerting for the medium who may see your loved one getting younger as they return to a time when they enjoyed life the most.

Why do some people see spirit all the time?

There are two strands to this answer. In the first instance, if someone is seeing spirit all the time this may not be a problem as long as they are able to distinguish between those who are spirit and physical beings. However, you should be able to control when you see and hear spirit. All you need to do is to be quite firm and tell them to leave you alone until you are ready to work with them. If a person is seeing and hearing spirit all the time without having consciously invited them to communicate, it is possible that at some time the door has been opened between the two vibrations and this person was not ware of it. If you ask them to leave you alone and they do not then its possible that they are not spirits of light. This is especially true if they are telling you things that are not pure or that make you feel uncomfortable. This is one of the dangers of trying to communicate with spirit without protection.

It may also be that in the case of voices, it is not spirit that you are hearing but the thoughts of those around you. One way of checking this is to see if it is as bad when you are away from everyone. If it is not, then you are very sensitive on a psychic level and need to begin by learning how to protect yourself. However, there are no easy answers.

If spirit is around us all the time why do mediums not see them all the time?

Some mediums are aware of spirit around them most or all of the time, but most only 'see' when they tune in. There are several reasons for this.

If you were aware of spirit around you all the time it could be quite distracting. As we have just said, the spirits that work on love and light work with you and will allow you to control when you can work with them. This is because they appreciate that you live on the earth plane and that, first and foremost, you have a physical life to lead.

Secondly, because spirit exists on a separate and distinct vibration to our physical being it usually takes a conscious effort to see them - hence the need to 'tune in'.

Can all spirits communicate with mediums?

All spirits can communicate with spirit and as we are all spirit the simple answer is yes. But not all spirits choose to communicate with mediums. It is only a small proportion of spirits who choose to work with mediums and those developing their own abilities.

It also takes a certain level of development because communicating through the vibrations of the earth can cause all sorts of difficulties. As we have seen just translating from one language to another is hard enough let alone communicating through different vibrations.

Spirits will also use different methods of communicating. The most basic is the visual communication which is easier to master and is less affected by distortion. Verbal communication is harder to master because it is done through thought waves. Obviously as spirits we do not have vocal chords as these are a physical attribute. Learning to communicate thoughts and ensure they are interpreted correctly is a long process and is dependant on the development level of both the spirit that is communicating and the medium who is receiving the message.

'Destiny is no matter of chance. It is a matter of choice: It is not a thing to be waited for, it is a thing to be achieved.'
William Jennings Bryan

'Peace comes from within. Do not seek it without'.
Buddha

Chapter 10

Some General Questions and Answers

How do I know it is safe to meditate on my own?

It is always good to learn to meditate in a group as this gives you protection. But that is not always practical. It is perfectly safe to meditate on your own as long as you follow some basic rules. First always begin by using your white light and then ask for protection. Ask that only the highest, the purest and the best come through. You will always get what you ask for so if you start a meditation by worrying (which is a negative emotion), you are more likely to have problems. It is no different from worrying about things normally. You are sending out this subconscious message that this is what you want to happen.

How do I know that it is the highest, purest and the best coming through?

Spirits that work on those vibrations will only give you constructive messages. The first 'pure' thought is the one that comes from spirit. The rest should be discarded because they come from somewhere else – either your own mind or if they are really not nice, somewhere else entirely. Finally use your spiritual instincts. If it doesn't feel right then it probably isn't. It's a bit like coming to see a medium and asking whether your partner is the right one for you. If you have to ask they probably aren't. But this doesn't mean disregarding something just because you don't like what's being said. If you feel instinctively that it is the truth, however hard that is to accept, then it is probably right. Trust your own judgement and have faith in yourself.

How can I protect myself from the negative energy around me?

This is a big question! First ask for protection and then use your white light. You can then surround this white light with a blue light as this enables you to stay within your white light without sending out a beacon to anything else because you are hidden beneath the white light. Visualise yourself in a waterfall of cleansing water and light. Do all of these or as many as you think necessary. If this doesn't work then try and work out where the negative energy is coming from. If you are dealing with negative people all the time then it is probably time to change your job/work/partner. If it is coming from something over which you have no control (ie: an ex partner, friend) then also cleanse and protect your house.

Begin by leaving your negative energy in the car. When you get home from work sit in the car for a couple of minutes and let all the negative things of the day float away. Once you have got out of the car bombard it with white light otherwise you will pick it all up when you get back in it again.

Once indoors sit as if in meditation and spark your white light. Then use it to fill your home. Once your home is filled with this white light and it is spilling outside the walls you can then go round and put protective symbols on each of the windows, outside doors, satellite dish and chimney. You can use either a Christian cross, a Muslim crescent, an Egyptian Ankh or the Eye of Horus. You can use anything that symbolises protection and safety to you. It is the intention more than the actual symbol you use.

If the negative energy is coming from someone who is either unconsciously or consciously sending it to you it may manifest itself in different ways. It will aim to affect you by finding the weak spot. If you suffer from headaches these will increase, if you smoke you will suddenly find it harder to stop, if you are inclined to overeat you will find it harder to control this.

It is then simply a case of gritting your teeth and refusing to let it stop you doing the things you know that you should be doing. When you first become spiritually aware you may find that you will have periods when you feel depressed or lethargic or unable to do your meditation etc Try to overcome these feelings by using the light and just persevere. If you have an off day, don't worry, just tell yourself tomorrow is another day and remember what we said about self forgiveness.

Can someone send attachments to you?

If someone wishes you harm who has already used an Ouja boards and/or knows how to use black energy then the answer is yes. They may not always be conscious of what they are doing but all that powerful negative energy they are feeling will be used by stronger darker energy forces as a way of getting at you. This is especially exacerbated if they are using drugs or drinking. It is possible for them to attach an invisible chord to you that allows them to link into you. This is similar to how we would send love, light and healing to someone who is ill, except they do not wish you well.

Again its results can manifest itself in different ways. You will either experience the things previously mentioned or if you are more spiritually aware you may even be able to feel the attachment. The best way to get rid of these chords is to close your eyes, ask for protection, use your white light and use your psychic ability to visualise the chord and then cut it with golden scissors. Unfortunately, you will probably have to do this regularly as they will try to reattach it once they realise it has been cut. You may have to do this several times until they move on and find something else to occupy their lives. Of course there are those who will never move on and the only answer is to keep cutting the chords and becoming stronger. Soon you will know instinctively that this is what is happening and will be able to cut them instantly.

There is also a train of thought that suggests using black energy in the same way you would white light and just hurling it back to wherever it came from. We would suggest taking advice on this as you will need to cleanse yourself afterwards.

How do the colours you wear affect your mind body and spirit?

The colours we surround ourselves with both affect our moods and also reflect our moods. It is now accepted that the use of certain colours in institution settings is very important. Pastel shades of green and lilac are very restful and calming whilst fire engine red can incite and inflame passion. Of course, like everything else, each colour has a positive and negative aspect to it. Whilst red can indicate anger and rage which is very negative, it can also indicate passion and the drive to change things for the better which is positive. We are all drawn to particular colours at particular times and often the colours we wear have nothing to do with the current fashion but more to do with how we are feeling at the time. Many people say that they find it quite difficult to choose clothes for a future occasion because when it comes to wearing them on the big day they have changed their minds!

Should you give up your job to work for spirit?

We are all here to travel our own pathways. You do not need to give up the day job to successfully work for spirit. In your day job you may be meeting many people and passing on the spiritual message to them. This can be more important than only passing on the message to those who are already converted. There is also a danger that if you are totally reliant on spiritual activities to fund your lifestyle you could lose sight of the reason behind your work – that of passing on the message of love, light and healing. This isn't to say that devoting your whole life to working for spirit is in any way wrong just that everybody can do this in different ways. There is no one right way to do so. But it is important that money does not become the motivating factor because when that happens spirit goes out the window and the message seen by other people is not that originally intended.

Like all life it is important that a balance is maintained. If you are doing a day job, you are not only passing on the message but you are also able to ensure that your spiritual work is not just for financial reward. But if it is your only source of income you need to make sure that you are charging a realistic amount to allow you to live. If you are unable to pay your bills you will not be able to concentrate and will not be offering a proper service. People also have a strange attitude to services that are offered for free or very low cost. For some reason they do not think it is worth having unless they pay large amounts of money for it. The amount you charge should be realistic and reflect both your professionalism and your experience. You should also consider that you are giving up your time and you have probably also paid for your training

The only other minor point to make is that if spiritualism is a way of life you have to participate in life to make it your way of life. If you are only mixing with the converted then you could miss an awful lot of life and there is a danger your views could become parochial and blinkered. But, as with life, there is more than enough room for a myriad of different approaches and if someone is working full time they are not able to offer such a comprehensive service and will not always be available.

It could be argued that we are using these books to fund our lifestyle. But, at present, both David and I work full time and the money from the sale of the books funds his visits to churches around the country and allows him to accept a minimal amount in expenses. It also allows us to run development circles, to provide clairvoyant evenings at very low prices and pays for the upkeep of The Saahera Centre where we hold our healer and mediumship training evenings at minimal costs to those who genuinely wish to work for spirit. It has also allowed us to subsidise the SWA until it is in a position to fund itself. Working full time also allows us to speak to many people in many different walks of life. This is our choice and the way that we have elected to work for spirit. But that doesn't mean that this is the only way people can work for spirit. It is certainly not for us to judge other people's choices.

Should you close your eyes when you give healing?

Whether you have your eyes open or closed makes no difference to the quality of the healing energy. You are just the channel, the healing energy is not coming from you so it really is just a case of doing what feels right for you and that also allows you to concentrate the most. However, if you are in a public place it is best to keep your eyes open at least some of the time so that you are aware of what is going on around you.

Do you need to touch someone to give them healing?

Again it seems to make little difference to the quality of the healing. After all, if you needed to touch someone to give them healing, absent healing wouldn't work. However, it does appear that sometimes the person who is receiving healing feels it more if you lay your hands on them. It might also help for more localised problems, like tumours, to actually lay your hands on the area involved, provided of course that it is not in a delicate area. Again this is something that you have to decide on an individual basis. Sometimes you will feel really strongly that you do need to lay your hands on a particular area, other times you will feel quite happy to just heal through the aura.

Why does it sometimes feel that the healing has stopped only to suddenly start again really strongly?

We all have lots of healing guides that work with us, including those who, like us, are learning. When we go to give healing to someone and we do not think they are benefiting as much from our healing as they could, we often refer them to another healer. Some healers also find that they specialise in particular areas so many of their clients have similar problems because they are the specialist in that area. Our specialisms often relate to the experiences we have had on the earth plane. If, for instance, we have suffered domestic violence, we may find that many of those who come to us for healing, as well as those we meet in our normal earthly existence, have also suffered from this. This is because our role as healers is not just to act as a channel for healing but to also use our experiences to help others. We use both our earthly understanding and our spiritual understanding of this to help others. Thus those who need help in this area will come to those healers who have similar experiences to them. This is usually a totally unconscious decision made by their spirit because it is their spirit that is drawn to the particular energy or aura of that particular healer.

It is the same in spirit. We start giving healing and the guide who is working with us suddenly feels that something different or stronger is needed. This may be because our guide is not advanced enough or just feels that the client would benefit more with healing from another guide who may specialise in this particular problem.

It could also be that the aura of the person you are giving healing to needs to absorb a certain amount of healing first before it becomes more intense.

Does this mean we will always have clients with the same problems?

As we progress spiritually we move away from some of the problems we have had. This is because our progress entails that we have dealt with some of our problems otherwise we will not progress! Thus having progressed because you have dealt with certain issues, new issues will come along and you will learn to deal with them. In the meantime your client base will change because you have changed. There is a very famous saying that 'like attracts like'. This is true spiritually as well as physically.

Why do our guides become guides?

Like all the questions there are many answers to this. First and foremost our guides become guides because they have chosen to do so. They were also probably our guides and teachers whilst we were in spirit and we would have agreed for them to work with us whilst we are on the earth plane. It is also entirely plausible that we would also work with them when they return to the earth plane as this means our learning process is continuous.

They are not necessarily related to us or though they can be and they are also unlikely to be 'us' in a former life although there is nothing to say that can't happen.

Our guides would also have to be similar to us otherwise it would be quite difficult to work together. If we are quite impatient they will probably be the same and if we like to learn slowly they will also be the same. This ensures harmony.

Our guides will often be people who were on the earth plane many years ago and many of them may have started their learning process at a time when healing and mediumship were considered a normal part of our lives. Mediumship would have been a great help in allowing us to be aware of potential dangers. We would probably have used our spiritual instincts to protect us. Healing would have been invaluable as medicine would have been in its infancy or non existent.

But perhaps healing would have been enough. The energy of the earth whilst humankind was still hunter gatherers would have been much purer. As we saw in Chapter 2 there is evidence to show that there was little fighting before the Indo-Europeans arrived with their male Gods and war. Life would have been simpler as the only things that really mattered were life, family, health and happiness. With an absence of material things there would have been much more positive vibrations. Generation after generation lived this simple life and healing and mediumship would have been passed from one generation to the next. As all had these abilities it was considered neither special nor heretical. The purer energy of the earth would have also ensured that the healing and mediumship of the people was much stronger than it is now. Because they were all practising it and there was none of the emotional and physical pollution, the vibrations would not have been so distorted.

It may also be that our guides were never human. It would be very arrogant to assume that we are the only planet in the universe that is occupied. This could be why we sometimes find it hard to see them.

But although it is interesting to know why are guides are with us it is important to remember that it is the message that is important not the guide or the person that is passing it on. We have seen what happened when the messenger starts to take precedence over the message. Both Jesus and Mohammed originally carried the same message. But unfortunately it became the messenger who was worshipped not the message. The same happens today sometimes with celebrity TV mediums and can be seen with Evangelical groups. This may not always be the fault of the medium or the evangelical leaders. The media promote them instead of the message. In this way the message becomes mixed up with the personality of the messenger and starts to take on their personality and characteristics. St. Paul promoted celibacy even though there was nothing in the scriptures preceding him to say that this was what God wanted. This angered many Romans and led to another interesting story – that of Thecla.

In the Acts of Paul and Thecla, Paul was described as handsome with a face like an angel. Paul gave his sermons about virginity and celibacy and Thecla, who was a young virgin, was entranced. Her fiancée, Thamyris, became concerned that Thecla would follow Paul's demand for chastity, and had him arrested. Thecla visited him in prison and she too was bought before the Governor. Paul was sentenced to beating and expulsion and she was sentenced to death by burning, but escaped because of a miraculous thunderstorm apparently sent by God to put out the fire.

They then travelled to Pisidian Antioch where a nobleman offered Paul money for Thecla. Paul claimed not to know her and the nobleman attempted to rape her. Because she fought him off, and despite the protests of the women of the city, she was sentenced to death and thrown to the lions. She was again protected as the female lions refused to let the male lions near her and she then asked Paul to baptise her. He refused because she was a woman so she threw herself into a shark infested pool and baptised herself, emerging totally unscathed.

However, this story is not in the Bible. First, the idea of celibacy would not have gone down very well with the Romans of the day. Secondly, as Paul preached marital celibacy as well as single celibacy the church would not have lasted long because there would not have been anyone born into it! Thirdly, female equality was not a proper image of women and was seen as a threat to the male dominated church. Finally Paul does not emerge from this story in a particularly good light as he appeared to be the cause of the problems but escaped relatively unscathed.

But Paul's interpretation of the message, that of celibacy, has endured. In 1322 Pope John XXII insisted that priests could not be married. If they were married the consent of their wife had to be obtained for them to be divorced. As it was unlikely a wife would want to give up marital rights this eventually led to priests being unmarried.

Although this may have had more to do with the church being unwilling to take financial responsibility for wives and dependants rather than any theological reason, it was the theological reason that was given and it was only because it had been included in the Bible that they were able to cite it. It caused considerable hardship amongst wives and dependants and many priests continued to have 'wives' and dependants that they kept secret.

Paul's view of women has also endured. Because they were not worthy to be baptised the church has always considered women to be second class citizens even though much of the church's work could not have been carried out without women. Any women who did not adhere to the early church's view of women and who are mentioned in the Bible are normally portrayed as either licentious or evil or both. But this is not based on a theological reason either.

The idea that Mary Magdalene was Jesus' wife was around a long time before The Da Vinci Code came out. Unfortunately she was a woman so either she would have to be airbrushed out of history or her character blackened. The question is why?

The Christian Church has long had a problem with sexuality. The reasons for this are unclear but if we accept that those who edited the texts of both the Old and New Testament were human we can only assume that, for whatever reason, they felt threatened by female sexuality and therefore chose accordingly. Men have long had double standards as far as women are concerned. Whilst heterosexuals would like all women to be available to them personally, this does not apply to their availability to other men. If a women is available to them, then she is available to all men, therefore she is not to be trusted.

But it seems to go deeper than this. Men seem to fear female sexuality because they see it as a form of control that women have over them that they are powerless to prevent. Whilst this seems a strange way for men to want to portray themselves, it is only comparatively recently that the rape laws were changed. Before this, men were able to successfully argue, that if a situation had reached a certain point, they could not stop themselves. They were, therefore, not guilty of rape because the girl had led them on.

This attitude to women prevailed at the time the scriptures were written and is thus part of our culture.

Can the spirit of your relative/friend still talk to you if they have been reincarnated?

We can see no reason why not. Spirit can be in more than once place at a time as can be seen when giving absent healing. You can project your spirit to someone else to give the healing. You can also project your spirit to other places to 'remote view'. If you can do this on the earth plane where you are restricted by the physical body and by all the earths vibrations then once you are in spirit it would be much easier. Although your relative comes through to you in the form they were on the earth plane (or you wouldn't recognise them), they are projecting their spirit into that form.

We are all spirit primarily. Therefore, it is perfectly feasible that although we are on the earth plane now our spirit is projecting through a medium somewhere in the form of a previous incarnation. This may sound a little far fetched but we have to remember that we are currently in a physical body so find it quite difficult to understand with our spiritual 'brain'. Or put another way, things that we would understand easily whilst we are in spirit we find very difficult to comprehend whilst we are in physical form. If it were easy then there would be no evolution because we would know all the answers and there would be nothing to gain from being here.

Would our relative tell us if they had been reincarnated and would they tell us who they were?

Again there is no reason why they would not tell you if they had been reincarnated. However, it would be doubtful if they would tell you who they were. This is for several reasons. First their new incarnation may not have the memory of their previous incarnation. Second their new incarnation may not have any connection with the people with whom they were reincarnated previously, although this is not always the case.

We are often reincarnated with a particular group of spirits that we have already worked with before, hence the recognition that we sometimes have when we meet certain people. It's a bit like being at school. We go up with our class to the next level and sometimes the people who were our friends before are no longer our friends and sometimes people we didn't get on with are now our best friends. We are also always meeting and encountering new spirits that we haven't met before because they are at different levels. Again it's a bit like school where we may play quite happily with other children of different ages and abilities.

To return to the question, the other reason they would not tell you who they were in their next life is that if they were someone who had been very close to you there is a danger you could become obsessed with them. However, we do sometimes feel a strong sense of recognition when we meet someone and often they may remind us very strongly of the person we knew.

We could well be right but it's probably not wise to say anything to them. Apart from the fact that they may think you a little strange, they are here to live a totally different life and they are the person they have chosen to be. Telling them you think they are someone else may cause them anxiety and a sense of confusion as to their own individual identity. Nor is it a good idea for you to think too much about it for the reasons mentioned above. On the other hand if it gives you comfort and you do not change your behaviour to this person because of your feelings then there probably isn't any harm in it.

Is there a time limit before you come back to the earth plane?

No is the simple answer to that. You will come back when you are ready. The more healing and spiritual awareness you gain whilst you are here, the quicker you will be able to come back because you will not need so much time to recover in spirit. On the other hand you may still not come back for a long time because you do not need to or because you may simply choose not to.

Do you sometimes come back too early without proper preparation and is this why people commit suicide?

Unlike here, where we are continually doing things that we are not prepared for, we are always fully prepared for our lives here. We do not know all the reasons that we are here, nor do we know all the lessons that we are here to learn. This may make it appear to our earthly selves that we are not prepared or that we have come back too soon but this is just the perception of our earthly selves. Our spiritual selves know exactly what we are doing. (Good job somebody does!)

If we commit suicide it is either because this was something we were always going to be tempted to do or it is something that happens because we have lost our way. Either way it is part of the lesson that we and our family and friends have chosen to experience this time. It is also a lesson for the wider community collectively as we all try to understand why things would feel so bad and the person would feel so alone that they felt death was preferable to their life. If we have just lost our way and were not meant to have committed suicide then we will come back at a later date and have another go. But this time we may well be aware of the pitfalls and when they come along our spiritual instincts will steer us away from them.

It is worth distinguishing between this and another type of suicide. This is when people are duped into thinking that killing themselves and others is going to reap them physical rewards in heaven. Apart from anything else you could not reap physical rewards in heaven because you would then be spirit and have no need of physical things. These are very misguided young people who are vulnerable and have lost their way. They have been manipulated by evil people who because they themselves are cowards, indoctrinate others to carry out these atrocities. Presumably they are perfectly aware that they are talking rubbish which is why they do not act themselves.

Why do I keep seeing a white light in my bedroom when I first wake up?

This seems to be quite a common thing with people when they first start to become aware of spirit. It is probably spirits way of protecting us. Once we become aware and start to open up to spirit we need to protect ourselves with white light otherwise we do not have any control over who we are opening up to. But until we know about this spirit will usually do it for us. We may associate this with a relative who has recently passed or someone close that has passed that we have started to think about quite a lot. It may also be that we have just begun to think about spirit or we have had healing for the first time. Having healing can sometimes stimulate our own spiritual awareness. It is a bit like suddenly waking up and realising that everything is not quite how we thought it was before because there is a new dimension to our lives. Quite simply we have begun to change our perceptions or who we are and why we are here.

As soon as we begin to ask questions about spirit they will come close. We are not always aware of this as our rational brain will always seek to explain things in a rational way relating it to the experience and understanding that it has stored away in its memory. Asking spiritual questions works on our spirit in the same way. It awakens the spirit within us and this is when those in the spirit world begin to communicate with our own spirit. It begins to reawaken our spiritual memory. But until we are more in tune with our own spiritual energy those in spirit, like our relatives and guides, will do their best to protect us and point us in the direction of those that can help us develop our own protection.

But it is really important that once we know this that we begin to take responsibility for our own protection. Remember that we are here to learn lessons, so if we ignore the signals and just leave it up to our guides, sooner or later we will let something come close that we would prefer not to! This is not normally a major catastrophe as long as we then seek help to send it to the light. Unfortunately we often do not realise for quite a long time that we do have a problem. As like most things, prevention is better than a cure, it's much easier to make sure that we take control as soon as possible then this situation does not arise.

What other ways are there of knowing spirit is close?

There are many different ways that people become aware of spirit drawing close. Many people feel a tight band round their head, rather like the medieval head dresses that people used to wear. Others will feel itches or feel like they have cobwebs on their face and neck. Others will feel tightening in their throat or a feeling of electricity in their hair. This list is not exhaustive and some will feel all those things and others maybe only one or two or none. The important thing to remember is that every one of us will experience spirit differently. There is no 'norm' as such.

Is spirit able to see the physical world or does it just see the spiritual part of the physical body?

This is a really good question and certainly made us think. To make sure we had the fullest possible answer we asked our guides. One of these decided that he was actually not as developed as he had thought as he found it very hard to explain it terms that we, in our physical form, could understand!

Spirit does not see the physical because spirit does not see in the sense that we, as physical beings, see. Seeing through our eyes is a physical experience. Spirits see with their mind the same as they communicate with their minds. Simply put, the mind is how our spiritual selves process information. The brain is how our physical selves process information. Spirit does not have a physical face so therefore would not have a physical mouth or eyes as we know them. Just as some mediums see spirit through their mind this is how spirit 'see' the earth plane. They 'see' our spiritual selves in the same way that they 'see' us or we 'see' them when we are in the spiritual realm. This is by identifying and recognising the signature emitted by energy. Everything on the earth plane emits energy of some kind and it is this energy signature that spirit is able to recognise and identify. It can also distinguish between negative and positive energy by recognising the signature of the energy that is emitted. One way it is able to do this is by recognising and identifying the colours emitted by the aura. This is one of the ways it is able to assess whether healing is needed or whether a person is 'dis-spirited'.

Are our loved ones sitting 'up there' and watching us in our everyday lives?

We think that is probably most unlikely – think how boring that would be – hardly heaven! As 'spirit' we also communicate on a psychic or telepathic level so our relative or loved ones in spirit can pick up on our thoughts, which again is a form of energy. This could explain why our loved one may comment on our change of hair style. It is not because they are sitting 'up there' watching us in our everyday lives but because they are able to tune into our thoughts in the same way we tune into them or to other spirits on the earth plane.

However, just as some mediums see spirit as a physical presence rather than with their mind perhaps some spirits do see the physical as a physical reality. We continue to develop on the spiritual plane so perhaps this is one of the ways in which we develop. Or it could be the opposite? Perhaps it is the more developed spirits that only use their minds to communicate and see with. We would love to hear your views on this.

Finally, it could even be argued that as the physical exists purely to allow us to express our spiritual selves, the physical does not actually exist in any real sense. It only exists as an extension of our imagination! Thus as spirits we would not be able to see the physical because it is not there!

Do the stars have a spiritual connection?

As people sometimes say that the stars are a relative who has passed over we were curious to know whether there was any connection between spirit and the stars. The answer is both yes and no. Your loved one is spirit and as such can project themselves in any form that they choose. If you ask to see them as a star then this is how they will project themselves to you, in much the same way that you might see them in a butterfly or a particular flower. But in a general sense, no, your relative is not a star.

But there are other ways that stars could be said to have a spiritual connection. Stars are very evocative and aspirational. They are viewed as a very positive element in our earthly lives as we often strive to reach the stars or see the stars as the embodiment of what we are trying to achieve. Others see the stars as gateways to different dimensions or as stepping stones to other galaxies.

Stars are a form of energy, like everything else. They can emit both positive and negative energy and like all energy can retain the imprint of past existences, past lives, past experiences.

Modern astronomy can tell almost everything about a star by its initial mass. This includes its luminosity and size, evolution, lifespan, and even its eventual fate.

It is now believed that many stars are between 1 and 10 billion years old. Some may even be close to 13.7 billion years old. This is the age that the universe is considered to be. The oldest star that has been discovered so far is called HE 1523-0901 and is estimated to be 13.2 billion years old.

Stars have always been important to every culture. The ancients used to look to the stars because this was where they believed their gods had come from. These gods had shown them how to map the heavens and how to read the patterns in the stars. These patterns pointed to future events that would affect them so the stars became an important part of their connection with God. This is why stars have been used in religious practices. Ancient sky watchers associated these patterns with particular aspects of nature or their myths. Twelve of these formations became the basis of astrology. Many of the more prominent individual stars were also given names with Arabic or Latin designations.

Stars were also thought to be the souls of the dead or gods which is where we derive our association between our relatives and the stars. One example is the star Algol, which was thought to represent the eye of the Gorgon Medusa.

To the Ancient Greeks, some "stars," known as planets (Greek πλανήτης (planētēs), meaning "wanderer"), represented various gods. They took the names of the planets to name these gods hence the gods Mercury, Venus, Mars, Jupiter and Saturn. Uranus and Pluto were not visible to ancient civilisations so they were given the names of Greek and Roman gods by later astronomers.

But stars have not just been used for religious practices they have also provided an important navigational tool for travellers at night and the motion of the sun against the background stars was also used to create the calendars by which they and we live. Thus they played an important part of ancient culture and this has helped endow them with the many spiritual qualities we associate with them today.

What is the difference between a soul and a spirit?

Another really interesting question and, like most things spiritual, with no simple answer. When we asked this question in development circle we came up with several answers. Essentially both your soul and your spirit are necessary for your chosen pathway. Although they are separate they are also connected as you could not have one without the other. If you did you would not function properly. One of our group's guides suggested the following analogy: the spirit is like the gears and steering on a car whereas the soul is like the engine. In other words your spirit is the essence of you and it is your driving force. It is your spirit that makes the decisions and your soul that provides your conscience. I suppose you could liken your soul to the part of your spiritual instincts that tell you whether something is morally right or wrong.

Of course your main spiritual instincts guide you in many ways and will allow you to make the right decisions for you, but you also need to have that extra instinct that tells you whether your decision is in the best interests of everyone and not just you. Any decision that is made in the best interests of everyone will always be the right decision even though others may not agree.

In a physical sense, if you can describe something that is energy in that term, your spirit is the aura that surrounds you, whereas the soul is an energy that is located within your physical body.

Finally, the term spirit can be used to describe many things. It could be used to describe the Great Spirit (God) or individual spirits. We also talk of people returning home to 'spirit' or talk of a spirit when we mean a ghost. The word spirit is also a collective noun. The word soul however, is an individual noun and is only used specifically to refer to your soul and the sense that it is your conscience.

Do souls go to purgatory?

This would seem to be yet another misunderstanding or misinterpretation of the message. Historically, the church stated that you had to be baptised or your soul would go to limbo or purgatory when you died. Baptism is a physical cleansing but it is more likely that it is a spiritual cleansing that is needed. People that receive lots of healing before they die are able to pass over much easier. Spirits that do not go over are often trapped within the earth plane. This could be described as a limbo or purgatory. But it certainly does not apply to babies who are so close to spirit anyway that they return to spirit without any problem. This was just scaremongering by a church who boasted that if they had a child by the age of seven they would have them for life.

Telling people that you had to be baptised by a 'qualified' person or you would not go to heaven or your soul would wander indefinitely was another issue. It was more to do with deliberately misinterpreting the message to retain control. Spiritual cleansing can be done by anyone who chooses to do so. You can all do it right now by using your white light.

All you need to do is to sit quietly with your eyes closed and visualise that in the centre of your body is a small seed. This is your spiritual seed and it connects you to spirit. This seed is white and all you need to do is visualise it growing bigger and bigger and as it grows it becomes brighter and brighter. It continues to grow and glow brighter until it completely covers your whole body. Imagine that if anyone was looking at you all they would see would be a brilliant white light. Not only is this your spiritual protection, it is also your spiritual cleansing tool. You can use this white light to cleanse and protect your house, your car, your crystals, your workplace – in fact anywhere or anything.

Is there a spiritual connection with mirrors?

There are also a lot of superstitions around the spiritual connections mirrors are said to have. They date back before the Egyptians and are world wide.

It is the belief that the soul projects out of the body and into mirrors in the form of a reflection that underlies perhaps the most widely known mirror superstition: that breaking a mirror brings seven years' bad luck. It was believed that breaking a mirror also broke the soul of the one who broke the mirror. Because the soul was so cross at such carelessness and at being hurt, it took its revenge by exacting seven years of bad luck. This superstition goes back to the Romans, who were the first to make glass mirrors. They believed that life renewed itself every seven years hence breaking a mirror meant breaking one's health and this "broken health" would not be remedied for seven years. The bad luck could be averted, though, by grinding the mirror shards to dust so that no shattered reflections could again be seen in them. Early American slaves dealt with this bad luck by submerging the broken mirror pieces in a stream of south-running water. They believed that the bad luck would be washed away in seven hours.

In some cultures, the breaking of a mirror was thought to presage a death in the family within the year. This association of mirrors with death is common in folklore, and stems from the belief that the soul could become trapped in the mirror, causing death. For this reason, young children were often not allowed to look in a mirror until they were at least a year old. Mirrors were covered during sleep or illness so that the soul, in its wanderings, would not become trapped and unable to return to the body. In previous centuries, when bodies were laid out in the house for days before a funeral, mirrors were always covered because it was believed that if the person who had died saw themselves in the mirror their soul would be trapped in the house.

In Bulgaria, they believed that the soul of the dead person remained in its former home until the burial of its body and would carry off the soul of any living person whose reflection appeared in a mirror. Mirrors appear commonly as grave goods in Serbo-Croatia, particularly for those who die prematurely. These are the most "dangerous" dead, apt to roam from their graves and harry the living. Mirrors are believed to trap the soul of the deceased at the gravesite where it belongs.

The belief that the soul could be caught and trapped in a mirror appears in many other ways. The peoples of northern India considered it dangerous to look into a mirror that belonged to someone else. It was especially so to look into the mirrors of a house you were visiting: when you left, you would leave part of your soul behind trapped in the mirrors, which could then be manipulated by your host to his advantage. In 18th century India, women were seen to wave mirrors before the image of death goddess Kali, apparently to appease her need for human sacrifice with the reflection of a person rather than the sacrifice of a real human being.

There are also rituals that have developed around staring into a mirror and shouting a certain phrase. This is supposed to bring forth an image of the dead.

Another superstition that says if you look into a mirror on Halloween you will see an image of your future husband. This may originate from the strange 'fact' that we are apparently attracted to people who look like us!

Perhaps one reason mirrors are thought to have a spiritual connection is because people originally only saw their reflections in water. Water refracts light and this distorts the image. Gazing into water is also very calming, people would relax and this would sometimes allow them to see their aura. Water shares the mirror's reflective nature, and reflections in bodies of water appear at the root of much mirror lore. The soul was believed to be attracted to water. Macedonians leave a container full of water in an empty grave after exhumation to capture the soul and keep it in the grave, preventing it from following its bones, which have been moved to the church to allow its former grave to be reused. Jars of water are common sights in Bulgarian graveyards for much the same reason.

The ancient Greeks believed that water spirits, lurking in reflective pools, lakes, and streams, would drag the unwary reflected soul underwater, leaving the now-soulless person to die.

The Greeks' belief in malignant water spirits was probably the forerunner of the myth of Narcissus. This beautiful youth followed the hunt in the mountain forests, where the nymphs saw him and fell in love with his beauty. But he cruelly rejected them all. A nymph whom Narcissus had turned away prayed that he might some day come to know how it felt to be spurned. The gods heard her wish and granted it. One day, tired and thirsty from the hunt, Narcissus came upon a clear, unspoiled woodland fountain and stooped to drink. In the still, crystalline water, he saw an image of rare beauty that he took to be the fountain's resident water spirit, and he feel in love. He yearned after his love in the fountain's clear water, but received no response. Slowly, rejection overcame him, and he pined away and died. His body was never found -- in its place was the beautiful purple flower that now bears his name. It was told that when his soul crossed over the Styx, he leaned over the boat's edge for another glimpse of his love.

Finally, your eyes have often been described as the 'window to the soul' because the eyes, like mirrors and water, also have the capacity to reflect outwards. When you gaze at your own reflection in someone else's eyes you are not only seeing into the depths of their being, you are also seeing your self and you are a spiritual being. You can not only see the past, present and future in that image you can also see images of other relatives because of their similarity to you.

Are elementals also spirits?

Ancient civilisations considered that all things had spirits. They lived much closer to nature than we do and their lives depended on nature in a way that we do not now. They interpreted the energy that they saw in the elements as spirits. Thus they talked of the spirit in the wind or the trees or the tides etc. Everything does have its own spirit because spirit is a form of energy and everything has its own form of energy. However, these energies or spirits are not the same as the energy or spirit within us, the kind that takes a life. But this does not mean they are any the less important, they are just different.

The spirits of the elements are often the memories of things past. There have been scientific experiments that have separated out sounds and even voices from supposedly inanimate objects such as rocks and bricks. So the answer to this question is yes, elementals are also spirits but just not in the same way as we are spirits.

It is now time to look towards the future and see what the world has in store for us as spiritual adults. It's time to begin the last part of our spiritual journey

'I have come to the conclusion that politics are too serious a matter to be left to the politicians.'
Charles De Gaulle (1890 - 1970)

'We are made wise not by the recollection of our past, but by the responsibility for our future.'
George Bernard Shaw

The End

We have now reached the last part of our spiritual journey. We have travelled from spiritual childhood to spiritual adolescence and we have finally reached spiritual adulthood. Our world too has travelled from its physical, political and religious beginnings through its political, religious and scientific middle years to the present day. But adulthood is not always everything that we thought it was going to be. Many of the things we thought we would do with our lives have not happened. Many of our dreams have not materialised and often we settle for what we have because we no longer have faith in our ability to achieve our dreams.

But it is important that we continue to have dreams because it is our dreams that create our reality. Without our dreams there is nothing to aim for, nothing to hope for and if we are without hope we have nothing, because it is hope that sustains us through the dark days when it seems as if there really is nothing to live for. If we have hope we can see an alternative reality, one that is filled with light and is the future that we are choosing for ourselves and our children.

When we are children or adolescents are thoughts are full of hope and our dreams for the future. They might change ten times a day but they are a constant sustaining force in our life. If things go wrong we are able to change direction and set ourselves new goals, new dreams. When we are young we find hope quite easy to sustain. We have an in-built optimism that things will always work out and that we have the ability to change our lives.

As we get older, this becomes harder to do. Cynicism sets in and because we have become frightened of change and our ability to manage it, it becomes easier to settle for what we have, however, unsatisfying it may be. Things have to become really bad before we decide to do anything and it is only then that we dare to dream that things could be better. It is at this point that we begin to make that choice to change the situation.

It may just be a tentative, fleeting thought and we may not even be really conscious of it, but once it is there the seeds of hope have been sown and it is only a matter of time before it takes hold. It is a feeling within us that there has to be more to our lives, or that we are somehow missing out on something that is important. We may not be able to articulate this to start with but once we are aware that this gap is there we will find ourselves looking to fill it. It is then that our spiritual self awakens and begins the search for its pathway. This is where our dreams come in because we will begin to visualise different scenarios to see if they are what we are looking for. This may be as simple as making minor adjustments to our lives like looking for promotion or starting a new hobby or it may mean making major changes such changing career or deciding to leave an abusive relationship.

One in four women suffer an abusive relationship at some time in their lives. It is the one area in our world in which men have ensured that women have total equality of opportunity. It is an experience shared by women that transcends all political, religious, cultural, economic and class boundaries. But although it is a shared experience it is not experienced in the same way because the responses of the societies in which women live vary considerably. Societies that have begun to grow up have finally realised that this kind of behaviour is unacceptable; societies that have progressed little over the past two thousand years continue to treat women in ways that are totally unacceptable. But even those societies that do accept that it is wrong and do seek to help women in these situations do little to address the underlying causes. Attention is centred on reacting to events and punishment of offenders instead or being pro active by re-educating their citizens at an early age about this kind of behaviour. Recent research shows that many young people, including young women, still think that certain situations give men the right to hit women and that there are some situations where 'women ask for it'.

The most dangerous time for women is when they decide to leave. Many are attacked and some are killed. In the UK alone two women die each week as a result of domestic violence. Some men even resort to killing their own children as a way of 'punishing' the woman for daring to leave. In the last section we saw how our insecurities, low self esteem and fear of change as individuals impacted on our communities and how they reacted to other communities. Domestic violence in all its forms is also a result of all of these things and is something only we as individuals can change. Society cannot change without us as individuals having the will to change things.

At the beginning of the last section we looked at how the two hemispheres of the brain were divided into left and right and how these had been labelled into masculine and feminine. The reason for this was quite simply that those who did the labelling saw the spiritual qualities of compassion and gentleness as a weakness and the earthly materialistic, physical qualities as strength. The prevailing norm at the time was male orientated so the compassionate, caring qualities were labelled as feminine whereas the earthly materialistic qualities were labelled as masculine qualities. It would seem that having left the world in the charge of the earth centred left hemisphere of our brain for the last few thousand years may not necessarily have been a good idea. Perhaps it is time we all re-engaged with the right side of our brain and allowed our spiritual side to re- emerge and become the dominant factor in our decision making.

The other problem with allowing the earth centred materialistic hemisphere to dominate is that it has fundamentally altered the energy of the earth itself. It is now out of balance because of the lack of the right spiritual centred energy of the right hemisphere.

Unfortunately to try and re- establish some kind of equality women have also increasingly had to allow the left hemisphere of their brain to become the dominant force behind their thoughts words and actions. But this has only resulted in us all concentrating our energy in the wrong direction. The equality we should be seeking is to re establish the predominance of the right hemisphere and its compassionate, spiritual qualities. At the same time the left hemisphere should gradually become more subordinate. All this means is that the qualities of gentleness, compassion, love and peace should be the norm that we all strive to achieve. This should be the benchmark we are aiming for and should take priority over everything else. Materialistic, earth centred decisions, taken without these qualities have resulted in the world as we know it - a world from which these spiritual qualities have been exiled.

The last section of this book looks in more detail at the world as it is today. As with the last two sections there is a certain amount of science, politics and religion. And as with the last two sections you do not have to remember every word. The facts and figures are there to support the theory and explain certain points; the book would make little sense without them. Our earthly home now depends on science, politics and religion more than in the past and because the world is now such a small place they are more entangled and entwined than ever. Because of this they are an increasingly important part of our spiritual journey especially as we are now approaching the end of that journey and finally thinking about coming home.

'Science is organized knowledge. Wisdom is organized life'.
Immanuel Kant (1724 – 1804)

Chapter 11

Coming Home – our planet

The state of the environment is now high on the agenda of most of the world's politicians. There are a few notable exceptions, namely the USA and China. Unfortunately the USA uses the highest percentage of the world's energy resources per head of population and is responsible for a large percentage of the world's carbon footprint. China is developing so fast they will soon be using the highest percentage of the world's energy resources and they are also responsible for much of the world's carbon footprint.

In Britain, after years of ignoring it, politicians are now scrambling over themselves to be the first to come up with environmental taxes. Unfortunately this is having an adverse effect. People who genuinely care about the planet feel that they have had their cause hijacked and cynically used as a means to raise additional taxes. This is beginning to alienate those who did care and those who didn't can just shake their heads and say 'see we told you it was rubbish'. Of course there are also a few sections of society who really have no interest in saving the planet and another section who are actively trying to bring about global warming as they think this will allow their prophesies to come true.

So what do we do about our planet? The planet has always heated up and cooled down throughout its history. The problems we seem to be facing now are not that this is unprecedented but that the process itself is being accelerated by our activities and lifestyles. As we saw in the first chapter, if change happens slowly we can adapt to it. If it happens suddenly we can find it much harder to adjust, adapt and survive. It would appear the planet is much the same. If our lifestyles were only causing minimal changes and these were happening slowly the planet would have time to adapt. But we have inflicted massive changes on the planet in a very short time scale and we have assumed that the planet will adapt. Unfortunately, this does not appear to be the case. It is not only physical changes we have inflicted on the planet, we have also inflicted changes to the fundamental energies of the planet and it is this that is causing many of the problems. We saw in the first chapter that the planet is a living organism and as such can evolve. This is what is happening today. The planet is evolving in an attempt to survive the massive changes that we are inflicting on it.

The planet has been steadily evolving for millions of years but has always down so at its own pace. The difference now is that we have changed the pace and the planet is struggling to keep up. It is the carbon dioxide in the greenhouse gases that come primarily from the burning of fossil fuels like coal-burning power plants that scientists and environmentalists say is to blame for warmer temperatures, melting glaciers and rising sea levels.

The United Nations organized a summit to create momentum for the December 2007 annual climate treaty conference in Bali, Indonesia, when Europe, Japan and others hope to initiate talks for an emissions-reduction agreement to succeed the Kyoto Protocol in 2012. The 175-nation Kyoto pact, which the United States rejected, required 36 industrial nations to reduce carbon dioxide and other heat-trapping gases.

The following information was taken from the Associated Press website on October 2nd 2007: 'At the United Nations on Tuesday Island countries from around the world warned that despite debate over global warming and the potential for a significant increase in sea levels, there has been little concrete action to stem the climate changes that threatens their existence.'

"The international community has convened numerous conferences and summits at which it has agreed on wide-ranging plans and programs of action," Foreign Minister of the Maldives Abdalla Shahid, told the U.N. General Assembly. *"However ... all*

too often the reality of implementation has failed to match the ambitious rhetoric."

One of the real fears of global warming is that the melting of the ice caps will increase sea levels. This will cause flooding on an unprecedented scale to many low lying areas and some islands that are already below sea level are in danger of simply disappearing. The Maldives is a low-lying island nation consisting of a number of atolls in the Indian Ocean. As the flattest nation on earth — with an average height of only 7 feet above sea level — it is considered particularly vulnerable to the perils of global climate change. Climate researchers say that many of its islands will disappear over the next century as the seas rise. Shahid's warnings were echoed by other speakers at Tuesday's General Assembly session.

"We view associated problems of high frequency of abnormal climate, sea level rise, global warming and coastal degradation as matters affecting the economic and environmental security of all small island states," said Timothy Harris, foreign minister of the Caribbean nation of St. Kitts and Nevis.

Charles Savarin, foreign minister of nearby Dominica, said that rising sea temperatures were causing the death and bleaching of corals and a decline of fish stocks.

"Climate change is the most pressing environmental problem humankind has ever faced," he said.

And Sonatane Taumoepeau-Tupou, foreign minister of the Pacific kingdom of Tonga, urged developed nations to implement emissions reductions and help developing nations to do the same. The alternative could be that the poor will suffer more than most, because they are often living in low lying areas most of risk from floods. There are many reasons people live in flood plains but it is often because this is where the land is most fertile.

But it is not just island nations that could disappear. The UK also has problems with coastal erosion as the east coast of England is gradually sinking into the sea. Furthermore, the managed retreat policies that are currently in progress are accelerating the process.

We also seem to be at more risk from floods than before. After the recent unprecedented floods in the midlands and south west of England there is much talk of restricting development on flood plains. Flood plains are, after all, exactly what they say they are – they are there to let the river overflow and drain onto the flood plain. But the government has dismissed this as unworkable and instead has insisted that councils do more to prevent flooding. Does this mean councils are now responsible for stopping it raining? Of course there is a distinct lack of affordable housing in England. If they continue to build on the flood plains no one will want to buy them so they will come down in price and the less well off will be able to afford them. This will solve the problem of providing more affordable housing. But is this really the solution to the housing crisis?

Although it is accepted that we need more housing the biggest problems are where to put them. In the north of the country many houses are not being sold and the number of private lets is increasing. But the real problem is in the south of the country. This may seem a strange question but why do we all want to live in the south of the country? Why is our economy centred on the south of England? It is here that the infra structure is in danger of breaking down. Not only are our roads congested, our reservoirs are inadequate if we have too little rain, our drainage and sewage systems are creaking and our land fill sites are gradually filling up. If we build even more houses in the south, these systems will collapse.

But it is not just Britain that has seen unprecedented rain this year. The monsoons in India have killed hundreds and thousands have lost their homes. This is an annual event in Bangladesh where large sections of their country face these problems year after year.

In Greece, they have the opposite problem. Lack of rain and soaring temperatures have led to fierce forest fires they have struggled to contain.

In South America mud slides have resulted in areas where the trees have been removed and in the USA and Caribbean the seasonal hurricanes are becoming more violent, year after year.

Our food industry seems to also be facing continual crisis. It seems chickens can cause salmonella poisoning, poultry can possibly give you bird flu, beef can give you CJD and Foot and Mouth has reared its head for the second time in five years, leading to mass slaughter of livestock, the threat of food shortages and at the very least price increases. Blue tongue disease has now come to Britain for the first time ever. Carried by midges and previously confined to Africa, it is believed that the increase in global temperatures has allowed it to migrate and it has now crossed Europe and come to our shores. Unfortunately no one has yet come up with a vaccine, although they are now increasing their efforts. Perhaps the reason they did not already have a vaccine for a disease that has been around for years was because there was little profit in making vaccines for people in countries that cannot afford to buy them.

Intensive farming methods and the constant use of insecticides is wreaking havoc on our countryside and its food production. Farmers are now finding it uneconomic to produce milk because the supermarkets have such a monopoly that they are in danger of putting farmers out of business. The same applies to the production of other animal foodstuffs. The recent flooding has wrecked the harvesting of vegetables and whole crops have been lost. European subsidies have failed to arrive in time to prevent some farmers going out of business and yet are paying other farmers fortunes to leave their land fallow.

The seas are also threatened by over fishing and several species of fish that are staples in our diet are threatened by extinction. However, the limits on harvesting fish of a certain size and the need to stick to fishing quotas have had unexpected side effects. Whilst fishing for species that are not covered by quotas fishermen inadvertently catch those that are covered by the quotas. Because they are not allowed to land them they throw back tons of dead fish at a time when so many people are starving. There are also reports that Norway is now facing a parasitic attack on its fish and has to resort to poisoning an entire river in an attempt to stop it spreading.

Hand in hand with council's attempting to make us recycle more goes an increase in penalising people for putting out too much rubbish thus criminalising members of the population for not recycling enough. Other councils have reduced rubbish collections to fortnightly. Whilst this might sound a good idea, most of the population see it as a way of councils' saving money (even though the savings are not passed onto us, the consumer), the government trying to ensue all the population is on a giant criminal DNA database, and the states increasing control over the minutiae of our private lives. Other problems include an increase in the rat population and the appalling smell, especially in the summer which presumably constitutes a health hazard. It's also worth bearing in mind that much of Europe still collects its rubbish daily. With landfill sites nearly full and the location and building of waste incinerator plants hotly contested, we seem to be fast running out of options.

It seems there is also now a scramble to see who can claim the territory under the North Pole where exploration is now easier because of the melting of the ice caps. This is not to actually own the land but to own the resources that are said to be there. Russia has symbolically staked its claim by planting a one meter high titanium flag on the Lomonosov ridge, which Moscow claims is directly connected to its continental shelf. This has heightened tensions in the international community because a quarter of the untapped reserves of oil and gas are said to be under this area – an estimated 10bn tonnes.

In the last chapter we mentioned the idea that the energy of the earth was much purer thousands of years ago. Even if you disagree with this you would probably agree that the air and the atmosphere were certainly free of the pollution that is present now.

Oil is now fast running out and the world needs to look for alternative sources of energy. These will need to be greener than those we have been exploiting over the past few hundred years. But what are those alternative sources of energy? At the moment efforts are concentrating on wind turbines, solar panels and wave power. But these will never be enough to replace the oil fields or coal that has fuelled our lifestyles for many years. There is also talk that an alternative form of unlimited free energy has been found in the so called 'empty space' which surrounds us. This space is, of course not empty but full of atoms and other electrical elements. However, there is no visible proof that this source of energy has already been developed, although lack of visible evidence does not necessarily mean that it hasn't given that it is apparently free and unlimited! The only other possible fuel source that could come close is nuclear power and commissioning a nuclear reactor building programme is fraught with problems, not least that no one wants to live next door to one, however safe it is alleged to be. So, either we have to look for other options and/or change our lifestyles dramatically.

Many engineers and researchers consider that it is only by taking dramatic steps that we will be able to save the world from the catastrophic changes global warming could bring. They argue that despite 10years of international negotiations aimed at reducing carbon dioxide levels by 60-80%, global emissions are still rising. The only other way forward is to invest in geo-engineering projects that change the planet, alter its oceans and/or reshape its cloud cover.

The Intergovernmental Panel on climate change published its latest assessment report earlier this year. It considered three suggested options that could reduce the sunlight reaching the earth. These were orbiting mirrors, sulphur particle schemes and projects for enhancing cloud cover. Because carbon dioxide would be left in the atmosphere it would stimulate plant growth and reductions in sunlight would prevent temperatures rising even if the C02 levels continued to increase. However, opponents argued that it was technology that was responsible for the current problems and more intervention would just make matters worse. But some ecologists agued that although there were dangers in intervening, doing nothing could be even more dangerous and geo- engineers argued that greenhouse gasses were already causing massive changes to natural ecosystems anyway.

The following are just some of the suggestions that were discussed. Although not all of them are likely to be tried it would be nice to think that they were going to consult with the world's populations before going ahead.

Ocean Pumps: vertical pipes could pump deep cold water to the sea surface. Cold water contains more life forms and these are vital for absorbing CO_2. They would absorb the CO_2, die and sink to the ocean floor, storing the carbon away for millennia. Marine biologists objected to this because of its effect on creatures such as whales and porpoises.

Sulphur Blanket: when major volcanoes erupt the earth often cools significantly as a result of the sulphur ejected into the stratosphere. It's been suggested filling hundreds of rockets with sulphur and blasting them into the stratosphere. But opponents point to the risks of acid rain and ozone depletion.

Mirrors: scientists want to fire two giant mirrors into space. It wouldn't completely block sunlight but would filter out infra-red radiation. The problem with this idea is the prohibitive cost and the fact that they wouldn't know whether it would work until they had tried it. To produce a 1% cut in solar radiation would require the mirrors to have surface area of 600,000 square miles.

Cloud shield: this is one of the cheaper options but would need global commitment and any tampering with weather patterns carries all sorts of risks.

Synthetic trees: these would not grow leaves or flowers but would adsorb carbon dioxide. They would apparently look like goal posts with Venetian blinds but would be able to remove about 90,000 tonnes of carbon dioxide a year.

Forests of the seas: plankton and algae absorb carbon dioxide so if the number were increased they could absorb more. The opposition to this idea centres on the dangers of using iron fertilisers to stimulate the growth which could damage marine life. This method is already being trialled.

But what has all this to do with our spiritual journey? Well, our spiritual journey can only take place in a physical environment. Although, as we have mentioned, you can evolve in spirit, it is the physical experience that allows us to evolve in a more balanced way. Experiencing the physical is also a way of putting the theory into practice and speeding up the process. If we have nowhere to experience the physical, our evolution will slow down considerably and we will have nowhere to try out our theories. We would be like scientists who came up with theories but had no idea whether they would work in practice – a bit like the above example of the firing of giant mirrors into space.

But would this be such a bad thing? Our physical journey through life is often 'solitary, poor, nasty, brutish, and short' to paraphrase a quote from Hobbes. (Hobbes was a 17th century British philosopher who wrote a book called Leviathan in 1651). But that, of course, is why we choose to undertake our spiritual journey in a physical body – to give us the experience that we need to create the perfect world. Once we have achieved this our need to experience pain and suffering will diminish because we will have all finally evolved past that stage. That is one of the reasons it is so important to help others on their journey. By helping them you are using your gift of selfishness in a positive way.

Hobbes, writing in the 17th Century, concluded that man is not naturally good and most of his actions are guided by self interest which if left unchecked would have very destructive consequences. His answer was the need for a form of arbitrator. He did not think it mattered whether it was a state or government as long as it had the monopoly on violence and had absolute authority. Hobbes also considered that concepts like morals and values had no eternal meaning – they would change and evolve throughout time. History has proved him right as many things that were once acceptable are no longer so.

The same applies to the way we see our world. In the past it was seen as a resource to be exploited. But because we have now evolved the way we see the planet has also evolved. We are now able to appreciate that it too is a living breathing organism and that this is the only planet we have. We cannot continue to consume as if there were three planets. But why do we feel the need to continually fill up our lives with material items?

What do we really need to exist? We need warmth, light, food, water and love. Without the latter the others mean nothing. The same applies to all the material possessions that we have. They mean very little without someone to share them with. But we seem to have forgotten how to love unconditionally and instead we fill our lives with material possessions that have become our substitutes for unconditional love.

Unconditional Love

One of the gifts we all bring with us is our ability to love unconditionally. But this is also one of the gifts that brings us the most problems because it is only effective if it is balanced and it is this balance that we find so hard to achieve. If you love someone unconditionally but they do not love you in the same way you will become a victim because they will use your love to control you. Loving unconditionally only works if everyone understands how it is supposed to work. Learning how to express love is something we learn as children and if that opportunity is lost we will all reap the consequences because part of unconditional love is respect – respect for ourselves and others. If we accept that the planet is a living organism then we have a duty to show it the same respect that we show towards every living organism on the planet including each other.

If we look at the concept of respect, one major part of self respect and respecting others is the ability to say no. Many people find it extremely difficult to say no. They are worried that if they say no, others may think less of them or like them less. Saying no is a two way thing. It is the request that is being turned down, not the person who is making the request. If we could all accept this it would make life a lot simpler because people would be able to be honest with each other.

What is the point of saying yes to something that you don't want to do? You will not do it to the best of your ability and you will resent doing it because it was not your choice to do it. If you are continually saying yes to things that you do not want to do you will eventually resent the person who is asking you.

Conversely, continually asking someone to do things that you know they don't want to do, will only encourage that person to resent you. As a means of control, like all means of control, it will only last so long before they do say no. The problem with saying yes all the time is that when you do decide to say no people take offence because you have always said yes. They have got used to you always saying yes so they expect it. When you suddenly, and for no good reason (as far as they are concerned), say no they can't understand it. This is because they have taken your acceptance for granted and your sudden refusal makes no sense to them. You are changing the parameters of your relationship with this person without warning. This makes them react in a negative way. Subconsciously, they had lost respect for you because you always did what they wanted. By the same token, you had also lost your self respect because somewhere, along the line, you gave control to that person. By asserting yourself you are taking back control.

If you are honest with someone life becomes much simpler. Not only do they know that when you do say yes, you mean it, they also know that you are being honest. If they take offence because you have said no then it is they who have to deal with that. Why do they find it so hard to accept rejection? You are not saying no to them, just to their request. Perhaps it is worth making this clear when you say no to people.

On the other hand, why are you saying no? Do you have a genuine reason or is it really because you can't be bothered? Saying no because you have been working all day and are tired is being honest. You have a duty to respect yourself and if this means making a choice between soaking in the bath at the end of a long day or going out then you have to decide which is the honest thing for you to do, not what will make other people happy. You have a right to be happy too. That is what self respect and unconditional love is all about.

The same applies to the way we treat the planet. Spiritually we are all one and as the planet is a living organism we are also one with the planet. Respecting the planet means learning to say no to consumption. We can only wear so many clothes, watch so many DVDs, live in one house at a time or drive one car at a time. Public transport is a credible alternative but only if it is affordable and accessible. Britain is one of the few countries in the developed world that does not have a publicly owned transport system. This means that, despite some subsidies, bus and train routes are restricted, in the main, to the routes that make the most profits. Many country areas have few buses and some have none at all, thus travelling by public transport is not a viable option. If we want to encourage people to use public transport it needs to be cheap, quick and convenient. It also needs to be in place before people are penalised for using their cars, not the other way round.

There should also be incentives for people to fit energy efficient technology in their homes. At present, if you fit energy efficient technology, you are likely to be penalised through the Council tax system because your property is seen to be more desirable than a property that does not have this extra fittings. To reap the outlay costs on many of these items would take several years.

We do have to make changes; not only to the way we live, but also to the way we view our lives here. But these changes will not happen over night and we will need help to make the transition. And it is not just the way we treat our environment that will have to undergo changes. The way we view religion and politics also has to change if we are to regain our self respect and avoid making the same mistakes we have made in the past.

'A cult is a religion with no political power'. Tom Wolfe

'With or without religion, you would have good people doing good things and evil people doing evil things. But for good people to do evil things, that takes religion.'
Steven Weinberg (1933 -), quoted in The New York Times, April 20, 1999

Chapter 12

Coming Home – Our Religions

The last chapter considered the environmental condition of the world. In this chapter we take a look at the religions of our world. Religion is big business. In America over 81% of the population consider themselves to be religious with 76% of those calling themselves Christian. But Christianity is not one homogenous group. There are, and always have been, many variations of Christianity. These include not only the more mainstream sects but a variety of smaller cults, many of whom are perfectly harmless but some of whom are potentially very dangerous, not just to the individuals that join them, but also to the world at large. Many are apocryphal in their outlook and some of these are quite prepared to start Armageddon purely to ensure their own place in heaven. We looked at the End Timers in Chapter 6 as just one example. But what makes a cult different from other forms of religious groups.

Cults

The definition of a cult according to Wikipedia is: *'a cohesive social group that is devoted to beliefs or practices that the surrounding culture considers outside the mainstream, with a notably positive or negative popular perception. In common or populist usage, "cult" has a positive connotation for groups of artistic and fashion devotees, but a negative connotation for new religious and extreme political movements. For this reason, most, if not all, religious and political groups that are called cults reject this label.*[13] (Wikipedia). But this is just one definition.

Cults are only seen as negative because by cults we normally mean the dangerous religious ones who fall into the following category. This following list is not exhaustive but from the point of view of this book the cults or sects we are referring to are those that impose all or some combination of the following over their members: physical, emotional, mental, financial and/or sexual control.

They are normally led by a charismatic figure who considers him/herself to be either god or the chosen messenger of god. They exercise control by first providing the individual with things that they perceive to be lacking in their own lives such as love and family and belonging. They provide the individual with an identity. Once the individual feels part of the group they begin to exert the control, subtly at first, then with more force. This is no different from the way the dominant person in a domestic violence situation exerts their control over their partner. And the reasons underlying the cult and the dictatorship are the same as the reasons that underpin the behaviour of the person who abuses his partner/child/friend. The charismatic leader, like all dictators, is insecure and needs to continually satisfy his/her desire for adulation to feel loved.

They begin by isolating members from outside family contact and then they often exhort their members to give all their worldly goods to the 'church' or brotherhood'. This is not just a way of making money although most insecure people feel money gives them the security they lack from relationships. By depriving the member of their money they become dependant and thus easier to control. There then follows a period of sexual abuse of the member. By this time the member has no one to complain to and no money to escape, even if they wanted to. Like the victims of domestic violence they often put up with it because they feel

---

[13] Wikipedia

that it is their fault or they have been brainwashed into believing that this is normal behaviour and therefore acceptable.

So how can you distinguish between a religious cult and a genuine belief?

This is an interesting question. Most religions would have started out as cults or at least they would have been seen as cults by proponents of the mainstream religions at the time. Christianity started out as a cult and might well have remained so without the intervention of Constantine. When he used Christianity as a way of uniting the Roman Empire he elevated Christianity beyond a cult and made it a mainstream religion. A belief has to have something that appeals to people over and above the belief they already hold. One of the things Christianity offered was a better life after death. This is also a spiritual belief that had been around for centuries. When the Jewish people left Egypt with the idea of multiple gods, they also left with the idea of an after life.

Jesus stuck very close to the teachings he had been bought up with, it was his interpretation that was slightly different. Virtually all his teachings are taken from earlier Jewish writings. Even baptism is a Jewish custom. He selected certain teachings and emphasised their positive message rather than their often negative dictates. He gave each individual a self belief in his own self worth, he emphasised that there was a purpose to life and that helping others was the real way to greatness and that human relationships should be characterised by good will. This is the true message from spirit. It appealed to so many people because it gave them a purpose, it made sense and their own spiritual instincts told them it was the truth and that it was genuine. Unfortunately, the message became reinterpreted by others and used to justify all sorts of things that Jesus never meant. Jesus was a spiritual messenger, a prophet as both the Jewish people and the Muslims believe. He was no more or less the son of god than we are. In the sense that we are all spirit we are all Gods children, the same as Jesus. The other problem with the way that the message was interpreted was that dying for the faith suddenly became a good idea.

Why martyrdom?

If the after life is so good then why are we all waiting down here? Why are we putting up with all the suffering and pain when dying will release us all from this?

The definition of heaven or the afterlife differs depending on the religion that is describing it and the time the description was written.

The Greek idea of heaven was that it was situated outside the nestled spheres that surrounded the earth. This was where the gods lived. It was a garden, an Elysian garden, in a divine realm in a pure light and was defended by winged angels. The Romans adapted this idea and increased the criteria needed to attain heaven. Philo Judeaus combined Greco – Roman ideas and saw heaven as existing just outside the Greek spheres. It was the Christians that unified the idea of God with heaven. In the Islamic faith God does not have an image and heaven is portrayed as a beautiful garden filled with myriad fountains and flowing water. It was Dante who introduced the idea of heaven being bathed in white light and Spiritualists who introduced the idea of an active heaven.

Buddhists have 30 heavens and 30 hells. They believe that we are reborn many times and it is our thoughts words and actions (karma) that determine which we are in. Nirvana is when you have reached enlightenment and have no further need to be reborn or exist on any plane.

In the early days of Christianity there were many different religions, cults, beliefs and gods. Every religion or belief system needs a selling point. This is something to make it stand out and to attract the attention of others and also to publicise the fact that it exists and that it is different. There are theories that the early church used martyrdom as a way of providing political and social cohesion amongst its members. Those involved in public relations would say that there is no such thing as bad publicity.

When people were executed for their faith others wondered why. What was so special about this faith that people were prepared to gladly die for it rather than give it up? If you add to this the fact that the Jewish people were an occupied people who were used to being under the yoke of Roman rule, then it seems to make more sense. When people are oppressed they look for any way in which they can rebel. One way of rebelling is to take away the power of the oppressor to kill you. If you do not fear death then you have taken away that power, that control. If you appear to gladly welcome death then you have taken away even more power and control from your captor. Furthermore, word of your death is circulated to others and so on. Thus martyrdom was a unique selling point.

But what does the word martyrdom mean?

The word martyr comes from the Greek and actually means 'witness'. It usually means a person who is put to death or endures suffering because of a belief, principle or cause. Though often religious in nature it can also apply to someone who dies in a secular cause, someone who dies for his country, those who die in battle defending a cause and those killed in struggles for civil rights or freedoms.

In Christianity, as we have seen, a martyr was an innocent person who is not seeking death but is put to death for their religious beliefs. They often refused to defend themselves because they saw this as imitating Jesus willing sacrifice on the cross.

Islam has a much broader view of martyrdom and includes anyone who dies in the struggle to defend the faith. However, there is much dispute within Islam as to whether so called 'suicide bombers' are really martyrs. It is against Islam to kill innocent people but just like those early Christians the deaths of suicide bombers make good publicity and this has been used to good effect by Muslim Fundamentalists.

But those who send young men and women to kill and maim others in the name of Islam are not true Muslims. They are no different from the fascist and communist dictators of the 20thCentury. They have just found a different way to terrorise people. Their aims are also no different. They too wish to stop freedom of thought and freedom of expression. Freedom of thought and speech is a threat to fascists and fundamentalists alike. Suppression of knowledge allows them to gain power because when people are ignorant they believe what someone else tells them. If they have no access to an alternative point of view they willingly believe all the lies that are told them. That is why the education system is so important. Knowledge is power because knowledge will allow us to refute the lies. Knowledge is power because it will allow us to explain why there are divisions within our societies. Once we understand why there are divisions and that these divisions are the result of misunderstandings and misinterpretations, some of which are centuries old, we can begin to rebuild the trust between nations. Once we have achieved this we can achieve peace. But peace is not the aim of fundamentalists.

We have talked about those who come here and choose their lives purely to cause pain, chaos and destruction. Many of them are in positions of power and many have control over the minds of others. This is because we have become lax. Because religions have remained stubbornly stuck in previous centuries many of us have lost our faith. By not changing or adapting, by trying to keep knowledge from us, religions have begun to sow the seeds of their own destruction. The world's major religions have so much to offer by way of spiritual messages. This is their role. The time for controling populations through the fear of the wrath of God is long gone. It is time for religions to let go of the past, embrace the future and send out the messages of love and light they were originally given. It is time they reread the Scriptures and took out the passages that are patently there because of someone's prejudices.

Looking to the future

The Bible was written in a time and culture where women had very little control over their lives. Many of the passages reflect this. We are told that marriage is for life. But this is not a spiritual message, it is a religious message intended to allow men to live their own lives and ensure that women did as they were told. It is also tied in with male insecurity about the parentage of their children. By ensuring women were tied to one partner and the penalties for adultery were severe, men could ensure their children were the ones who inherited the family silver! This is a physical instinct that stems not from our spiritual selves but from our physical selves. Spiritual teaching tells us we are here to experience life and to learn. If you are tied in a relationship with a violent spouse and you cannot leave then you cannot learn anything because you are not free to live your life.

Marriage is not for ever, any more than anything else in life. Everything changes. However happy you are with your partner, the chances of you both dying together are pretty remote. Social studies now seem to confirm that we have, on average, three partners throughout our lives. The first is to have fun with, the second to have children with and the third to grow old with. By telling people that marriage is for ever, the churches have condemned many people to living lives of abject misery. Furthermore, by refusing to marry divorced people in church they have not only alienated a large number of people, they are also setting themselves up as moral judges.

But it is not just the bible that needs to be up dated. The Qur'an was written after the Bible but was still written in a different time and culture from today. Early passages of the Qur'an seem to show that Muslim women were actually treated much better and had many more rights than Christian women. It was the Muslims who were the vanguard of freedom and enlightenment across the ancient world. Whilst Christian Europe was surviving the dark ages and knowledge was suppressed in an attempt to keep control, Islam was centuries ahead in science, medicine, and learning in general.

The Moorish invasion of Spain is portrayed by the Christians as something terrible but they were actually welcomed by many of the towns and cities because of the level of culture and knowledge they bought with them. Isabella and Ferdinand's re conquering of Spain in the 16th Century, far from being a war against the Moors, was actually a civil war as many of those fighting on both sides were Spanish. It also bought terror as they introduced the Inquisition and 20,000 Muslims and Jews had to flee the country.

The Crusades

The Crusades are also an area that history has rewritten. The Muslim presence in the Holy Land goes back to the initial Arab conquest of Palestine in the 7th century. Pilgrimages were allowed to continue and western Europeans were less interested in the loss of Jerusalem than with the invasion of other non Christian invaders such as the Vikings. However, the Muslim armies' successes were putting strong pressure on the Eastern Orthodox Byzantine Empire.

The Crusades were, in part, an outlet for an intense religious piety which rose up in the late 11th century among the lay public and was further strengthened by religious propaganda that advocated a Just War to retake the Holy Land from the Muslims. The remission of sin was also a driving factor. This provided men who had committed sin, with a way out of eternal damnation in hell. It was a hotly debated issue throughout the crusades as what exactly "remission of sin" meant. Most believed that by retaking Jerusalem they would go straight to heaven after death.

However, there is considerable controversy as to what exactly was promised by the popes of the time. Another theory, based on the speeches of Urban II was that you had to die fighting for Jerusalem for the remission to apply. This meant that if the crusaders were successful, and retook Jerusalem, the survivors would not be given remission. A further theory suggested that if you reached Jerusalem, you would be relieved of the sins you had committed before the crusade but you could still be sentenced to hell for sins committed after the crusades.

The immediate cause of the First Crusade was Alexius 1st appeal to Pope Urban II for mercenaries to help him resist Muslim advances into territory of the Byzantine Empire. There is considerable controversy as to why Pope Urban did come to the aid of Alexius 1st. The reasons suggested include that he saw political and economic gains for the Western Church and that it was a way of healing the divisions between the eastern and western church. However, whatever the reasons behind the crusades they are rooted in history and should have no bearing on the 21st Century.

But the problem is that the word 'crusade' has two separate meanings that are dependant on your heritage. For Muslims the very word still provokes terror because of the appalling way the crusaders behaved. Yet the word 'crusade' for westerners is just another word for a campaign, is used in a variety of ways (crusade against drugs; crusade against speeding drivers etc) and holds no such associations.

From being in the forefront of exciting scientific and medical knowledge Islam slowly stagnated. This is purely because Mohammed is seen as the last prophet. If there cannot be any more prophets it means that the writings of Islam can never be updated. Any attempts will be met by accusations of false prophecy.

As with the Bible it is essential that the Qur'an is reread and updated. It is full of spiritual messages that are just as relevant now as they were then. It is the messages that are quite obviously time specific that need to be updated and modernised. Fighting holy wars went out hundreds of years ago. The Qur'an contains so many beautiful passages of love and spiritual upliftment, it is those that we should be concentrating on. God could not possibly tell us to kill or hurt others because these are human frailties. God, by very definition, cannot have human frailties otherwise he/she could not be God – he/she would be human. It is the fact that these passages have not been updated and modernised that the fundamentalists find it so easy to corrupt the Qur'an and use it for their own ends.

One example of this is the Taliban. Their interpretation of Islam is a far cry from the spiritually uplifting verses that Mohammed wrote as a message of upliftment and encouragement to his people. They are a fundamentalist Sunni Muslim and ethnic Pashtun movement that ruled Afghanistan from 1996 – 2001. Although they were removed from power by American ariel bombardment and Northern Alliance ground forces, smaller groups are still engaged in fighting with NATO troops and the current government. Whilst they were in power they enforced the strictest interpretation of Sharia law ever seen in the Muslim world. They became notorious for their treatment of women who were forced to wear the burqa in public, not allowed to work or be educated after the age of eight and then they were only permitted to read the Qur'an. Women who did seek education were forced to attend underground schools where they and their teachers faced execution if caught. Because they were not allowed to be treated by a male doctor without a female chaperone many illnesses were left untreated. Any violation of the Taliban laws was punished by public flogging in the street and public execution.

This is hardly the way a God of love would want half of his population treated and only the most insecure male could want to see his mother, sisters or spouse treated in this way.

Because of its human rights' violations there were only three states who granted the Taliban diplomatic recognition. The United Nations and many Islamic states including Iran, India, Russia, Turkey and most central Asian Republics refused to recognise it and actively supported its rival – The Afghan Northern Alliance.

Culture or Religious tradition?

Many British Muslims are now calling for sharia law to be part of this country's legal system. The idea of sharia courts in Britain is likely to cause considerable controversy, but religious courts already operate in this country to serve other faith communities such as the Jewish rabbinical courts and have limited powers of enforcement of their rulings. However, the majority of British Muslims seem perfectly happy with the way British society is. It could be argued that many came here in the first place because of the way British society is.

Interestingly enough only 37% say that the Muslim Council of Britain and Muslim religious leaders reflect their views. This seems to correspond with the equally small number of citizens who actually voted for the government. It would seem that religious organisations are apparently no more representative of their members than the government is representative of the citizens of the country.

More importantly perhaps, 86% believe that is unacceptable for religious and political groups to use violence with a further 69% believing it was right to inform on people who they thought might be involved in terrorist activity.[14]

Of course this means that 14% do think it is ok to use violence and 31% would not inform on suspected terrorists. Furthermore 55% thought schools did not have the right to dictate dress codes of pupils and 44% thought they should have the right to dictate school uniform policy in Britain and that girls should be allowed to wear the hijab to school.

But is this really a religious custom or a tradition that was started for other reasons and has now become synonymous with religion?

Circumcision was common in most hot countries probably because it helped prevent infection. Because it was widely

---

[14] Statistics taken from Dhimmi Watch

practiced for a physical reason did it gradually become to be seen as part of or associated with a religious tradition?

Did the tradition of Muslim women covering themselves begin for a practical reason such as protecting their skin from the intense sun and the drying air in the desert, not to mention the adverse effect of the sand. Women's skin is much softer than that of men's and needs more protection. Did men then see this as a way of claiming ownership of women because only their husbands saw them without the protective covering? Is this how it developed?

Buddhists find the idea of killing any living thing abhorrent. Is this why they shave their heads – so they do not get head lice and then have to kill them?

The cow is sacred to Hindus because it from the cow that life comes. The cow gives them milk and the bull works the fields and the tow together give them more cows etc.

Robes are symbolic of many religions. Nuns and monks wear the habit, first and foremost, because the material used to produce them was cheap. The wearing of these identical robes gradually marked them out thus the robes bestowed on them a specific identity. It was this identity that later came to symbolise their humility and uniformity, but all this came about because of the practicalities of providing cheap clothing.

Many of the food restrictions that religions place on their members stem in part from the limited access to certain foods in different seasons, but primarily the inability to store food in hot weather. As this food was likely to go off very quickly in hot weather and would make anyone who consumed it either extremely ill or die, it would make sense not to eat it. Thus a tradition that stemmed from a totally practical reason became synonymous with a religious belief.

The Celtic Cross is iconic of the Celtic Christian religion. The original cross on Iona was a normal cross on which the arms were too heavy and kept breaking. To stop this happening supports were added which has given us the Celtic Cross.

These are really just examples and suggestions of how certain rituals and traditions either have or may become associated with religions when in fact the original reason behind them may have been simply practical. If this is true then it shows just how easy it is for behaviour to be misinterpreted and then used to justify other behaviours in the name of religion.

Religion has now reached a crossroads and has a choice as to which direction it should go. If it chooses its spiritual path then the world will be able to evolve and move forward. If it chooses control and dogma the world could once again regress. But a religion is only the sum of its members and it is those individuals who have the power to change the direction of their religion.

One of the ways democratic government was supposed to have differed from previous governments is in its separation of religion and the state. However, as we have seen, this was only applicable in certain democracies. Many countries have never been able to separate the two and it would now seem that religion and politics are once more becoming entangled in many more countries with possible unfortunate consequences for the world.

'Change your thoughts and you change your world'.
Norman Vincent Peale (1898 – 1993)

'I know not with what weapons World War III will be fought, but World War IV will be fought with sticks and stones'.
Albert Einstein

Chapter 13

Coming Home – Our Politics

In the last two chapters we have seen how our world seems to be perilously close to catastrophe. Not only are we depleting our home by our over use of resources, we are also poisoning our atmosphere, the seas, the oceans and the air that we breathe. We can then add to this the growing political problems, many of which seem to stem from religious wars that should have been finished with centuries ago. It would seem that religions, like individuals, find it very hard to forgive, to let go of the past and to move on.

On the other hand there is much talk of 2012 as the magic date when the world is going to end. We have already looked at the cults and sects whose philosophy is based on prophesising this and in some cases who are actively seeking this apparent apocalypse. But what does it actually mean when people talk of the world coming to an end? What does' the coming of the kingdom of God' really mean?

Like everything else it is a matter of interpretation. Does it mean that the planet is going to disappear with a big bang or into a black hole, or just that the world as we know it is going to change beyond all recognition? If it is the latter is that such a bad thing? The coming of the kingdom of God could simply mean that we are all going to become much more spiritual in our outlook and the way that we live. The kingdom of God could actually be here on earth. It does not have to mean we are all going to be 'raptured' or beamed up to some mythical heaven.

We have the power to make our world a heaven or a hell. For many people our physical lives on the earth plane could accurately be described as a form of hell as the world over the last few centuries has lurched from one crisis to another, from cycles of violence and destruction to yet more devastation. On the basis of this evidence it would seem that the world is long overdue for some change. But what kind of change – that is the 60 million dollar question!

In the introduction we summarised some of the major problems facing the world at the moment. We will now look at these in some more detail. This is not to depress you but rather to continue one of the themes of this book that not all change is bad, even if we initially think it is. It is rather to suggest that any changes that may or not be coming in 2012 could actually be positive changes and changes that we should be welcoming – not fearing. However, to look at this issue in a positive light we first have to see why change could be welcome. The only way to do this is to look at the way the world is now and see if it really is the perfect place that we think it is when we start to worry about any possible future changes.

Economics

We started by highlighting the problems with the financial institutions. Our financial systems are very complicated and as we are not financial experts we do not intend to turn this into a lecture about economics. That said we do have to look at the way the systems work in order to understand the reason they are so precarious and also the ways in which they could change for the better.

As individuals we pay our taxes to the government. We pay taxes on our earnings and on what we spend. Every time we buy anything there is tax paid on it. This even applies to things that do not have any direct tax or duty on. For instance, we do not pay VAT on food (yet) but farmers receive subsidies from various European funds and to fund these subsidies we pay a certain amount to the European Community. We also pay duty on most things that come into the country from outside, either through subsidy systems or import duty.

The taxes we pay on our earnings goes to fund welfare, defence, national policing and all government departments and Quangos and the wages and pensions of all those who work for these organisations. They also give money to local councils to fund services. This money is paid by means of a system of complicated subsidies to the council tax. The aim of these subsidies is to control the amount of money by which local councils put up the council tax each year. This sounds good, but in reality it often results in councils cutting services in an attempt to fulfil all their statutory duties and provide the statutory services, which are often increased each year as more and more legislation is bought in. (Statutory just means duties and services they have to provide by law).

We then pay an additional contribution, through the council tax, to fund all the local services including refuse, highways, housing, the police and fire service and the wages and pensions of all those who work in local and county government. Thus, essentially we are paying twice for the same thing. However, whilst the first contribution we make is related to how much we are earning, the second contribution is related to the size and condition of the property we live in and the area in which this property is located.

There is considered to be a point at which the proportion of taxation becomes unsustainable. This is when it becomes economically unviable to go to work. Unfortunately this point has nearly been reached for many people as they face increasing bills for council tax, energy and housing costs.

Councils are not allowed to borrow money but governments are. The Government borrows money from the IMF – The International Monetary Fund or the World Bank. There is a tacit agreement between the United States and Europe that the World Bank's president is always a US national whilst the IMF is always headed by a European. However, when the government borrows money form the IMF they impose economic conditions.

Rather like when you go to your bank for a loan they want to be sure they are going to get it back. These economic conditions are about how the government runs its economic policy. Therefore, if the government owes money to the IMF, which most governments do, the economic policy of the government is essentially governed by the IMF. Thus it could be argued that a group of unelected people, who most of us have never heard of, run the economic policies of a large proportion of the world and are controlling all our lives.

This can be seen most clearly in many of the poverty stricken countries of Africa. In the past the loans they were given were dependant on them following certain economic policies. For instance, many were encouraged to grow cash crops to sell to the more developed countries. This led to then growing less food for their own consumption leaving them with a need to purchase food from abroad. This was obviously more expensive than growing it themselves. When there were droughts they were unable to grow as many cash crops so were unable to afford to buy in food. This has led to terrible famines. The following information was taken from http://www.africaaction.org/campaign_new/debt.php:

'Africa's over $200 billion debt burden is the single biggest obstacle to the continent's development. Most of this debt is illegitimate, having been incurred by despotic and unrepresentative regimes. African countries spend almost $14 billion annually on debt service, diverting resources from HIV/AIDS programs, education and other important needs. The U.S. and other rich countries have resisted calls to cancel this debt, instead proposing partial solutions that are inadequate and impose harsh economic policies on indebted countries'. It goes on to cite the following:

- 'Sub- Saharan Africa receives $10 billion in aid but spends $14 billion in debt repayment;
- while more than 80 million Nigerians live on less that $1 per day, in 2005 Nigeria agreed to pay over $12 billion to

the Paris Club of Creditors in exchange for partial debt cancellation;
- in 2003, Zambia spent twice as much on debt repayments as on health care. But partial debt cancellation allowed the government to grant free basic healthcare to its population in 2006.

If we borrow money we have to pay interest on it. The rates can vary but are linked to the interest rates charged by the financial regulator of which ever country you are in. In the UK this is the Bank of England. These directors meet each month, look at the economic figures for the past month, decided what they think is going to happen in the future and set the rates accordingly. Their calculations are also influenced by what other countries are doing. If borrowing money is cheaper in one country than another, large borrowers will get their money from that country and this could result in a devaluation of the pound thus making the money in our pockets worth even less. All financial transactions affect the economic growth of the country so it is important interest rates are not too dissimilar from other countries. On the other hand, the higher the rates, the more money the banks will make, providing the investment is secure.

Domestic interest rates rise, we are told, to keep down inflation. But often the inflation is caused by the rise of the price of things over which we have no control, like oil. Furthermore, every time oil prices rise, the government makes more money because tax is charged at a percentage rate of the price. Thus if oil goes up by 20% the amount of revenue the government gets goes up accordingly. Because the price of oil has gone up our energy prices go up and this puts inflation up. The Bank of England then responds by putting up interest rates. This increases the price of borrowing money and therefore the cost of our mortgages. Because our mortgage costs have gone up this also puts inflation up and so the Bank of England puts up the interest rates in an attempt to hold down the inflation which is partially caused by the policies they have implemented. This is obviously a simplified view but reasonably accurate, none the less.

One final point to make about inflation is this: the inflation rate at which interest rate rises are calculated against is not the same as the inflation rate that is used to calculate salary increases. For some reason this is always lower that the rate of inflation used to calculate rate rises and other tax rises. They don't call us 'rip off Britain' for nothing!

In the meantime because interest rates have risen the banks are making record profits which they lend to the IMF and World Bank to enable them to lend money to governments. But the profits the banks are making are based on credit. It is not real money. We use our credit cards to pay for things which we cannot afford to pay for in cash. Thus we are borrowing money which we can pay off monthly, either in small instalments or in full. As interest rates rise so does the cost of this credit. It only needs one large investment fund or bank to over stretch it self or be unable to repay its loan and the whole thing will come crashing down.[15] This has now happened and the world's economies seem to be in free fall. We only have to look at what happened in the world when the Wall Street Crash of the 1920s happened. In an attempt to avoid history repeating itself governments around the world are now busy nationalising the banks to ensure they do not fail after making some spectacularly bad investments and loans.

Many companies used the low interest rates to borrow vast sums of money to buy other businesses. When interest rates rose many struggled to pay back this money. These are businesses that are high street names. When businesses are unable to pay back the money that they owe they are faced with stark choices. They make staff redundant to cut back costs and/or raise their prices to try to increase their income. If they raise prices this affects the inflation index which could result in interest rates rising again. If

---

[15] At the time of writing unsustainable lending policies in the US led to a run on Northern Rock in this country. This was because the debt had been shared out to different companies all round the world in an attempt to reduce the risk.

they cut staff these people will be unemployed. Not only will they claim benefits (to which they are entitled), which is an additional cost to the tax payer, but they also have less spending power. As more people spend less, more businesses are likely to face economic problems. When firms face economic problems they cut staff etc. This is called a crisis of supply. When firms are unable to sell their goods huge surpluses accumulate. This can send countries into recession.

The other crisis that can hit countries is when there is a crisis of demand. This happens when there are not enough goods produced so the prices rise accordingly. This increases inflation which affects the inflation index and interest rates are raised in response in an attempt to bring down prices. Managing the economy is like walking a tightrope. Governments have to try and balance supply and demand and if they get it wrong it affects us all. When too many firms face an economic crisis shareholders begin to sell their shares in the company. If a lot of shareholders start to sell their shares, this can cause a panic on the stock market. This happened in the 1930s and is currently happening again.

In the 1930s it led to the rise of fascism in Germany and economic misery and hardship for millions round the world. Eventually it led to a world war. Our economic systems are much more entwined and closely linked that they were then. Many of the predictions for 2012 talk of World War 3. But is this just scaremongering?

Politics

Fascism is by no means dead in Europe, nor is the racism that seems to go hand in hand with any kind of totalitarian regime. In Russia there are now several youth organisations reminiscent of the Hitler Youth of the 1930s. The Nashi, a youth movement run by the Putin's Kremlin have become a central feature of Russian life. Those who join the Nashi and the other youth movements not only find a sense of purpose and excitement they can also improve their educational prospects and thus their employment prospects. The alternative is a corrupt education system and the prospect of a dead end job. They have an annual camp where they are encouraged to breed to increase the dwindling Russian population. But more insidiously they are being taught to hate democracy.

Like the population of Germany in the 1930s, the Russian experience of democracy has not been a positive one. Similarly, the people are now beginning to accept a return to state control of the media, economy, politics and society. Although racism and prejudice are lurking beneath the surface of the Nashi, other groups in Russia are much more openly racist. This is going hand in hand with a complete rewriting of history. Stalin is no longer seen as a paranoid megalomaniac who slaughtered over 25 million of his own people. Instead the common consensus is that he actually did more good than harm. The new history guide for teachers describes Stalin as 'the most successful leader of the USSR'. The real villain is now seen as Yeltsin who is now denounced for his weak pro democracy policies. Thus the education of the first generation to grow up in a Russian democracy is not teaching them how to value their freedom and the duties of citizenship, it is re educating them back to the age of authoritarian rule with all the dangers that this spells for the other democracies in the world. The world is yet again in danger of ignoring the warning signals.

But it is not just Russia that seems to regressing back to the past. Many African nations have also struggled to cope with the democracy that has been imposed on them.

In Rwanda between half a million and a million were massacred from April to July 1994. Extremist political groups organised the killings which were primarily directed at the minority Tutsi ethnic group and those from the Hutu majority who opposed the killings. The slaughter ended when rebel forces of the Rwandese Patriotic Front (RPF) overthrew the genocidal government. However, ongoing political tensions, guerrilla warfare and massive refugee movements have continued to sow political instability and humanitarian crises throughout the Great

Lakes region, including in neighbouring Burundi and the Democratic Republic of Congo (formerly Zaire).[16]

Sudan is the largest and one of the most diverse countries in Africa, home to deserts, mountain ranges, swamps and rain forests. It has emerged from a 21-year civil war between the mainly Muslim north and the Animist and Christian south which is said to have cost the lives of 1.5 million people. Southern rebels said they were battling oppression and marginalisation The UN says more than two million people have fled their homes and more than 200,000 have been killed. Pro-government Arab militias are accused of carrying out a campaign of ethnic cleansing against non-Arab groups in the region. The conflict has strained relations between Sudan and Chad, to the west. Both countries have accused each other of cross-border incursions. There have been fears that the Darfur conflict could lead to a wider, regional war.[17]

Zimbabwe is slowly being suffocated under the government of Robert Mugabe. His government has been criticised for corruption, the suppression of the political opposition, economic mismanagement and the deterioration of human rights. Thousands, if not millions, have starved and the inflation rate is set to hit 1.5 million percent by the end of the year (2007). There is now an outbreak of cholera which has spread to neighbouring countries. The United Nations Economic Commission for Africa has named them Africa's worst economic performer with unemployment rates at 85% and interest rates at 70%.

The recent power sharing deal brokered by the South African government seems to be unworkable as Mr Mugabe refuses to concede any power despite signing an agreement saying he would do just that. The whole situation is reminiscent the 1930s and Hitler signing agreements saying he would not encroach on any more territory and then doing exactly the opposite. The reason Hitler was able to do this was because he knew the world did not

---

[16] www.globalsecurity.org
[17] BBC News 24 1st June 2007

really care enough to step in and do anything constructive about it.

But, again, it is not just Africa that has problems. The following is an extract from Human Rights Watch World Report 2007: 'Human rights conditions in China deteriorated significantly in 2006. Authorities greeted rising social unrest—marked at times by violent confrontation between protesters and police—with stricter controls on the press, internet, academics, lawyers, and nongovernmental organizations (NGOs). Several high-profile, politically-motivated prosecutions of lawyers and journalists in 2006 put an end to any hopes that President Hu Jintao would be a progressive reformer and sent an unambiguous warning to individuals and groups pressing for greater respect for the fundamental rights and freedoms of Chinese citizens. Domestic observers believe that these constraints will remain in place at least through the 2008 summer Olympics being hosted by Beijing.

The Chinese government continues to use a vast police and state security apparatus to enforce multiple layers of controls on critics, protesters, and civil society activists. Such controls make actual arrests—which draw unwanted international attention—less necessary in silencing critics. The system includes administrative and professional pressures, restrictions on domestic and foreign movements, covert or overt tapping and surveillance of phone and internet communications, visits and summons by the police, close surveillance by plainclothes agents, unofficial house-arrests, incommunicado confinement in distant police-run guest houses, and custody in police stations. Many are charged with vaguely defined crimes such as "disrupting social order," "leaking state secrets," or "inciting subversion." Some 100 activists, lawyers, writers, academics, HIV/AIDS campaigners, and human rights defenders were subject to such treatment in 2006, indicating a new crackdown'. [18]

---

[18] Human Rights Watch World Report 2007

The following is taken from The Burma Campaign UK site: http://www.burmacampaign.org.uk/ 'Burma is ruled by one of the most brutal military dictatorships in the world; a dictatorship charged by the United Nations with a "crime against humanity" for its systematic abuses of human rights, and condemned internationally for refusing to transfer power to the legally elected Government of the country – the party led by Nobel Peace Laureate Aung San Suu Kyi.'

In 2007 the world watched as weeks of peaceful protests led by the Buddhist monks came to an end when the military junta began firing on innocent protesters. This was followed by weeks of overnight raids on monasteries and thousands of arrests. A further five monasteries were raided in Rangoon and about 36 monks were arrested overnight on 3 October, after receiving beatings from soldiers. "The raids in the North Okkalapa monasteries started around 10 p.m. and ended in early morning," said Nilar Thein, a leader of the 88 Generation Students group. "Monks requested soldiers not to use violent acts on them. But soldiers neglected their requests."

The raids on monasteries in South Okkalapa Township began at midnight and ended at dawn. Everyone in the monasteries, including laymen, women and children, were taken away. Dissidents in Rangoon estimate there are 1,200 monks detained among an estimated 3,000 people arrested during the mass protests in Burma. Monks are currently detained in Insein Prison, the Government Technology Institute and Kyaikkasan Stadium in Rangoon. Many monasteries in Rangoon remain locked up, and monks are unable to go out for alms, say Rangoon residents[19].

However, it appears that is not just countries that are intent on ruling by totalitarian means. There are a group of people who meet once a year, by invitation only, called the Bilderberg Group. The invitees are powerful people from countries around the world and the meetings are held in absolute privacy. Although the place

---

[19] Source: Irrawaddy

and time of the meeting is known, no press are invited, no minutes are ever released to the world and security is extremely tight. It is believed that their intention is One World Government. Apparently the idea is to give each country a political constitution and economic structure organised to place political power into the hands of the chosen few and eliminate all intermediaries, to establish a maximum concentration of industries and suppress all competition, to establish absolute control of the prices of goods and raw materials (The Bilderberg Group already has this control through its grip on the IMF, World Bank and World Trade Organisation), to create judicial and social institutions that would prevent all extremes of action.

This is **not** a Jewish conspiracy but a consortium of very rich and very powerful people, including the members of the Bank of England who control our interest rates. The alleged aim is to bring about a *'single global marketplace, controlled by a One World Government, policed by a United World Army, financially regulated by a World Bank and populated by a micro chipped population whose lives are governed by materialism and survival, all connected to a global computer that monitors our every move'*.[20]

This sounds totally far fetched until you consider it in the light of the increasing use of surveillance that we mentioned previously, the increasing use of legislation to control everything we do, the suppression of freedoms we have taken for granted, the increasing use of our news broadcasts to bombard us with trivia and the way we live our lives in general. If you would like more information about these issues there are several websites you can visit including: www.democracynow.org; and www.nexusmagazine.com

However, if we take a step back from this proposed physical materialistic One World Government and consider the idea of a One World Government in a spiritual sense, would that be such a bad thing?

---

[20] Daniel Estulin quoted in Nexus August – September 2007 pg 24

The United Nations was set up to replace the League of Nations. This was an international organisation founded after World War 1 as a result of the Paris Peace Conference in 199-1920. Its goals were to ensure that the world's problems would never again result in the type of carnage seen in the WW 1. This would be achieved by disarmament, and preventing war through collective security. Disputes between countries would be settled through negotiation and diplomacy. It also set itself the task of improving global welfare. The diplomatic philosophy behind the League represented a fundamental shift in thought from the preceding hundred years. Because the League lacked an armed force of its own it depended on the Great Powers to enforce its resolutions, keep to economic sanctions which the League ordered, or provide an army, when needed, for the League to use. However, they were often very reluctant to do so. Benito Mussolini stated that "The League is very well when sparrows shout, but no good at all when eagles fall out."

Although it did have some success it ultimately proved incapable of preventing the Second World War. It was replaced by the United Nations after the war which inherited a number of the agencies and organisations founded by the League.

Along with its primary aim of preventing wars, its stated aims are to facilitate cooperation in international law, international security, economic development, social progress and human rights issues.

There are now 192 United Nations member states, encompassing almost every recognized independent state. Its headquarters are in New York City and the UN and its specialized agencies decide on substantive and administrative issues in regular meetings held throughout the year. The organization is divided into the following administrative bodies: The General Assembly which is the main deliberative body; The Security Council which decides resolutions for peace and security; The Economic and Social Council which assists the promotion of economic and social co operation; The Secretariat which provides information, studies and other facilities needed by the UN and The International Court of Justice which is the primary judicial body.

There are also additional bodies such as the World Health Organisation (WHO) and The Untied Nations Children's Fund (UNICEF). The Secretary General of the UN is its most visible public figure and the current incumbent is Ban Ki-moon of South Korea who took up the post on January 1st 2007.The UN has six official languages: Arabic, Chinese, English, French, Russian and Spanish and is funded by member states.

On the face of it the UN is a very forward looking organisation and its aims could be considered to be very spiritual in nature. However, this does not really appear to be the case. The UN is made up of individual nations, each with their own vested interests and ways of viewing the world. These perceptions of the world are a result of each nations' unique individual experiences and history and it is these that colour the way each of these nations votes on major issues. As with individuals, nations find it very difficult to encompass the idea of one-ness. Nations, by their very definition, are separate states and the politicians of all these individual states are there to further the interests of their individual nations. It would be very difficult for an individual politician of one nation to embrace this spiritual one-ness and see the world as one whole and base his/her vote on that unless he/she could be sure that all the other members of the UN were also doing this. So where do we start?

As with anything new, someone has to make the first move and suggest a new way. Unfortunately, it would seem that the world at present has still not evolved sufficiently for this to be a possibility. For all the world leaders to work together there will either have to be some kind of major threat or catastrophe that compels them to realise that it is all their interests to work together or the individuals of all the nations of the world will have to change their perceptions of why they are here.

As the first is hopefully unlikely this leaves us with the second option. It is us, as individuals that have the power to change the world we live in. Presumably you do think there is room for improvement or you would not have read this far. The next step is to pass this message on – the message that it is our spiritual selves that need to evolve to the highest that we can be, not our physical selves.

We are not in competition with everybody else on the planet. Any material gains and possessions are fleeting as we cannot take them with us. The only thing we will be taking with us to our spiritual home is our spirit. Everything else we achieve here we will leave here when we die. Wouldn't the best achievement be to leave a world that has finally evolved and is finally at peace? Not the false sense of peace that we have now but a true and lasting peace: A world that is our heaven and not our hell. It is this which is within our grasp if we only have the courage to reach out and take it.

We need to understand history to ensure that the mistakes made then are not repeated. But history is history – it is past – it is gone. Just as we, as individuals, must let go of the past to move on countries must do the same. If we continually berate ourselves for something that happened years ago we are in danger of reopening past injustices. Furthermore, we will not only never heal the wounds, but we are also unable to look forward because we are too busy looking back. Looking back at the past is for enjoying the happy memories, learning from the mistakes and then using the experiences of the past to help plan a better future.

Unfortunately, countries, like people seem unable to do this. The world is still fighting wars over things that began centuries ago. Politicians of failing governments continually refer to the glorious past of their counties as a way of uniting their populations. This can provide a sense of national identity that might otherwise be lacking. However, this type of nationalism can be extremely dangerous. Often some of the territory that the country held is no longer theirs and the population may now be of a different ethnic mix. The next step is often to bolster this national unity by excluding a section within the country. This is done by scapegoating a particular section and blaming them for all the countries problems. When that fails to work expansionist policies that blame other countries often follow.

We have now seen that it is not just countries that use these tactics or that are fighting over issues that have their origins in previous centuries. Religions, because they are rooted in the past, also use these tactics and as we have seen, some of the most devastating wars and crime against humanity have been committed in the name of religion.

Thus it would seem that the real problems facing us now are two fold: the world's resources are running out which could result in wars over dwindling material resources; and secondly, religious states, secular states and members of populations in both of these are increasingly using religion as an excuse to try and control the world's populations. Furthermore, both religious groups and secular groups are using similar forms of fascist extremism to achieve their aims. The simple answer to both these problems is that we all need to change our perceptions of the world and why we are here. The difficulty is putting that understanding into action.

The world's economic systems depend on consumerism to keep going. If we all suddenly stop buying things the system would collapse. This would have catastrophic effects on the world's populations. The trick is to reduce consumerism to the minimum without destroying the system. In other words we have to find the right balance between consumerism and abstention. Saying no, as we discussed in the last chapter, can be difficult. Working out the right time to say no and finding that balance between being assertive and being selfish is exactly the same as working out when to buy something and when not to. The way to achieve both is to listen to our spiritual instincts instead of our physical animal instincts. The ability to distinguish between them is part of our ongoing spiritual development and something that is a major part of all our spiritual journeys. The quicker we can learn to make decisions based on our spiritual instincts and not our physical animal instincts the more we will evolve whilst we are here.

But we have not quite reached the end of our journey yet. Spiritually, we have gone from children to teenagers, but physically we are now approaching the end of our journey and we need to look at how we can evolve in to our spiritual adulthood. After all, the future is the responsibility of us as spiritual adults.

'Diamonds come from deep below. They are the result of evolution from one form to another. This is what death is.'

'The supreme irony of life is that hardly anyone gets out of it alive'.
Robert Heinlein (1907 - 1988), *"Job",* 1984

Chapter 14

Coming Home – Spiritually

As we said in the last chapter, we have now reached the end of our physical, political and religious journey. We have also progressed form our spiritual childhood through our spiritual adolescence. To progress to our spiritual adulthood we either have to evolve here on the earth plane or when we have reached the end of this part of our evolution, we have to leave our bodies, our home here, and go back to spirit to prepare for the next stage. This means going home to consider our journey and the lessons we have learned on the way. But before we finish our journey in this body there is just one final aspect to look at and that is the end of our lives in this body and the return of our spirit to our spiritual home. This is rather similar to us finishing our holiday, (even if it has been the holiday from hell) and then returning home.

One of the many issues that face us towards the end of our physical journey is how much control we have over our time of passing. There is considerable debate about whether euthanasia should be allowed and much of this debate has its origins in western religions and the way the original message was interpreted. If we look at the middle ages for instance there was little that could be done to ease suffering in those who were dying or in considerable pain. However, religions were busy telling everyone that god was omnipotent which left them with a quandary. If God was great and loved everyone how could he allow such suffering? The stock answer was that committing suicide is a sin and it is only God that has and should have the power over life and death. (This, as we have seen, has led to God being blamed for all the suffering in the world when in fact it is we who are responsible for the suffering in the world not God.)

People were also told that your suffering would enable you to enter heaven and that it was God's will. But is it? Does a God of love want you to suffer unnecessarily? But how do we decide what is unnecessary suffering? Much of our journey on the earth plane could be described as being full of unnecessary suffering if seen from our earthly perspective. But as we saw at the beginning, our spiritual choices probably bear no relation to the choices we would make from our earthly perspective. If we allow ourselves to go sooner that we would have if we had died naturally, there is a danger that we might not do something that we came here to do. On the other hand, once someone is incapable of communicating that would seem to be very unlikely. We also have access to many drugs that can prolong life beyond what we would consider to be the natural life span with that condition. On the other hand part of our spiritual journey here involves using our abilities and talents and for some people this will mean developing new drugs specifically to prolong life and reduce suffering. So how do we decide whether euthanasia is right?

The simple answer is that the only way to decide whether it is right for someone to choose this path is for them and those closest to them to listen to their spirit, their inner voice, and to make the decision from a spiritual perspective not an earthly perspective. Your spiritual perspective is only concerned with the best interests of all involved and these will only be fulfilled when all those involved have had the experience that they came here for. That was the easy answer. The difficult bit is deciding when that is. To do this you have to distance yourself from any earthly perspective and be able to see the situation only from a spiritual perspective. This means literally seeing the situation form the outside. Only when you are sure that you and everyone else have done this are you in a position to make a decision.

The final thing to remember is that the ultimate decision should always rest with the person concerned because it is a choice that they have to make. Of course, like anything else you can always ask spirit for help, but you cannot use them to absolve yourself of responsibility. You are ultimately responsible for the decisions that you make while you are here. It is making decisions that make you strong. However, many of our decisions are based on our innermost feelings and it is these that are based on our spiritual intuition. And learning to listen and interpret our spiritual intuition is one of ways that helps us to evolve.

What happens when we die?

As we do not remember our previous deaths with any clarity and are yet to reach it in this life time, this is quite hard to answer. However, when asked, spirit dictated the following in semi trance, hence some of the flowery language. We did consider editing it but thought it should be left as it came through from spirit. We hope you enjoy the answer.

This is quite a complex question and depends on many different factors such as whether you are already enlightened or whether you have any knowledge of spirit. For those who have no knowledge of spirit the following is usually the order of events:

You are first met by your relatives and friends. This is to reassure you that you are safe and there is no need to worry. You are taken through the tunnel of white light by your gatekeeper. Your gatekeeper has been with you since you first drew breath even though you may never have been aware of him/her. As you draw your last breath you will become aware of a wonderful feeling of peace and a release of all your earthly cares and worries, no more pain or discomfort just a wonderful feeling of love surrounding you. You will see in front of you a really bright light. This is the so called tunnel. You will feel yourself drawn to this tunnel and you should allow yourself to be drawn in this way. There is nothing to worry about, nothing to fear.

Normally it is those who go suddenly who panic and try to resist. Those who have had time to prepare feel nothing but this sense of love and happiness and peace. Time is no longer relevant and it may feel like everything is moving in slow motion. There is time if you wish to visit your family, wherever they are, as your spirit leaves your body and the earthplane behind. This again takes no time at all because there is no time now. Time is an earthly concept and is no longer relevant to you. You are now spirit only but because of your long time on the earthplane you will still feel physical and emotional sensations. Rather like someone who loses a limb but can still feel it. It is this continuation of feeling that prevents those poor souls who wish to remain from leaving the earthplane and going through the tunnel. But it is also this continuation of earthly feeling that allows you to feel the peace and love and that conversely allows you to feel no fear.

So now you have accepted the pull of the light and you are moving through the tunnel. The light is getting brighter and brighter and pulsating round you. As it pulsates round you feel it cleansing you as it does when you use it in your meditation but a million times stronger and more powerful. As you ascend higher and higher the feelings of love and peace increase and you look up you see those that you love waiting for you. You have to remember that all this happens in a millisecond of earthly time so for all intents and purposes you are in fact able to see your relatives and friends before you draw your last breath. Many people talk of seeing relatives before they go to the light. Although science tells you this is purely a physical reaction of the body shutting down it is also true that it is this physical process of the body shutting down that allows your spirit to override all the reactions that are controlled and manipulated by your physical body and it is this that allows your spirit to reassert itself again. We use the word again because this is how your spirit was before it took physical form and for the few years that it was able to be the primary sense before the other earthly senses took precedence.

When you are at the end of the tunnel you will be surrounded by so many of your friends and relatives that the sense of wellbeing will overwhelm you. Then there is so much to catch up on that you will spend eons of your earthly time greeting those who have come here before you and who have eagerly awaited your presence. You are also, if you wish, able to see your friends and family who remain on the earth plane as they mourn your passing. Although this is necessarily a sad experience it will also comfort you as you see that despite their grief at your passing they are able to carry on without you as of course they must. The more enlightened will be able to communicate with you. But this is dependant on both you and they being able to understand how to do this.

The problem for so many of you is that you either do not believe or you are not able to focus enough in your grief to hear the responses of those who have gone to the light – those who have gone home. They will speak to you and they will tell you that they are well and happy and healthy but very few of you are able to hear them at this stage because you are not listening. This is nothing to be ashamed of, nothing to worry about, it is perfectly normally to feel this way and in fact it is part of your earthy existence that you are emotionally attached to the other spirits around you so find this period of loss almost unbearable. But having read this we hope that you may be able to remember this so that through your sadness and pain you know deep down that your loved ones are fine, they are with you whenever you wish them to be and although they will leave you for some time while they carry on to the next part of their homecoming, they can come to you whenever you need them. Of course the quicker you are able to accept this the quicker they are able to move on to the next stage and once they have been to the halls of healing and been cleansed of their earthly pain and suffering they will be able to come through to you more clearly. Again there are several reasons for this.

Firstly, healing removes the emotional pain and suffering as well as the physical residues of the earthplane. One cleansed of this the spirit is restored to its beautiful purity, strengthened and empowered by the experiences that it has successfully traversed on the earthplane and in this state is able to communicate more clearly with the medium on the earthplane. Secondly, once a certain amount of time has elapsed the person on the earthplane is able to accept the message without becoming overwhelmed by emotion. There is a saying that time heals and this is true even if it only means that with time you learn to adjust and to live with your loss. Of course once you are able to communicate with spirit you need never really loose touch with those who have gone back to spirit. It is just like learning a new skill and adjusting to a different form of communication. Rather as when your relative moves to another country. You may not be able to see them but you can still telephone them, write to them or email them. Before this technology was available communication was only by letter.

If you are overwhelmed by emotion you will not be able to fully appreciate the message and it would be distressing for both you and your loved one in spirit. Because they would not yet have been to the halls of healing they would not have that emotional detachment that the healing will give them. Life on the physical plane is painful enough and returning to spirit, whilst overwhelmingly joyous, does also have its sadness as those who pass to spirit are aware of the suffering that their loss has caused. So allow those who have gone to spirit time to heal as you too need time to heal and then your reunion with them when they do return to communicate with you will be a more fulfilling experience for both of you.

So you have arrived and you have met up with those who have gone before. All around you are other spirits also reunited with their kith and kin, but although you can see and hear them you are not disturbed by them. This is because as spirit you are not afflicted by earthly problems such as distractions and interruptions. This is your time to rejoice and realise that there is life after physical life. For some this is a great shock. So many do not believe that this is happening! For so long they have thought this to be rubbish that it is indeed such a shock!

But once over the shock, the joy is unrestrained. Although sometimes tinged with a little sadness as the realisation that they spent so long with a closed mind and wasted opportunities to speak to those who had gone to the light before them. But no matter, this was the experience they chose to have so no blame should be attached to this.

It is now time to free yourselves of the earthly pressure and residue so it is time to go to the halls of healing. This is a large hall on many levels. (Home is on many levels and you will return to the appropriate level and receive your healing on the level that you have attained. Progress through the levels is done both on the earth plane and in spirit.)

The length of time you spend in the halls of healing depends on the amount of enlightenment and the amount of healing you have had on the earthplane.

Again this is nothing to worry about. It is like being in a deep sleep and when you wake you feel wonderful as you are then fully restored to your spiritual self without the physical, and emotional residues of the earthplane. Your spirit is you and you are all beautiful spirits and it is this that you again become.

When you emerge form the halls of healing you will go to the library. There you will review your life. This is not a judgement on what you did right and what you did wrong but a gentle assessment of your every thought, word and action and the consequences, many unseen, of all these. As you can imagine this will take some time but it is not a painful experience but a learning experience. As you revisit different times and events you will understand the processes that lead you to consider certain courses of actions and the events and actions of others that caused events to happen in your life. It sounds very complicated but this is because you think as an earthly being not as spirit so you will find it hard to comprehend these things. You also have to understand that time does not exist so unlike the earthplane you will not tire or grow weary, you do not need to eat or drink or do your laundry or your housework! Time is for you to learn and to evolve into the understanding that you need to progress to the next level. You do not always need to come back to the earthplane to address some errors of judgement or things that you perceive to be errors of judgement.

Understanding is everything because once you understand the reasons for things you do not need to do them to remember them. There are however, many things that you may need to repeat even if they are in different circumstances than those you faced before. If they were exactly the same you would recognise them instantly so would not repeat them. Very much like on the earthplane you may experience an abusive relationship and then go from one to another because you do not recognise it as such. Abusive relationships, like so many other things, take many different forms and are therefore not always recognisable. Hence the need to experience several different sides of the same coin until eventually your instincts, your soul, will recognise all types and you will no longer have to experience them.

During this time of assessment you will be able to communicate with those who are still on the earthplane. Because you are still evaluating your life there the emotional ties will be still be there but they will be different. You will be able to view things with a certain detachment. You will be able to give encouragement to those who are still there but because you are able to see the full picture you will know what is appropriate to tell them. This is why messages that come through mediums to you from those in spirit are only ever messages of support, encouragement, love and guidance. They will never tell you what you should be doing because they would know that to do that would be first to remove your free choice but more importantly remove your opportunity for growth and evolution. Whilst advice is always helpful, whether you take that advice is always up to you and spirit will only ever offer guidance, never orders!

Once the review and evaluation has taken place and you have understood the consequences and ramifications of every thought word and action not only of yourself but of all those who were part of your story on the earthplane it will be time for you to progress to the next phase. For this you will return to the level in spirit that is appropriate for you. This may not be the same level as those friends and family who first met you on your return. But this is not a matter for sadness. Remember, you are now spirit so those earthly ties and attachments that you had with those spirits no longer exists. When you all gather to speak to someone on the earthplane you will all congregate as you would when you were in your physical bodies but that is only because the person on the earthplane would not recognise any other kind of formation. For these instances you would appear as you did when you were on the earthplane else how would the medium be able to describe you to your loved one in a way that they would recognise?

Because you are spirit in a physical body this is very hard to understand but once you are in spirit your level of understanding will be that of a spirit and will be from the perception of spirit. Because this is different from that of your earthly perception it will then make perfect sense! It is rather like trying to understand the concept of infinity or indeed some of the theories that this book has discussed to which we will now return.

If you think back to the first chapter we discussed how the Sumerians described the beginnings of the earth in their book the Enuma Elish. Let's return to that and look at some surprising facts and suggestions.

'Peace is like a flowing river, it is not until it stops that you realise how gentle and relaxing it was'.

'Could we change our attitude, we should not only see life differently, but life itself would come to be different. Life would undergo a change of appearance because we ourselves had undergone a change in attitude.'
Katherine Mansfield (1888 - 1923)

Chapter 15

Conclusion

We have set out to argue that personal interpretations about our physical, political and religious beginnings and the doubts they have caused are responsible for the past few centuries of wars, destruction and misery. Because the spiritual message was interpreted by people who wanted to put their own slant on it the true message never really made it. Furthermore, the messengers were always turned into 'gods' or gurus and it became they who were worshiped not the message they were trying to impart. That is one of the reasons there are so many messengers here now trying hard to impart the spiritual message. There is supposedly safety in numbers. If there are a lot of people all saying the same thing there is less danger of them being idolised and more chance of the message getting through. At least that is the theory.

The problem is trying to work out which are the impartial messages and which have personal interpretations attached. Unfortunately it is totally impossible to be completely impartial, however hard you try. This is why we have said repeatedly that you should not accept our version either unless you feel that it is your truth too. It is also why we took such pains in The Re-Enlightenment to suggest that you meditate so that you can ask your own questions and find your own answers.

But let's return to this book and look at one more theory

about our origins. Section One suggests that although most religions and belief systems would accept the idea of reincarnation of the soul or spirit, one theory suggests that we can now take this a step further and ask have we really all been here physically as well? This theory is also explored in a book that suggests that the moon was built and placed in position by us in the future.

According to this book evidence from the moon suggests a catastrophic event 3.8 billion years ago. The evidence also points to the moon having both earthly material and material from another source. This is generally assumed to be another planet that has impacted with it. However, it has now been suggested that, in fact, the moon was actually built and placed in position. The moon is positioned at exactly the right distance from the earth to enable the eco systems on earth to thrive. This could, of course, be a natural phenomenon. But it has been suggested that the moon is hollow and was, in fact, placed there by us in the future![21] So just how far fetched is this theory?

We often hear that the full moon has adverse effects on people. Is this true and if so, why? There has been quite a lot of research into whether this is true and some police forces have even changed the way they deploy officers by increasing provision on the nights of full moons. This is because they see a clear correlation between a rise in crime and a full moon.

If we take it that there is some truth in this then the obvious question is why? We have two major natural energy sources in our world, one is the sun and the other the moon. We rely on the sun for our warmth, our light and our food. Without the sun nothing would grow and if nothing grows then we could not exist. The world would be a very dark place.

But we also rely on the moon. The moon is also a source of energy even though we may never have thought of it like that. We know that the moon controls the tides. But as Christopher

---

[21] For a more detailed account of this take a look at 'Who built the Moon' by Christopher Knight and Alan Butler

Knight and Alan Butler explained in their book 'Who built the moon', we could not exist here without the moon. It is in exactly the right place to perform its function which is to control the movement of the earth's water. Without control the tides would either be non existent or would continually over run the earth. But this is not the moon's only function. Ancient people used to worship the moon. Why? They were not necessarily aware that it controlled the tides so they did not see its significance in this way.

Other theories suggest that ancient civilisations worshipped the moon because it is the moon that energises the lay lines of the earth. It was these lay lines that provided the energy they were able to harness and utilise. Remember, originally the lay lines were pure and emanated positive energy around the earth. This resulted in peaceful communities who lived in harmony with their surroundings and the neighbouring communities. This in turn ensured that the energy of the lay lines remained pure because the energy around the lay lines was also pure. At the full moon the energy of the moon was at its most powerful and it was then that it re-energised the lay lines.

Because we have corrupted this source of energy when the moon sends out its most powerful emissions, at the time of the full moon, it also re-energises those lines that are negative. This increases the flow of negative energy around the planet. Just as some people are more susceptible to picking up spirit, others are more susceptible to the negative energy of the earth. Thus, at the time of the full moon, they get a surge of negative energy which causes them to act in certain ways.

Yes this again sounds far fetched, but proponents of this theory suggest that we should think about it from another angle. Physically we are 70% water so when the moon affects the water on the planet it also affects us. It affects our chemical structure in much the same way as it would if we added some orange squash to water. It is no longer just H_2O, it becomes something else. When our chemical structure changes it affects our hormones and this affects our emotions which in turn affect our thoughts, words and actions.

Religions tell us that we are supposed to be created in God's image. Another theory asks what if this is physically true? We have had the ability to clone human beings for many years now. Gene splitting, the ability to add or remove genes has also existed for some time. Cell fusion is the ability to create a new hybrid being and is also being currently investigated. Once the research is complete humankind will be able to create beings in his own likeness and if we went to another planet we would be able to cross breed with the inhabitants. So is this what happened? Are we indeed created from cloning, gene splitting and cell fusion? Are we indeed created in god's likeness?

If this is the case is it also possible that the earth was actually seeded twice? The first time was with Neanderthal man. As previously mentioned he was there to carry out the tasks allocated to him by the gods. When they needed a more advanced workforce the gods created a more advanced version. The genetic code is the same for both so the source of both must be the same.

As proponents of this theory point out - a hundred years ago this would have seemed in the realm of science fiction but much of the necessary scientific knowledge now exists. We can clone, we can split genes and we can now use cell fusion to create hybrids. We are doing it all the time with plants. The idea of forced genetic intervention is not so strange now as it would have appeared 100 years ago.

They go on to argue that the facts do not square with the idea of our evolution from apes. If mankind indeed descended from the apes there should be evidence to prove it. But it appears that the evolution of humankind cannot be explained in the same way the evolution of other species is explained.

So is it possible that it was our future selves that came here originally to seed the earth? As previously mentioned the technical and scientific ability is now there to do this and who knows whether it is already being done somewhere. Following on from this, did we, when our scientific ability had increased sufficiently, come back and genetically modify the species that had evolved here ie: Neanderthal man? Is this what really happened? Did the gods (us) arrive and start messing about with the genetic make up of original man? Messing about with things that they didn't really understand?

We know this may sound like something out of science fiction and maybe it is. But advocates of this theory ask is it really so far fetched and in any case, what is science fiction? Many things that were written in the past under the guise of science fiction are now part of our every day lives, including, some would say, George Orwell's novel '1984'! As bizarre as this may sound we do now have the technology to find a planet and plant the right genetic material to enable us to actually live there at some time in the future. At the moment it would still take millions of years for an alternative planet to become habitable but technology and science are advancing in giant leaps all the time. Who is to say that in the not distant future that the time frame would be considerably shorter? Add this to our ability to clone humans and some very interesting possibilities arise.

They argue that before dismissing this you should try imagining that you lived in the deepest jungle and had never come across anybody other than your fellow jungle dwellers. Because of your remoteness to civilisation you have had no contact with the outside world and your world is still the same as it was hundreds, maybe thousands, of years earlier. Suddenly a helicopter lands in a clearing near your home. What would you think? How would you describe the people who climbed out of the helicopter with their mobile phones, Ipods and various other modern devices? How would you see or understand their medicines, weapons and their modern machines? Is it that impossible that you would imagine these people to be Gods?

In Chapter 2 we spoke about the Elohim who are now believed to have predated the Sumerians and who are believed to have influenced the development of many ancient cultures. Elohim is a Hebrew word which expresses concepts of divinity. It is apparently related to the Hebrew word ēl, and, in a linguistic sense, consists of the Hebrew word Eloah (הולא) with a plural suffix. In the context of Islam, some scholars have highlighted that the divine name Allah, used in the Qur'an, has a linguistic relationship with the word "Eloah (הולא). The word "Elohim" is also found in the late Bronze Age texts of Canaanite Ugarit, where it was used to mean the family of the creator God. In some denominations of the Latter Day Saint movement, such as the Mormons, the term Elohim (also spelled "Eloheim") is often used to distinguish God the Father as a distinct member of the Godhead. The plural sense of "Elohim" is generally recognized by the Latter Day Saints Church as meaning "the council of the gods" in the creation story.

It has been said that the problem with 'god' is that man has created him in his own image. Maybe that statement has more truth than previously thought. It would explain why the gods of the Old Testament are full of anger and vengeance instead of love and light. If there is some truth in this theory and it is accepted that man has indeed created god in his own image it would explain why there is so much human frailty in the gods that are described in religious teachings. It is simply because it is us in the future that are the gods that our religions are based on. This is why the gods of our religious teachings are not always full of love and light because they are not based on Spirit, but on us with all our faults and human frailties.

Scientific theories such as String theory and M theory suggest that space in general has about 10 or 11 dimensions but we, as humans, can only really perceive up to the third dimension. Although we have knowledge of the fourth dimension – time - we can see nothing past that. However, it is entirely possible that one of these dimensions is the spiritual dimension and that our spiritual selves can therefore perceive this spiritual dimension. If you would like to know more about scientific theories such as String Theory or M Theory, there is plenty of information on the internet and there are several books that will explain them. We have only included them to show that time is another dimension that we know exists but cannot necessarily understand. Thus, although the way time works within the different dimensions cannot yet be understood either, it does not mean that it cannot work in the way that has been suggested.

In the first book we explained that there is no time in the spiritual dimension. But you are also spirit in a physical body and as such this is also true for the spirit on the earth plane. For your spirit there is no difference between the past, the present and the future. They are simultaneous. Time is circular not linear. It is rather like a large round spindle that is full of paper and just goes round and round. There is no beginning, no middle and no end. It goes on indefinitely. Each piece of paper is dependant on the one before and the one after, layer upon layer.

So, some theorists would suggest that not only is it possible that we have created god in our own image, it is also possible that god did create us (in a purely physical sense), just as the Bible says.

Is it really worth killing over?

Of course this is just another theory. The physical, religious and political history of our planet is fascinating. The religious history of our planet has been so well hidden that it may never be really possible to find the answers whilst we are here. But whilst there are almost as many theories, arguments and interpretations as there are people, is it really that important? We may dismiss this last theory as totally ridiculous but would we start a war over it? If not why is it any different to go to war over the religious interpretations about our origins?

Whilst history is important because it gives us our sense of identity and because it should allow us to stop repeating previous mistakes, is it really worth fighting over now? Theorising about the past is an interesting diversion on our spiritual journey because it makes us question things that we have been told. Questioning allows us to open our minds to new possibilities and allows us to find truths that are acceptable to us. But is it really that important? Investigating our past is just like life. We spend ages following a particular path and then find it did not really get us anywhere, or what seemed important at the start is no longer important. We often feel that we have then wasted a large part of our lives. But this is not really true. Every experience we have here is a part of our spiritual journey. Sometimes the reasons for doing and experiencing things are obvious, at other times they are totally obscure. But they are never wasted. It is these experiences that make us who we are.

We can now return to our spiritual journey and leave the past behind. Unfortunately the rest of the world seems unable to do that. The rest of the world is still fighting wars over things that supposedly happened thousands of years ago because they are being told selective versions of history that back up the regimes and religions that are not brave enough to allow their people to ask questions.

The point we are trying to make is that it really is time we stopped wasting our all our spiritual energy on fighting the battles of 2000 years ago and concentrated on the reality that is now - the present – our gift to ourselves. Whether Jesus was the Son of God or whether Mohammed was the last prophet may have been important 2000 years ago but is not relevant to the way we live now. The message they gave to the world then has steadily been corrupted and eroded, but the message is still just as simple as it was then – unconditional love and peace. But unless we leave the past in the past we will never achieve this.

Earlier we compared ourselves to spiritual children. As such we liked playing and one of the things children like playing is war games. But children begin to grow up and have other things to occupy their minds. Teenagers have a lot of energy and have lots of new ideas. They make mistakes but that is part of the learning process. In the second section we looked at the world as it has been over the past couple of centuries. We examined our world's political, religious, scientific and spiritual journey at the same time as we examined our own individual political, religious, scientific and spiritual journey. We showed how our individual thoughts words and actions and our sense of individual identity impacts on our communities and eventually on our world. We also looked at the earth's energy lines and the suggestion that these were now pulsating negative energy around the planet instead of the positive energy that was intended.

If there is any truth in some of the more 'outlandish' theories then could it also be true that it was us (our spiritual selves) in the future, who encoded and encrypted the secret of how to harness the power of the energy lines. On the other hand, even if there is no truth in this, there could still be truth in the suggestion that there is an untapped energy source in the ley lines. If this is the case then it is possible that we also have the knowledge of how to unlock this power. The big question would seem to be that if this is true is human kind ready to have access to this power?

However, this section also showed how we, as individuals, can use our spiritual gifts, in particular our gifts of insecurity and fear of change, in a positive way. This can have a massive impact on how we live our own lives, and on the lives of those around us and even to the extent of affecting our return home when we die. It can also help to add to the positive energy within the earth plane.

We suggested in The Re-Enlightenment that we needed to find a new identity, one that could exist alongside all our other identities and yet be universal in its appeal. It would also need to be big enough to include everybody and yet small enough to keep its personal appeal. It would be an identity that all could subscribe to without losing their individuality and an identity that all could subscribe to through choice without feeling any outside pressure to embrace it. They would choose it because it is logical, practical and reasonable. They would choose it because it gives everything to everyone and does not exclude or demonise others. They would choose it because it chooses them because it is already within them. They do not need to look for it too deeply, they do not need to find it because it is not lost. It is already part of them and a part of everyone else so it is already shared and universal. We argued that this identity is our spiritual identity.

But what is our spiritual identity?

As we grow older we gain in self confidence. We worry less about what others think and more about how we have used our lives and whether we have achieved all the things that we want to. Our spiritual identity is the mature, confident, unafraid, balanced spirit that we all have the ability to find if we try hard enough. We have already argued that most of the world's problems stem from our insecurity and our fear of change. But this insecurity is a physical emotion that we do not have to embrace. We can let it go and see ourselves as confident individuals embracing change and the opportunities for personal, national and international growth that it brings. It is this spiritual identity that we need to teach our children. We need to give them the confidence that all too many of them lack - the confidence that the world is their oyster and they can do anything they set their minds to do. The future is theirs and they have the ability to create any future they want. They just have to find the self belief that comes with confidence. This is the greatest gift we can give our children.

Our spiritual identity is essentially our ability to see our selves as one part of a whole. Spirit is one soul or consciousness and we are all a part of that one soul or consciousness. This acceptance that we are all one allows us to emphasise with others because their problems are our problems. We have already seen that the world is now such a small place that this is true physically anyway. But the ability to overcome this separateness that is part of our earthly physical identity is what it truly means to embrace our spiritual identity. If you accept that we are all part of a whole then any attempts to dehumanise or demonise others would, of course, dehumanise and demonise us. If you accept that we are part of one soul or consciousness then it becomes impossible to make someone else an 'outsider' just so that we can belong because we all belong anyway.

But it is not just us, as individuals, that needs to embrace this identity. We need to collectively embrace this identity. Our communities also need to come of age and embrace self belief and confidence. We have already seen how our individual insecurities, lack of self forgiveness and lack of self belief leads us into behaving in ways that cause harm to other people. We have also argued that it as individuals that we come together to become political and/or religious communities. If we can find our spiritual identity, our communities will do the same. If our communities find their spiritual identity they will no longer behave in ways that cause harm to other communities. Yes it sounds idealistic but what is the alternative?

One of the questions we have asked repeatedly is why is it so important for us to evolve? The answer is quite simple - if we do not evolve we are in danger of going backwards again. We have already seen how advanced previous civilisations were and how we have subsequently gone backwards and regressed. We do not have to look far into history to see that periods of freedom and enlightenment soon dissolve into chaos if there is no balance between restraints and freedom. The Roman Empire was a good example of this. The people were unaware of the real problems threatening them because they were too involved in trivia. When populations have their attention focused on irrelevancies politicians are able to act without consulting the people they are there to govern. They often make decisions that are not beneficial to the population as a whole as they begin to only pay attention to those who are involved in the political process. This leaves large numbers of people disenfranchised or feeling excluded and threatened. When this happens there are always people who are ready to take advantage of the situation. We only need to look at Europe in the beginning of the 20th Century to see examples of this. History does not have to keep repeating itself any more than we have to keep repeating the same mistakes over and over again. We do have a choice, the same as we have a choice in our own lives. As a world community we have to change and we can only do that if we, as individuals, change.

One of the ways we can encourage individual and community growth is through meditation. Meditation allows us to reconnect with our spiritual one-ness. We are also able to connect to our spiritual teachers and healing guides. We explained how to meditate and how to give healing in The Re-Enlightenment so there is no need to repeat it here.

The final section examined the process of coming home at the end of our spiritual journey. It began by looking at how our planet is also getting old and how it is changing. It continued by examining how our political and social systems are also undergoing massive changes and how these affect us all. It finished by looking at how some religions have resisted change over the centuries leaving them stuck in a kind of time warp or limbo. This is rather like the spirit of someone who would not accept change throughout their life and now, through fear of change finds themselves unable to go to the light. Conversely, others have changed so much they are either no longer in touch with the people they are there to guide, or have split into innumerable factions. Some of these are not only predicting the end of the world, but actively trying to speed up the process. We also looked at the rise of inward looking cults and sects with charismatic leaders whose only intention is to control the members to feed the ego of a leader who believes they are God or at the very least God's chosen messenger.

We have not set out to alarm or worry or even to shock you, although that may have been the result. But as we have repeated many times, how we see things and how we interpret them is of paramount importance to how we react to them. This is not intended to be either an Armageddon or apocalyptic book but a book of Enlightenment, a book that looks forward to a time when the world is healed and becomes a place where we can come and actually enjoy our holidays!

There is an expression that you cannot make an omelette without breaking eggs. If we compare the world to an omelette we can see that the omelette is the whole, the finished product when all the ingredients are included and become one. The eggs are the separate ingredients that have to be broken down and added to everything else to make the whole. We are the eggs, our future is the omelette. But for this to happen there has to be big changes and whilst change is something that cannot be avoided it is also something that fills people with fear and dread. Even thought the world is such a sad place it is still the only world we know – at present. But that doesn't mean it has to stay like that. We have this incredible power within us to change our world for the better. Our thoughts create our future so what type of future do you see? What kind of future do you envisage for your children? Collectively we can make those dreams come true. Just as we get the governments we deserve so do we also get the world we deserve. We deserve so much better – don't you?

'How wonderful it is that nobody need wait a single moment before starting to improve the world.'
Anne Frank (1929 - 1945), Diary of a Young Girl, 1952

Appendix 1

Spiritual Writing

11ᵗʰ June 2007

The key in the urn is symbolic of the key that will open many doors. There are so many secrets in the world, not least the secrets of your beginnings. Not your spiritual beginnings specifically but your physical beginnings. These are gradual coming more into the open and you will continue this with your next book. You will also delve deeper into your spiritual beginnings. These too are part of the journey. After all a journey has a beginning middle and an end.

The key is gold because its worth is beyond measure. Knowledge is worth much more than precious metal. Knowledge of truth is priceless and can never be bettered.

The molecules of the human body have been subject to many changes over the centuries but none more so than from the first to the third civilisations. It is then that the changes became more ingrained and the regression took place. This regression has two forms – the physical and the spiritual. Whilst the physical regression is now repairing itself, the spiritual regression is beginning to take hold. There is the beginning of a polarisation of the spirit between those who are evolving at a great rate and those whose spiritual regression is accelerating. This is not coincidence – it is deliberate. You wish to know why you are here to evolve. In part it is to prevent the acceleration of spiritual regression amongst the population currently on the earth plane, because there is, of course, a link between those spirits who are there and those who are at home. There is great concern about this and it is so very important that the message of love and light is taken far and wide. We will explain more when it is time for you to write the next book but we do not wish to give you too much too soon or you will be unable to finish the current book.

It is as always a battle between good and evil. Is that not what the world is about?

14th June 2007

There comes a time when it is your time to pass over and join us but often people will find it very hard to let go. It is not god that allows you to suffer it is you. You are the people who have made the laws that make it illegal for you to help your loved ones progress on their path. There are many reasons for this but one is of course the protection that your law provides to the old, frail and vulnerable who otherwise might be assisted or persuaded to go before their time for the benefit of others. But there are times when it is perfectly obvious that it would be a kindness to allow someone to cross to spirit. This is when the situation becomes very difficult. There are often disagreements within families as to the best course of action but it remains the decision or the choice of the person concerned. As with everything on the earth plane you have a choice. Do you remain and suffer or should you choose to go? We cannot answer that because it is different for each person. Seen from a spiritual perspective there is no difficulty in coming to the right decision because your spiritual perspective is of course different from your earthly perspective and has no interests other than the best interests o the person concerned.

Going to spirit is an act of love not an act of violence. Thus if you choose to go to spirit it must be for the right reason. Remember that death is not the end but the beginning. If you do not die how can you evolve?

Diamonds come from deep below. They are the result of evolution from one form to another. This is what death is.

Expectancy

There is a great air of expectancy in the world as it awaits the changes that spirit is bringing to the world far and wide.

Expectancy is freedom for to expect only the best creates only the best. Conversely if you expect the worse it is the worse that will happen.

Truth is the result of your expectations because the truth of your reality is created by your expectations. And only the truth can set you free. This is why expectancy is so eagerly awaited.

Hope is the sustaining lifeblood of humankind. Without hope there is nothing. If you have hope you have expectations and you are creating your reality and it is a positive reality because it will set you free of your bigotry and prejudice and from the lies that have caused the divisions amongst you.

We see a future bright with anticipation and clear in its direction. Expectancy is the word of spirit and it will make you free. It will bring with it the responsibility to open the closed minds and once this is achieved it will bring the responsibility that freedom always brings. The need for education and teaching that explains how you should use your freedom.

Just as the expectant father awaits the birth of his child so do we await the birth of a new humanity – one that is spiritual first and physical second – one that loves first and last and that creates the most beautiful future for all the citizens of the world.

Faith and Trust

Trust not those who would give you false words, those who corrupt the words of god and turn them into words of hate. Faith in god does not and cannot mean hate because god cannot conceive of hate. God is only love so if you place your trust and faith in those who would tell you otherwise you will not evolve much beyond your current level of awareness.

It is for those present to interpret the word of god through trust and faith and to take this word far and wide. We trust that you will do this. This is why you have come here is it not?

Faith, they say can move mountains. This is true but the mountains that faith must move are those mountains of evil, of mistrust, of anger and of hate. Those black mountains are the thoughts of mankind. When these thoughts coalesce they become these dark mountains and it is these mountains that faith must move.

Trust is the trust that you are interpreting the word correctly and that is what mankind will hear in your words because they are our words – the words of god or spirit, however, you wish to say them. These are the words that form the faith that will move the mountains and earn the trust of mankind.

We would also like to add that it is your faith and trust in us that gives us voice and allows us to give you the words. For this we are most grateful for soon we will be returning to the earthplane and we would wish it to be better than it is now.

Faith and trust is within you. It is trust and faith that you need to allow us to speak through you. It will not be long now.

Trust is like the rain, it starts slowly then encompasses you with its full glory. When you live in the desert a little rain is a wondrous thing. So it is with your world – it is so barren that a little trust and a little faith is indeed miraculous. Do not allow the minds that are dry of meaning to blow the seeds of faith away.

Trust is belief in what you cannot see, faith is knowing it is there.

Forgiveness

Forgiveness is the most beautiful word for it is forgiveness that makes you free. It is easier to forgive others than it is to forgive ourselves. We forget that we are too are human so we too have faults. We make mistakes – if we did not make mistakes we would not learn. But why do we find it so hard to forgive our own mistakes as we forgive the mistakes of others? If we do not forgive ourselves we cannot be free and if we are not free then we cannot progress and move on.

There is nothing so bad that you cannot be forgiven. To not forgive is to judge and to judge is such a human foible. Spirit does not judge you so why do you judge yourselves so harshly?

It seems that those of you on the earth plane either fail to forgive yourselves or at the other end of the scale, accept no responsibility for your actions. You will need to find the balance and in doing so accept the past and allow yourselves to move on. Forgiveness is truly divine and those who learn to forgive are also truly divine and that is what you are my children. You are all truly divine and absolute perfection in the eyes of spirit.

How can you be anything else for it is I that crated you and it is I that gave you the means to become truly perfect and truly divine. If you trust in spirit then you have no alternative but to accept the truth of this.

If you do not forgive yourselves you will allow the baggage of the past to slow you down. Like the man with many heavy bags who tries to walk across the desert he sinks into the sand and it is so with those who are unable to forgive themselves and who continue to punish themselves for things that they imagine they may have done in the past.

Guilt is a luxury that you cannot afford in that it allows others to control your destiny. Your future shines like the jewels in the desert and it is only your failure to let go that prevents you taking and receiving the gifts of the earth. The gifts that are waiting for you in abundance for you to collect them. See not your physical bodies, your physical forms, instead see your spiritual selves in all their glory. Let go, let God and move into the sun. Leave behind the clouds of despair for every time you allow those black clouds of despair to gather you add to the blackness that is your world. Forgiveness and the ability to forgive yourself is such a positive gift that is frees and enlightens all those who embrace its gifts.

Many people apologise to control others. Apologise to yourself and take control of your lives. Only by taking control of your lives can you become the person you wish to be. Do not hang onto your guilt or your fear – these will just hold you back. It is often those who are least likely to take responsibility for their actions that need the most self forgiveness. They cannot accept that others will love them if they appear less than perfect. Only those that are less than perfect expect others to be perfect. We give this message to those who wish to progress and trust these words will give you food for thought in the coming weeks. Thank you for listening to us.

Why do guides become guides – 6th August 2007

Guides come to be guides because simply this is their choice. But there are other reasons too. Many were healers on the earth plane and many were persecuted for their crafts. But this is those who were healers in the later years of the planet. Before the current age, the Common Era as you call it, healing was an acceptable art. There was no stigma attached to healing but nor was there anything special. It is here that many of the healing guides began to practice. When they practised healing the energy of the planet was not as corrupted as it is now so the healing was much purer. It did not have to be filtered through the pollution of your world today. We refer not just to the physical pollution of course, but to the emotional and mental pollution through which modern healers and mediums have to work. This is why it is so important for those who wish to be healers and mediums to meditate and cleanse themselves of this pollution.

We have chosen to be guides because we wish to help you return the earth to its original splendour. We, like you, believe the world is worth saving. Like you, in spirit, we agreed to work with you because we were also your guides and teachers whilst you were in spirit. Because of our experience of different ages we can give you different perspectives and different understandings. It is important that you and your guides are similar in nature. If you were not it would be an uneasy fit and neither of us would reach our true potential because we too are continuing to learn and progress. Often we too will ask our guides and teachers to come through for you if it is something that we are not entirely sure of.

It is important for you personally to have many different guides because you are a scribe and must be able to think with many different heads. For the purposes of the current book an

Arab Muslim and a Christian are invaluable guides. Once you are finished with this we will depart and new guides will come into write the next one.

Remember it is the message that is important not the guide.

Hope – August 14th 2007

Hope is the mainstay of our lives. Without hope we have nothing. For it is hope that takes us beyond the level of our physical being and hope that takes us to new heights. Without hope your world would not exist because hope gives strength to your lives and creativity to your thoughts and it is your thoughts that create your reality. Hope points us to a future that is bright, that is better than our current existence. A life without hope is grey because it has no colour. Hope gives colour to your lives as it taps into the creative energy within and it is hope that keeps vigil through the dark days of despair. It is hope that shines like a beacon and it is hope that will take you beyond the mundane and transport you to unimaginable joy. It is only hope that can do this because it is only hope that can transcend the drab and dreary and shine its light on us all. Let hope be your guiding light – let hope be your mantra – let hope take your world to a better place. Without hope there is nothing because hope is all.

Peace – September

The world is so much in need of peace. But it is not just the world that is need of peace. We too need peace in our hearts before we are able to appreciate the beauty that surrounds us. But it is difficult for us to find peace on the earth plane because we are constantly subject to negative vibrations and pressures that destroy our inner calm and inner peace.

To find our inner peace we have to have faith in spirit. We have to know beyond all doubt that spirit is always there and always has our best interests at heart. However bad we consider our problems to be that should not be allowed to destroy that inner peace and inner calm that comes from our certainty. Our certainty that this life is just an illusion. It is purely an expression of our spiritual selves. Our inner peace stems from the certainty that there is eternal life for our soul and it is this certainty of believe that gives us the peace we crave. For the world to have peace we must all find that inner peace. Once we all have that knowledge and security then the world too will begin to know peace.

Peace is like a gently flowing river. It is not until it stops that you realise how gentle and relaxing it was.

The Stars – October 8th

Spirit as you know can project into any form it chooses. If you wish to imagine a relative is a star then this is one way they will project themselves. Stars are, after all, energy, like everything else that exists. The energy of the stars may be positive or negative, the same as the energy of anything else. Stars contain energy from the past and within those energies are myriad forms and lives past. All forms of energy contain imprints of existence, stars are no different. Many were life forces in their own right and many gave life to many different energy forces.

What you see in the sky are the echoes of the past, echoes of lost civilisations, echoes of past energy, past conflicts and past lives. Spiritually therefore, they contain the energy from past events.

All the universe is connected spiritually as well as physically as you know so the stars have a spiritual connection. But as to whether they exist purely as your departed relatives. To this the answer is no, only if you wish them to project in that way, but in general terms no.

Ancient civilisations watched the movement of the stars because of the patterns there. These patterns held the key to their existence because it was from there that the gods came. The gods showed them how to map the heavens and how to use these maps to predict catastrophes and events that were of value or that would affect the future, such as invasions and wars. All is interconnected – the future, the present and the past. You have forgotten many things that the ancients knew, this is why your earth is in such turmoil. This turmoil began centuries ago when the gods forgot why they had come.

Colours – October 29th

Colours reflect your feelings as well as expressing your feelings. You are drawn towards colours that may be lacking within your life or you are drawn to colours that boost the energy of the chakras or the energy centres. We heal on many different levels. A healer whose words are wise may be drawn to the colour blue – the colour of the throat energy centre. But just as significantly the person who wears a lot of blue may be giving themselves healing as well as others. There may be many things that have been left unsaid, hence the need to wear blue – the colour of communication. Conversely the person who wears blue may be a great communicator. The significance of a colour is specific to that person at that specific time. At another time it may mean something else entirely.

We all need colour in our lives to enhance the colours of the energy centres and to encourage the balancing of the energy centres. There will never be just one colour and if there is it will be a transient time and it will soon merge with other colours. If there was a constant colour then this would signify a blockage of energy because the energies of the body would be unbalanced.

The aura is a swirling mass of all the colours and when it is so it is then that the spirit is perfectly balanced.

Colour shimmers like light over the drab corners of the world. Its energy can brighten even the dullest day. Use colour in your lives to help counter the negative energy of the earth.

Colour is one of the secrets that has been lost. The energy that comes from colours can be harnessed if you know how. The energy can be used to re-energise the lay lines too if you are able to understand this concept. It can be done through visualisation techniques like the techniques you use when healing or very similar to those anyway.

Solitude - November 10th

Solitude is the pleasure of the soul and the spirit. The world is so busy and noisy that it is only when we sit quietly that we are able to reach our inner most selves – our spiritual selves. Amidst the turmoil of our thoughts it is the silence and the solitude that allows us to travel beyond our earthly bodies and connect with our spiritual self on the spiritual plane.

Solitude allows the spirit expression; it allows us to hear the inner voice and to understand where we are going. All too often we speak without really knowing what it is we want to say. The value of silence and meditation cannot be stressed enough as it is this freedom from echoes of the world that provides us with the spiritual insight and wisdom that our earthly beings need and desire.

The sand storms of the dessert afforded us a peaceful haven. Not only were our enemies unable to find us but as we were cut off and sheltering we were able to connect with our guides who would share their inner wisdom with us. The ancients knew the value of one's own company. Nowadays solitude is frowned upon in the same way that peace and quiet are thought to be the province of the elderly. Without silence the world degenerates into chaos because no one has the time to work out their true pathway. Solitude is another of the free gifts we can give ourselves – and of course you are never truly alone because we are always with you.

Thursday 15th November

Everything has an energy so you could say that everything has a spirit This is because spirit is the essence of everything. It is spirit that is the energy in everything and it is spirit that leaves its imprint or signature on everything that is on the earthplane. The spirits of the trees and the wind and the sun are the way energy was interpreted by ancient people. They lived much closer to the land and as such they lived close to the elements. That gives rise to the spirit of the elementals. If you consider your spiritual philosophy you will remember that everything you do here impacts in some way on other spirits and this is also true of the other elemental spirits that exist within the movement of the tides and the wind etc. All these things have a spiritual energy. It is just a different type of spiritual energy from that of individual spirits. It is all about interpretation and interpretation is a very personal thing.

The following was written by Julie Millar in circle and she had kindly allowed us to include it.

Be not so arrogant as to assume your level is the only one given to the beings on the earth plane. The earth spirits are the guardians of the natural world. They are the first spirits or the simplest form of spiritual energy. But be not mistaken they are just as important to the realms of spirit.

The white light has its origins in the ancient oak groves of the ancients. When they saw the first cleansing rays of the morning sun come through the branches of those trees they recognised the power of the purity of light. It is that essence of purity you capture each time you put the white light to your heart. The oak tree is the symbol of eternal growth and renewal.

In the vastness of the high places the spirits of the rocks keep their vigil. In the darkness of the green valleys the wraiths of the pools and rivers are watchful and in the openness of the moors the spirits of the hills and fields are very present. All these beings have their place in the eternal order. Think not that you are the only guardians of the world. Their nature is not yours to discern. It is not one of progression ? but one of never ending patient stewardship.

2008
September

The dessert is timeless as are the realms of spirit. Time is irrelevant, it is a concept of the earth and is used to control. Natural time no longer has a place in your lives but it will do again. Time should be when you rise when it is light and sleep when it is dark. These are the natural rhythms of the earth and it is the natural rhythms and cycles that we must return to.

Inspiration is born of trust and love and will reach out to those who are seeking. The whole world now seeks knowledge on a deeper level than before. No longer is it possible to lie and pass false messages for it is the year of revelation. It is the year when falsity, hypocrisy and darkness is revealed unto the masses. It is the year when systems that are unstable and based on false premises collapse, it is the time for a new beginning. Out of the depths of darkness comes anew dawn. The sun is slowly rising in the east and with it comes an end to hypocrisy and greed, an end to the treachery of men.

The sands of time are gradually shifting to reveal the future in all its glory. Too long have you laboured in the dark, now is the time for the sun to shine through. Just as the sands shift to reveal the new pathways so will the world shift to reveal the new tomorrow. This new tomorrow brings ultimate joy, ultimate satisfaction and true creativity. This is the dawn of a new age and our message will finally be heard.

The eternal truth begins with the concept on one-ness. Only spirit can appreciate this fully for with the physical comes separateness. It is your spirit that must embrace and understand and project this outward.

October

The wisdom of the ancients is that which precedes the prophecy and accumulated knowledge of more modern times. It is the basis of all religion, the basis of all understanding, the basis of truth and the pathway we should be embrace. Understanding the wisdom of the ancients is a spiritual journey that will take you beyond current experience and which manifests itself as new or ancient because they are both the same and yet different.

Truth is often the hardest thing to find for it is buried deep within us, hidden by layers of lies, like the many layers of meanings. To understand truth you must write as you hear, not how you think.

Like gossamer the threads of wisdom are all around us but like the elusive fibres of a spiders' web they are often hard to grasp. This is because we try too hard to make things fit within our own frame of understanding. To truly understand we must first let go our earthly understandings and embrace our spiritual selves.

Appendix 2

The Light is For Everyone

The White Light of Protection

This is your connection to your spirit and it is this white light that is also your spiritual protection. It is very easy to protect yourself. All you need to do is visualise a white light in the centre of your chest. Visualise this white light getting bigger and brighter until it covers your whole body and you are cocooned in a pyramid or egg of white light so bright that it can be seen for miles! This white light covers you from top to toe and nothing can penetrate it. Cover the white light with blue and ask in your head for protection and that's it. You can do this at any time.

Sending White Light Around the World

The world at the moment is sorely in need of some light. The web site http:///.lightworkercount.com was set up to ask people all round the world to pledge 5 minutes every Saturday to send white light around the world. 5 minutes is no time at all yet if we all do this think how much light we will be sending. It doesn't have to be done at a certain time; in fact it is better if people do this at different times because this means a continuous stream of white light is being sent round the world.

All you do is to visualise the white light (as above) and them expand the light until it covers your house (or wherever you are) and then your street, village, town etc. As it grows it gets stronger and brighter until eventually you are covering the whole world with white light. Another way is to visualise the globe and concentrate white light on to this so that it is glowing with the white light. Just hold the image for 5 minutes. Don't worry if you find it hard to concentrate this long to start with. Just persevere and it will get easier. If you loose the image just start again; it is the intention as much as the action that is important.

Triangles

The Lucis Trust also concentrates white light around the worlds in a different way. Together with two other people, either in this country or in other parts of the world, you agree a time where you all will concentrate a beam of white light between you. This will effectively set up a triangle of white light in the area that you are concentrating on. For more information and to set up your triangle go to www.triangles.org

Inspiration

The inspiration for this book came from many different sources but the following may be of interest if you would like to explore some of the theories discussed further:

Zecharia Sitchin- The Cosmic Code: The Sixth Book of The Earth Chronicles
Graham Hancock - Fingerprints of the Gods.
David Rohl – The Lost Testament
Christopher Knight and Alan Butler – Who built the Moon?

Dedication

We would like to dedicate this book to the following people who have, at various times, inspired and encouraged us. Without them, our pathways would have been different and this book would not have been written.

Rev. Alan Bowley; Julie and Gary Fell; Ian Jones; Jim Mortimer; Sue Tyrrell; Steve Windsor.

About Us

Carole and David are co-founders of the Spiritual Workers Association, (SWA) an international umbrella group set in January 2008 to bring spiritual organisations and independents together across the world, to promote excellence and improve standards in the field of spiritual work. Membership is free and open to anyone who would like to join together with spiritual workers of all countries, creeds, faiths and beliefs to help raise world consciousness and make the world a more spiritual place.

Carole is a spiritual healer, Reiki master and teacher of spiritual healing and philosophy. She has an MA in Philosophy and BSc Hons and has had several articles published in spiritual magazines and newspapers.

David is a well known established platform medium, ordained spiritualist minister and spiritual healer and has also had articles published in spiritual magazines. Together they teach healing, philosophy and spiritual development at their home in North Essex.

They are also the authors of The Re-Enlightenment- A Spiritual handbook. For more information please visit www.theswa.org.uk Or www.saahera-centre.org

The Re-Enlightenment – A Spiritual Handbook

Who are we?

Why are we here?

Is there a god?

The world we currently live in is characterised by its conflicting cultures with their diverse political, social and religious views. Add to this the growing climatic problems and the increasing gap between those who have and those who have not and this world seems a very unstable place.

The majority of us not only feel powerless to prevent this, but also find it hard to accept some of the reasons we are given to explain this pain and suffering. Religions, spiritualism, politics and science have all provided competing explanations but have not provided any real proof. Furthermore, the world as we currently know it is a result of those competing explanations.

We are all citizens of this world and as such have a vested interest in its future. We all have questions about why we are here and we are all entitled to the answers. There is something in this book for everybody, from those who are not satisfied with the way the world is and think there has to be a better way, to those who just wish to know why we are really here.

www.ingramcontent.com/pod-product-compliance
Lightning Source LLC
Chambersburg PA
CBHW021834220426
43663CB00005B/239